Wingate and the Chindits

Wingate and the Chindits

Redressing the Balance

DAVID ROONEY

CASSELL&CO

Cassell Military Paperbacks

Cassell & Co
Wellington House, 125 Strand
London WC2R OBB

First published by Arms and Armour 1994
This Cassell Military Paperbacks edition 2000

British Library Cataloguing-in-Publication Data
A catalogue record for this book is available from the
British Library

ISBN 0-304-35452-X

Edited and designed by DAG Publications Ltd
Edited by Jonathan Falconer; designed by David Gibbons
Layout by Anthony A. Evans

Printed and bound in Great Britain by
Cox & Wyman Ltd, Reading, Berks.

Contents

List of Maps

Introduction

I wish, first, to express my sincere gratitude to Brigadier Michael Calvert DSO, and Lieutenant-Colonel Peter Cane MC, both intrepid Chindit leaders, who have generously put their vast knowledge of the Chindits at my disposal, and have helped in every way. Sadly, Peter Cane, who was the main inspiration for this book, died in April 1994. I respectfully dedicate it to his memory.

The primary purpose of this book is to describe in a readable form the remarkable career of Major General Orde Wingate; secondly, in a clear and concise way, intelligible to the general reader, to tell the story of the Chindit campaigns in Burma; and finally to unravel the murky background of how one man, in the privileged position of editor of the Official History, succeeded in denigrating Wingate and influencing generations of both authors and readers; if possible, I hope to rectify that injustice.

My interest in Wingate and the Chindits was aroused when I wrote *Burma Victory* (1992), which described the battles of Imphal and Kohima and touched on the Chindit issue. The most obvious problem centred on the almost universal praise, led by General Slim, which Wingate received when he was killed in 1944, and which contrasted starkly with the dismissive and highly critical view of Wingate which Slim put forward in *Defeat into Victory* (1956). This was followed by the vicious criticism of Wingate in the Official History published in 1961. These points just did not add up, and deserved further serious research. The tale that unfolded was more remarkable than could have been expected, and forms the final section of this book.

I am particularly grateful to the following individuals and organisations: Harold Hyam Wingate Foundation for a grant towards the expenses of my research; Lieutenant-Colonel Orde Wingate for access to the Wingate Papers; Colonel Jimmy White and the Officers and members of the Chindit Old Comrades Association who have strongly supported my project – they have generously furnished me with much valuable material, and I apologise that I have been unable to attribute it individually. Most of this is now in the Imperial War Museum; for assistance in my research I am grateful to my former colleague Dr David Chandler at the Royal Military Academy Sandhurst; Colonels Hugh Patterson and Kenneth Robertson; Pat Andrews and Richard Ponman at the Cabinet Office; Simon Robbins at the Imperial War Museum; the staff at the Churchill College archives, the Cambridge University library, the National Army Museum, and the Public Record Office Kew. Also to Michael Elliott-Bateman at Manchester University and the staff of John Rylands library; Major Klebanov and the Hagana Museum Tel-Aviv; Rika Shin for advice on the Japanese aspect; Brigadier Mead for his support; David Shirreff for his advice on the Ethiopian campaign; J Milner CBE; Douglas Fairbanks and *Dekho* magazine; Elena Tsatskis for solving all my computer problems, and Carol Cooper for her technical help. Finally my thanks go to our daughter Kathy Rooney for her work on my script, and to my wife for her support.

David Rooney
Cambridge, 1994

Prologue

On 24 March 1944, at the height of the second Chindit campaign in Burma, Major General Orde Wingate DSO and two bars, who had created and personally led the Chindits, was killed when the Mitchell bomber in which he was flying from Imphal to Lalaghat in Assam, crashed into a mountain side. Everyone on board was killed. Thus died a strange, lonely and eccentric man; and a brave, resourceful and brilliant soldier, who ranks among the outstanding military leaders of the Second World War. In the army he had been a difficult and abrasive colleague, who inspired deep loathing and resentment, and, at the same time, respect, loyalty and devotion.

His enemies considered him a vulgar upstart and charlatan, but an answer to that charge is given in the Order of the Day which he published at the launch of the first Chindit expedition in February 1943, and exemplifies the zeal, determination and deeply religious nature of his character:

'Today we stand on the threshold of battle. The time of preparation is over, and we are moving on the enemy to prove ourselves and our methods. At this moment we stand beside the soldiers of the United Nations in the front line trenches throughout the world. It is always a minority that occupies the front line. It is a still smaller minority that accepts with a good heart tasks like this that we have chosen to carry out. We need not, therefore, as we go forward into the conflict, suspect ourselves of selfish or interested motives. We have all had the opportunity of withdrawing and we are here because we have chosen to be here; that is we have chosen to bear the heat and burden of the day. Men who make this choice are above the average in courage. We therefore have no fear for the staunchness and guts of our comrades.

'The motive which has led each and all of us to devote ourselves to what lies ahead cannot conceivably have been a bad motive. Comfort and security are not sacrificed voluntarily for the sake of others by ill-disposed people. Our motive, therefore, may be taken to be the desire to serve our day and generation in the way that seems nearest to our hand. The battle is not always to the strong nor the race to the swift. Victory in war cannot always be counted upon, but what can be counted is that we shall go forward determined to do what we can to bring this war to the end which we believe best for our friends and comrades in arms, without boastfulness or forgetting our duty, resolved to do the right so far as we can see the right.

'Our aim is to make possible a Government of the world in which all men can live in peace and with equal opportunity of service.

'Finally, knowing the vanity of man's effort and the confusion of his purpose, let us pray that God may accept our service and direct our endeavours, so that when we shall have done all we shall see the fruit of our labours and be satisfied.

O. C. Wingate, Commander,
77th Indian Infantry Brigade.'

Wingate was the man of whom it was said 'He was a prince among men', or 'he was a thoroughly nasty bit of work'. He gained devoted admirers and ruthless enemies who traduced his memory – now is the time when a balanced investigation will bring out the truth.

PART ONE

WINGATE'S LIFE
AND
ACHIEVEMENTS

1
Early Life

Wingate's upbringing under the stern tenets of the Plymouth Brethren contributed substantially to his unconventional outlook. His early years were dominated by this dour sect. Started by a Protestant clergyman of the Church of Ireland in the 1820s because of the corruption of the Anglican Church, the Brethren believed that the whole of Christendom lay under God's stern displeasure because it had fallen away from the purity of the New Testament. This unrelenting attitude and a vivid fear of eternal damnation, certainly influenced Wingate as a boy, and although he later rejected many of the Brethren's beliefs, the melancholy consciousness of God's displeasure remained with him for many years.

Wingate's grandfather was a wealthy merchant who, when his young wife died, became deeply religious and spent several years with a Scottish mission to the Jews in Hungary. His son, George – Wingate's father – joined the army in 1871 and was posted to India where he, too, had a dramatic religious conversion and joined the Plymouth Brethren. His strong religious conviction caused some problems when, during a campaign in the Naga Hills, he refused to move his unit forward on a Sunday. In 1879, whilst on leave in England, he was introduced to a Captain and Mrs Orde-Browne, who were Plymouth Brethren, and who had six daughters and a son. For 20 years George Wingate wooed the eldest daughter and married her at the age of 46 when he was a Colonel, and she was 32. The Orde-Browne family who were deeply involved with a Plymouth Brethren mission in the East End of London, offered generous hospitality to the Wingates during their postings to India and back.

The birth of Orde Wingate on 26 February 1903 could hardly have been more dramatic. Stationed at Naini Tal about 140 miles north east of Delhi, in the Himalayan foothills and far from any specialist medical help, Colonel Wingate had sent cables requesting prayers for his wife during her confinement. This passed fairly easily, but was followed by a dangerous and alarming haemorrhage which could not be staunched. During the following night she lay like a corpse for hours at a time, and then in desperation Colonel Wingate suggested a hypodermic injection, and the doctor agreed. At about 4am, the Colonel noted a slight change, and 'knew his prayers had been answered'. (Letter from Colonel Wingate to Mrs Orde-Browne, 3 March 1903. Wingate Family Papers)

In July 1903, after the mother and baby had slowly recovered, the Wingate family with the infant Orde had leave in London, and then in February 1904 returned to India, leaving two girls and the baby with the Orde-Browne family at Blackheath. The following year, Colonel Wingate retired and was fortunate to receive a substantial pension which was nearly equal to his pay. He and his wife, though both devout Plymouth Brethren, were very different in character – he appears to have been dour and rather grim, while she was highly intelligent, cheerful and affectionate.

The family lived for some time in Worthing and Reigate, and the family papers give fascinating glimpses of a large and boisterous family – four girls and three boys. Although they were reasonably well-off, they lived frugally since the parents spent much of their time and money on missionary enterprises – especially the Central Asian Mission which Colonel Wingate founded. They also wrote and edited missionary magazines. It appears that because of the parents' strict beliefs, the family were deliberately kept away from other children, and from the dangerous influence of the outside world. Until he was 12 years old, Orde had hardly ever mixed with children of his own age. His upbringing was harsh and Spartan, dominated by his dour and puritanical father, and he lived with a daily consciousness of hell-fire and eternal damnation. This may to some extent explain Orde's later rebellious attitude towards authority.

Initially the older children were taught by their mother, and were expected to pass on the teaching to the younger children, but they then progressed to a governess and to a succession of teachers from the local Reigate schools. Every day had a strict timetable of work, including music, and a much-travelled uncle insisted that the schoolroom was decorated with maps of the world. Most of Sunday was taken up with meetings of the Brethren and the study of the Bible, including reading the Old Testament and learning lengthy passages by heart. At first Orde's brothers and sisters were quicker than him at reading and learning, but when his sisters Rachel and Sybil teased him about this, it appeared to provoke him into furious effort, and his reading developed rapidly.

In their large house and rambling garden, isolated from other children, the young Wingates lived in a fantasy world peopled with figures they knew from mythology, Grimm's Fairy Tales, the Arabian Nights, and many bloodthirsty episodes of Scottish history. In these escapades Orde began to show the positive side of his character.

In order to prolong his control over their children – to keep the outside world at bay, and to prevent the undermining of their religious beliefs – Colonel Wingate moved the family to Godalming in 1914, so that Orde could go to Charterhouse School as a day boy. He spent four years there from 1916 to 1920, an outsider and a loner who made little impact. He took no part in games, which in itself set him apart, and on games afternoons he went to the school chapel and prayed. This was considered eccentric, if not positively unhealthy, and it all created an atmosphere in which Orde felt unhappy, isolated and persecuted. Colonel Wingate considered that attendance at school chapel might undermine Orde's strict Plymouth Brethren upbringing, and he had many clashes with the school authorities. To be a day boy at such a school and not to take part in games, virtually ensured that Orde would be cut off from most of the benefits of the public school education of the period, and would become increasingly separate and alone. From his time at Charterhouse there emerges a picture of a lonely unhappy boy who did not share in any of the friendship or comradeship of the school, who developed a sense of antagonism to the normal groups among his peers, and who was too ready to challenge authority.

The only relief from the grim atmosphere of school seems to have been the frequent weekend cycling expeditions which his father led in the pleasant country around Godalming. These outings always had a serious object in view, such as a study of a Norman church and its history. Similarly, during family holidays at the seaside, lazing about and idling were forbidden. Instead, the children were given challenging objectives to encourage independent thought, initiative and self-reliance. One of Orde's sisters believed that his later exploits stemmed from this early training.

He left Charterhouse and, following the family tradition of military service, went to the Royal Military Academy Woolwich in January 1921 to be trained for a commission in the Royal Artillery. Woolwich had all the customs and ethos of the public school writ large, and

Wingate was ill-prepared for it. Initially, he made a poor impression, being scruffy and lonely and, because he took no part in games, was once more dangerously isolated from his fellow cadets. A sympathetic and sensitive description of Wingate at Woolwich is given by Derek Tulloch, a fellow cadet, who became Wingate's closest friend and finally became second in command (2 i/c) to Wingate in the Chindits. (See Derek Tulloch, *Wingate in Peace and War*)

In the severe regime of the Military Academy, discipline was largely maintained by the cadets of the senior year, and especially the Senior Under Officers. They could award punishments like extra drill, 'Confined to Barracks', or loss of weekend leave, and under this system Wingate collected many penalties. His natural tendency to challenge rules he thought were stupid meant that at Woolwich he had a fairly torrid time. He would never compromise, as others did, and again he had the feeling that he was disliked and despised. A contemporary cadet said 'Wingate was surly, he failed to respond to any friendliness, refused to conform, and refused any imposed discipline – a very unattractive character'. (Quoted Tulloch, p21)

Towards the end of the first part of the course, Wingate was so certain that he would fail the examinations that he tried and succeeded in making himself so ill that he did miss them, and had to be put back a term on account of sickness – preferring this to the disgrace of actually failing. This proved to be a very difficult time for him – he was disturbed, unco-operative, and in a turmoil about the religion in which he had been brought up and against which he was now rebelling. Other cadets found this difficult to understand, thinking merely that he had been extremely crafty to get out of church parades on religious grounds.

During this period of loneliness and depression he was introduced to riding and he rapidly developed a passion for everything to do with horses. He seemed to have a natural skill and soon became a very fine rider. This gave his confidence a considerable boost, but it also led to an incident which had a permanent effect on his outlook, and which illustrates his stiff, unbending character and 'his ability to create violent antagonism against himself by his attitude to authority'. (Tulloch, p24)

This critical incident started with a quite trivial matter. All cadets had to march down to the stables for their riding sessions, and this Wingate frequently refused to do. On one occasion, when the squad of cadets reached the stables, Wingate was there, had chosen the best horse, and was already mounted. The cadets thought this was intolerable and must be stopped. The matter was referred to the Senior Under Officers (SUO) of the senior term – ie, the term from which he had just been dropped – who decided that Wingate must be 'run'. This was a brutal and rarely used custom, carried out with the knowledge of the Academy adjutant, in which the offending cadet was stripped naked and made to run the gauntlet of the senior term, who were armed with swagger sticks, and then hurled into a pond. The senior term, armed with their swagger sticks, reported to the rugby pitch after dinner that night and formed up in two lines facing inwards. Normally the victim ran desperately down the line of cadets, but Wingate, his eyes blazing, walked slowly down the line, almost daring them to hit him, and then jumped into the water. He gained considerable respect for his calm demeanour.

This incident proved a turning point for him. His own term resented the way he had been treated by the seniors, wrecked the rooms of those they thought were responsible, and thereafter accorded him greater respect and comradeship. The Commandant reprimanded him severely for his idleness, his scruffiness, and his generally unco-operative attitude, and threatened him with expulsion. This, coming at the same time as the 'run', seems to have changed his outlook. Until then he had wasted a lot of time reading trashy novels and thrillers. He now destroyed all of these and devoted himself to military studies, to history, philosophy and economics. The main motive for this sudden change seems to have been his humiliation by the mob, which gave him a fierce determination to gain a position of power to prevent such a thing ever happening again. It also coloured his general attitude to life, and gave him a strong bond with the underdog. For the rest of the course at Woolwich he progressed reasonably well, though without any great success except at riding. Even so, a cadet who shared a room with him said 'I found him odd, anti-social... and out of tune with the rest of us'.

In August 1923 he passed out of Woolwich and was posted to the 5th Medium Brigade at Larkhill on Salisbury Plain. This was the start of the happiest and most carefree period of his life. He joined a happy and relaxed Mess where he took part in normal Mess functions, and the usual high-jinks of 'dinner-nights'. He very rapidly became involved with everything to do with horses, but also set himself a big programme of serious reading and music. A bookshop bill in 1925 shows that he had bought *War and Peace*, Shaw's *Arms and the Man*, the *Communist Manifesto*, and a book on Birth Control (Wingate Papers) – an avant-garde choice for an officer of that time.

Horses became his main interest and he was soon in the position to benefit from the army rule that if an officer owned a horse it could have free forage. An aunt left him a legacy (about £2,000) and soon afterwards he sent his groom to the west of Ireland to bring back a horse called Tatters that had been recommended. This horse was a tremendous success and soon Wingate was involved in hunting with South and West Wiltshire Foxhounds, with the Portman Hunt, and also in point-to-point races. In his first race on Tatters he won at 15 to 1. Ever the loner, he quickly gained the reputation for his skill during hunting, in finding his way across country, and particularly for finding suitable places to cross rivers. This earned him a nickname of 'The Otter', and it was a skill he used to good effect in later years in leading his columns over the Chindwin, the Irrawaddy and the Shweli rivers.

His parents were aware of the religious turmoil he had faced, and of his rejection of many of the Brethren's precepts, and his prowess at point-to-point exacerbated their differences. He took many tumbles, both in hunting and racing, and one of these was reported in the *Daily Mirror*. His father wrote 'It is a very unfortunate incident – Is it a warning from God? You have been brought up in the fear and nurture of the Lord. The fear of the Lord is the beginning of wisdom. Can you cut out horse-racing for ever. As a Christian it is the only safe thing to do. This time, in answer to our prayers, you have escaped – next time it may be a broken leg or concussion of the brain or something that will disable you for life.'

His mother, illustrating some other attitudes of the day, expressed her concern over the way he handled his money, because she feared that a Labour government would bring up men from the ranks and the future of existing officers might be in jeopardy. She, too, linked this fear to the religious theme. 'If your confidence was in the Lord I should feel easy, but what if he purposely lets you down to teach you your need of him?'. His father continued the gloomy political-religious theme in a letter of June 1926, 'Terrible judgements have fallen on Russia for her wicked persecution of the Jews, and so will judgements fall on England for turning back from the gospel lights to Roman Catholicism on the one hand and to communistic socialism on the other'. (Wingate Papers) These few quotations give a clear indication of the very strong and unusual religious pressure which was exerted on Wingate during the whole of his upbringing, and which continued even when he was an officer in his twenties. This, together with the grim curtailment of any social intercourse with youngsters of his own age, explains why he had such a difficult time at Charterhouse and Woolwich, and why he developed such a rebellious attitude towards authority.

His private letters at this time throw an interesting light on his life. The majority concern hunting, horses, dogs, dances and race meetings, but there are several concerning the Officer's Christian Union, and many dealing with money. In some ways he was generous. He offered to buy his sister a dress, and she wrote back to thank him, and to say it was £3 15/- and could she have it by return of post. He also sent some money to help his brother Nigel, who had gone up to Pembroke College Cambridge. A Sergeant Evans returned a loan of £5 from Peshawar; another sad letter was an appeal for help from a soldier who had been wounded, and then on leaving hospital was starving and stole a purse to buy food. He was arrested, was given six months in prison, and on his release was destitute again. He longed to get to India, because he had a good knowledge of Hindustani.

It was difficult in the 1920s for an officer to live on his pay, and Wingate's legacy was modest compared with most of his fellow officers. Surprisingly, he kept a large number of letters dealing with unpaid bills and demands for settlement. Phrases like 'much overdue', 'not the first time', or, from a letter to his CO, 'I can't get any money out of Wingate', constantly recur in demands from hotels, from the NAAFI, gramophone record suppliers, garages, and riding equipment shops. He appeared to be in fairly frequent trouble for not paying his Mess bill, and on one occasion was fined £1 by his CO for not paying on time. This is a picture of a young man whose social life and his passion for hunting and riding overstretched his finances, but who probably shared the view of his contemporaries that tradesmen could always be kept waiting.

Wingate's passion for hunting, and another important aspect of his mercurial character, are illustrated in a remarkable letter he wrote to an evangelical clergyman Dr Fothergill, explaining how he felt when he awoke at the start of a day's hunting:

'"Today" I said to my soul "You will forget this tawdry life of reality, this vulgar present, this banal undistinguished existence, for ever crowding with such trivialities as Liberty, Fraternity, Equality, humanity, evangelicanism, the dictatorship of the proletariat, and other dreary coarseness. Today, in the only world I will admit to be real, the world of dreams, of fancies, of departed glories, in this world in which we all have so much more power than in the one called real... Today I shall be like a God".'

He then describes riding to the meet, and concludes:

'And here were all sorts of departed glories – the glories of feudalism, of descent, of inheritance, of name and place brought high for today. Begone foul plebian, here is no place for you.' [Undated letter, Wingate Papers]

This remarkable mixture of arrogance and fantasy is a good indication of the restless imagination which he later harnessed to military issues.

Because of his outstanding prowess at riding, he was posted in January 1926 to the Military School of Equitation at Weedon in Buckinghamshire (considered one of the best equitation centres in the country. Here Wingate showed his rebellious side, frequently challenged the instructors and, to their chagrin, excelled at all he did – including a clear round on a specially constructed Olympic course. To the majority of the cavalry officers at the centre he was insufferable, boring them with long speeches about Karl Marx and arguments about communism, and showing off his superior knowledge and practice of equitation. Even when passing out in July 1926 he snubbed the Commandant – saying he intended to specialise in motor transport.

As he achieved more success in his military career, so his relationships generally improved. He corresponded cheerfully with his sister Rachel who was a missionary in Chinese Turkestan, and with his sister Monica and brother Nigel who were both up at Cambridge. His links with his parents, too, gradually improved.

Having excelled at Weedon, Wingate returned to his unit, but the attraction of endless days of hunting and riding seem to have palled and soon after his return he went to see Sir Reginald Wingate, formerly Governor-General of the Sudan and High Commissioner of Egypt, who was his father's cousin. Known to the family as 'Cousin Rex', he was to have considerable influence over Wingate at a fairly critical stage of his career. He gave him a positive interest in Middle Eastern affairs and in Arabic, and as a result of this Wingate successfully applied to take a course in Arabic at the School of Oriental and African Studies in London.

His stay in London seems to have been fairly relaxed although he worked extremely hard throughout the course, from October 1926 to March 1927, passing out with a mark of 85 per cent. He had lodgings with some fellow students first in Holborn and then in Camden, and lived a fairly quiet life except for an occasional outburst when, for example, he chased another officer up the down escalator at Piccadilly Circus, and was reprimanded by the GOC London District. He did so well at his Arabic studies that he was encouraged to obtain a posting where he could put his Arabic to good use, and perhaps obtain an Army interpretership. Here again Cousin Rex proved useful. Acting on his advice – and to some extent with his backing – in June 1927 Wingate obtained six months leave, in order to mount an expedition in the Sudan. Cousin Rex advised him to travel to Cairo, obtain travel facilities to visit Khartoum, and then try to obtain secondment to the Sudan Defence Force. (Wingate Papers) Thus by 1927 he had established himself as an able and enterprising officer, and he was about to embark on a challenging expedition.

2
The Sudan Experience

The help and advice of Cousin Rex, who as a former Governor-General still had numerous high-level contacts, enabled Wingate to proceed rapidly with his plans for a period of service in the Sudan, and in September 1927 he started his journey. He rejected the idea of going by boat or train and, instead, sent his luggage to Cairo, and then set off across Europe by bicycle. He had an eventful journey. After crossing France and southern Germany fairly rapidly – sometimes covering 70 miles in a day – he was robbed in Czechoslovakia, arrested in Vienna, and delayed by inefficient bureaucracy in Yugoslavia, where he eventually disposed of his bicycle for £5. With his usual colourful and arrogant views, he described slavonic officials as 'Dilatory, stupid, ignorant, self-important, and inefficient'.

He sailed from Genoa to Egypt, and then spent 10 days in Cairo before travelling down to Khartoum. He had no wish to join in the social activities of Khartoum, where little Arabic would be spoken, and he was delighted when he was able to spend some time with Vicar Miles, a District Commissioner in an isolated station. Miles found him a rather odd character, who seemed to challenge all the accepted ideas of the time, sometimes it seemed just for the pleasure of an argument. On one occasion Miles found Wingate sitting in the sun, claiming that he was testing his endurance – needless to say he was very badly burned and took several days to recover. While Miles enjoyed the arguments and the usual smile with which they concluded, two young colleagues in the station found him insufferable. (Christopher Sykes, *Orde Wingate*, p61)

Before he left England he had applied for a transfer from his regiment, and in April 1928 he was posted to the Sudan Defence Force where he was sent to The East Arab Corps to serve in the area of Roseires and Gallabat on the borders of Ethiopia – to which he was to return in 1940. He was to spend six years with the Sudan Defence Force, and used his time profitably. In the following year, 1929, he returned to England on leave and qualified as a first-class interpreter in

Arabic, which meant an increase in pay of £120 per year while serving in Arab countries.

He gained promotion in March 1930, when he was given command of a company, with the local rank of Bimbashi or major; he was now 26 years old. He commanded 300 well-trained soldiers, mostly Muslims from the Eastern Sudan, and he revelled in training and looking after these men and their families. He had very substantial powers, including the award of 25 lashes with a rhinoceros hide whip, 30 days solitary confinement, or 30 days loss of pay. He had his own slightly eccentric views on command and discipline . When two soldiers quarrelled over a woman, and one found the other asleep and hit him. The man died, but Wingate refused to send the culprit for trial with all the legal complications that would ensue, largely because he had a real horror of imprisonment for these primitive people.

His unit was stationed near Gallabat, and he frequently went into Ethiopia, where he became particularly interested in the Ethiopian people and their history, with its mixed Jewish and Christian background. His main responsibility was dealing with elephant poachers, and this occasionally led to armed clashes.

His diary recorded his shock when in a skirmish with a gang of poachers, for the first time in his life he saw a man killed, an incident which upset him profoundly. Unlike many young officers, he had a deeply spiritual side to his nature, and pondered at length about the meaning of life, about man's relation with God, and about death. This sombre side of his character was highlighted when he received news from home of the death of his sister Constance, which seriously depressed him. From time to time he became obsessed with the question of death. Sometime later, when he was on leave in London, he went to a film in which the hero – called Wingate – died a violent death. He left the cinema and was violently sick, and he confided to his girl friend that he had a foreboding that he would die a violent death. (Sykes, p70)

He enjoyed a period of extreme contentment when he was away in the bush with his own unit, for which he used his imagination to devise challenging training schemes, but when he had to be in the HQ Mess in Khartoum he tended to antagonise the other officers by his aggressive and argumentative ways. On one occasion his CO warned him that he must stop arguing about communism and 'other destructive ideas', or he would be sent back to his regiment with an adverse report. Wingate accepted the rebuke.

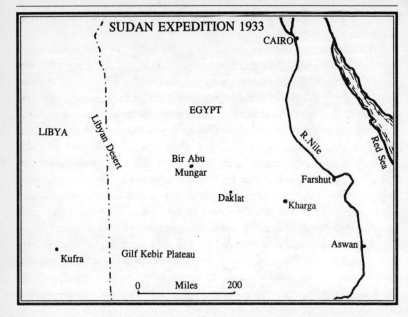

At the beginning of 1932 he planned an expedition into the Libyan desert, with two aims: to investigate the lost army of Cambyses – an army of 10,000 men engulfed by a sandstorm in 500BC – which was mentioned by Herodotus; and secondly, to seek for the lost oasis of Zerzura. For centuries Arabic sources had mentioned this oasis lying well to the west of the Nile, with green vegetation, sweet water and a great white city. That type of myth was common because sudden heavy rains in the desert did produce a brilliant growth of greenery and flowers which subsequently disappeared.

At this stage Cousin Rex again provided help and advice. He put Wingate in touch with Dr Bermann an Austrian archaeologist who was also planning an expedition into the desert, and who advised him to join up with the Austrian group in view of the danger of desert travel. The Austrians were investigating the possibility of basing their expedition on motor transport, but Wingate who had already decided to use camels, decided to go his own way. Then the whole project seemed to be in jeopardy when the Sudan Defence Force refused their permission, but again, through the good offices of Cousin Rex, they agreed. Wingate had planned his expedition very carefully, and was supported with equipment from the Royal Geographical Society, and from the

Sudan Survey Department. He even adapted a bicycle wheel as a mileometer to check the distances.

His expedition left Khartoum in January 1933, going north by train as far as Farshut, on the Nile. (Later he wrote an article for the *Royal Geographical Magazine*, April 1934, and most of the available detail for this expedition comes from that.) From Farshut he travelled westwards in a motorised trolley, the speed of which petrified him. From there he went on to Daklat which was on the edge of the Libyan Desert, where he met his guide and three companions, and the 13 camels he had hired. Some of the men were physically unsuitable for such an expedition, and the camels were not the type he had asked for. However, stuck on the edge of the desert he had no chance to change either of them, and had just to make the best of it.

For travelling, Wingate wore bush shirt and shorts, covered by a long Arab robe or gibbah, sandals and a turban. His sparse diet included dried dates, biscuits, cod–liver oil and a good supply of local grown oranges – bought at 100 for two shillings. He took three blankets, but found that the nights were bitterly cold, and at night he wore everything he possessed.

He immediately established a severe regime, and despite strong grumbles, he determined to travel by day in order to see and survey the country both for the Sudan authorities and for the RGS – normally, because of the intense heat groups travelled at night and navigated by the stars. From Daklat, he travelled westwards, and reached Bir Abu Mungar where he established a dump of food and water ready for the return journey. From there he led the expedition southwest towards Kufra through a bleak, grey and desolate landscape, which he described like being on the moon.

He had amazing powers of observation, and his journal is full of acute descriptions of the landscape, the soil, the rocks, the birds and any type of vegetation, and even the sand. While traversing the moonscape he noticed that there were fissures in the rock, and in these there were often small shrubs which were usually dead and made very good kindling for their fires. During this long and arduous march, he kept going on a diet of biscuits, oranges and cod-liver oil, and for the inevitable blisters on his feet he merely used Vaseline.

As they approached the area where he thought they might find the oasis of Zerzura, the party was hit by a severe sandstorm, and his companions told him the spirits of the place were warning them to keep away. They found nothing, and started their return journey, happy for the storm to have blown itself out. After a succession of long and difficult marches, on one day they thought they saw a herd of antelope, but this turned out to be a flock of crested cranes. On this part of the journey, too, they were tormented by hordes of rats which appeared well-fed and fat, and which his companions ate and pronounced as 'tasty'. Wingate could never work out how, in such an isolated area in the desert, they could find enough to eat, let alone grow fat.

After more days of gruelling marches they noticed something strange in the desert, and it turned out to be a motorcar. What a sense of humiliation and anti-climax! Wingate described it as 'the hated symbol of civilisation', but he was not seriously put out by this, for the search for Zerzura was only a part of his scheme. It was far more important as an opportunity to test himself in terms of physical endurance, and powers of organisation and leadership.

The party returned safely to base and Wingate went off to Cairo where he stayed with friends for several days. He was excellent company – bubbling over with vivid descriptions of his experiences in the desert. In his report he wrote 'no-one going forth in the spirit of adventure has found more joy and delight in the fulfilment of his enterprise, than I did in the failure of mine'. His report also dealt at some length with the important issue of the development of motor transport and the need to adapt both wheels and tyres to desert conditions, but also commented on the use of camels and the necessity of having the right type of camel, and the right type of pack saddle. He had been unfortunate in the supply of camels for his expedition, and his final comment was that the camels were 'an unfailing source of irritation'. His expedition had given him both experience and information which was to prove invaluable in future years.

3
Wingate in Palestine

The Special Night Squads

When Wingate was studying Arabic in London he had met Peggy Jolly and they had a warm and affectionate relationship. She was a calm and cheerful girl, and very different in character to him. Although they enjoyed deep and serious discussions she was aware of the melancholy side of his nature, and his occasional depression because he felt that he had not found a real cause to fight for. They were planning to marry when he returned to England after his service in the Sudan.

He sailed from Egypt in March 1933 and on the ship he met a Mrs Patterson and her daughter Lorna, who was 16. Some people thought the mother had fallen for him, but he and Lorna fell deeply in love. When he reached home he met Peggy. He looked absolutely wretched and she asked him if he had fallen in love with someone else. Acutely embarrassed, he admitted it, and she agreed they should part.

He was posted to Bulford on Salisbury Plain as a lieutenant and became heavily involved in retraining, as all artillery units were then being mechanised. He became messing officer and tried actively to wean men off meat and pudding, and convert them to fruit and vegetables. He also campaigned for more married quarters, so that men would give up homosexuality and brothel visiting, and VD would be reduced.

Two years later, on 24 January 1935, he and Lorna were married in Chelsea. They had a brief honeymoon in Devon and then moved to a spacious married quarter in Bulford. They lived here for nearly a year, leaving the domestic affairs to a servant and batman while leading a highly Bohemian life, and engaging in frequent spirited discussions on books, art, music and philosophy. Their household included a baboon bought from Harrods. At this time Wingate also returned to his love of horses and kept a favourite called Hannibal.

At the end of 1935 he was posted as adjutant and acting captain to a TA battery in Sheffield. The Wingates enjoyed their stay in Sheffield more than they had expected, and discovered a real empathy with the local people who were suffering dire poverty. That year he qualified for Staff College by examination, but was not nominated. Shortly after, when the Chief of the Imperial General Staff (CIGS) attended an exercise near Sheffield, Wingate strode up to him, ascertained that he was the Chairman of the Staff College selection committee, and referred to his Arabic qualification, his Sudan service, and his desert expedition. This did not result in a place at Staff College, but obtained a posting as Intelligence Officer to the 5th Division, about to leave for Haifa. They sailed in September 1936.

Captain Wingate, recognised as an Arabic expert, arrived in Palestine in September 1936, with HQ 5 Infantry Division. During that year, the Arab Revolt had resulted in over 300 people

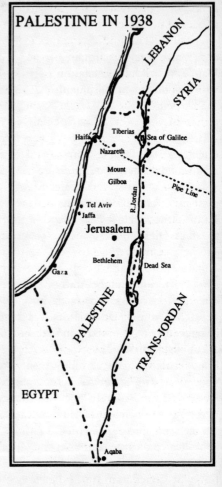

PALESTINE IN 1938

being killed in Palestine, but the British military action against this uprising proved to be ponderous and ineffective, even though there were two infantry divisions in the country.

Soon after his arrival in the country, he wrote home to his mother, 'it is amazing what the Jews have done... the desert really begins to blossom like a rose'. He wrote a lyrical description of the countryside and the wonderful flowers. He described his stay in a kibbutz, and how he had visited the Jordan Valley, Nazareth, the beautiful little town of Tiberias, and the Sea of Galilee where he saw fishermen pulling in their nets. For a man who knew much of the Old Testament by heart the impact of these visits was overwhelming.

The background to the problems then facing Palestine lay in the conflicting promises Britain had made at the end of the First World War. The Balfour Declaration of 1917 had stated that Britain viewed with favour the establishment in Palestine of a National Home for the Jewish people, but added that nothing should be done to prejudice the rights of the existing non-Jewish communities. At the same time, because of Lawrence's work with the Arabs, and their success in driving out the Turks, Britain promised the Arabs control of most of the area reconquered; then under pressure from France, it decided to divide the area up into 'Mandates', under French and British control. After such duplicity, it is not surprising that there are problems in the Middle East. Initially, the British Mandate in Palestine succeeded and under the first High Commissioner, Sir Herbert Samuel, supported by the wise and restrained counsel of Chaim Weizmann who had initiated the Balfour Declaration, the country enjoyed several years of growth and prosperity. A few minor Arab uprisings took place, but generally things remained peaceful and prosperous.

The Balfour Declaration had not envisaged large scale Jewish immigration to Palestine, but the situation changed dramatically after 1933 when Hitler came to power in Germany. The number of Jewish immigrants then increased to tens of thousands, and above all they needed land. The Jews saw land as the foundation of their Home-land, while in contrast, the Arab landowners were always ready to make the most of a seller's market. Often an absentee Arab landlord would sell land to a Jewish organisation, and then evict the existing Arab tenants from land they had lived on for generations. Fierce antagonisms soon grew up, and by 1936 Arab terrorists were making frequent attacks on Jewish settlements. From Syria, Arab leaders, helped by the exiled Mufti of Jerusalem, and by the increasing support of Axis agents, directed the attacks. The British tried to pacify the situation by establishing a Legislative Council, with a ratio of two to one in favour of the Arab population, but the Jews, not surprisingly, rejected this as it would place them in a permanent minority. Arab attacks increased rapidly during 1936, and night after night the crops and cattle of the Jewish settlers in the rural areas were destroyed. Even Arab headmen who held out against violence were themselves assassinated.

The British administration, backed up by the 5th and 8th Infantry Divisions, with 30,000 men, seemed powerless to prevent the regular atrocities, in spite of a policy of internment, collective fines, curfews, and virtual martial law. The Arabs, normally operating at night, would attack a Jewish settlement or ambush a police or army convoy. The army would then bring up reinforcements by road, or call for air support, but by the time either of these materialised the Arabs had melted away into the dark and, if a search was made, they appeared as normal peasants in their homes. Because of the sympathy of most Arabs for their cause, the Arab terrorists nearly always knew in advance when a British patrol was going out, and they knew too that it would never leave the road.

Although most of the action by British units took place against Arab attackers, British officers and soldiers alike tended to have a general sympathy for the Arabs, whom they saw as being dispossessed of their land by the Jews who had powerful and wealthy backers. One British officer at the time spoke of the almost total ignorance of both officers and men about the political issues of the day. In this situation, Wingate, who at school and in his early days in the army had had experience of being spurned and shunned, began to feel an affinity for the Jews and for the Zionist cause. 'He needed to follow the lone path which fitted to his strange combative character.' (Sykes, p110)

He soon got to know some distinguished leaders in the Jewish community, but many of them initially were surprised or even suspicious of his extreme views. Meetings were arranged with the leaders of Hagana, the Jewish underground movement, which at the time was pursuing a policy of cautious restraint, and they refused to believe that a serving British officer could possibly be a Zionist. They remained highly suspicious of him even though he could quote the Bible in Hebrew and the Koran in Arabic. Helped by friends who believed that his interest was genuine, he frequently stayed at an orthodox Jewish settlement near the Sea of Galilee, and here he absorbed more of their language, their faith, and their way of life. Once on a car journey, in a state of great excitement, he started criticising Saul for the way he handled his armies on the very spot they were passing.

Throughout his life, wherever he went Wingate seemed to have high-level contacts – encouraged initially in this field by Cousin Rex – and in November 1936, he and his wife Lorna were invited to dinner at the British High Commissioner's residence; unusual, surely, for a newly arrived young captain. At that dinner party, the Wingates met Chaim Weizmann, the long established leader of the Jewish Agency, and this started a long, deep and affectionate friendship which had significant results for the Zionist cause.

Wingate's intellectual powers were always remarkable, and they were illustrated again when in January 1937, after only a few months in Palestine, he wrote to his Cousin Rex giving what was a brilliant – but clearly an arrogant and biased – view of the whole Palestinian situation. He argued first that the High Commissioner was hopeless and should be removed; the British staff were pro-Arab, third-rate, and knew neither Hebrew nor Arabic; and the Arab revolt had been mishandled by official dithering. In contrast, the Jewish achievement was fantastic, 'such energy, faith, ability and inventiveness as the world has not seen, and they have been loyal throughout the uprising'. He believed the Arab states were not really concerned about Palestine, and their military power was negligible; if Transjordan supported the revolt 'the corrupt and slovenly Abdullah' should be removed and the country taken over; on the other hand if the Jewish people were armed and trained, it would be worth two Army Corps to Britain.

He outlined what he thought should be done: Britain should admit that bad administration caused the revolt. Then the Government should settle all land disputes, guarantee the economic future of the Arabs in Palestine, and guarantee in perpetuity the Holy Places of Islam.

Next, the Government should recognise the right of the Jews to migrate to Palestine, recognise Palestine as the National Home for the Jewish people, and forthwith should arm the Jews, and raise two Jewish brigades for the internal and external defence of Palestine. 'If we do this we shall secure Palestine for the Empire, and the Empire for the world. A war is coming and for pity's sake let us do something just and honourable before it comes. Let us redeem our promises to Jewry, and shame the devil of Nazism, Fascism, and our own prejudices.' (Wingate Papers)

This letter showed a clear grasp of the political and military issues facing Palestine, and shows how completely Wingate supported the Zionist cause. He spent most of 1937, still as an Intelligence Officer, but in Jerusalem where he and his wife rented a flat. He worked incessantly, building up his knowledge of the country, running courses – for which he was commended – and establishing many contacts. He spent much time at the Weizmann's home at Rehavia near Tel Aviv, and he met Ben Gurion; but he also studied the Arab cause and visited Abdullah, about whom he had been so dismissive and insulting.

During 1937, a Royal Commission under Lord Peel had been investigating the problems of Palestine and in June 1937 its report recommended the division of Palestine into British, Jewish and Arab zones. The Jews, with wider aims, were aghast at this, though Weizmann persuaded the Zionist Congress to accept it; most Arab leaders, except Abdullah, rejected it out of hand.

So often Wingate's incisive mind grasped military situations well ahead of all contemporaries – here, in Ethiopia and in Burma – and his ideas were already racing ahead of events; with monumental indiscretion – to say nothing of disloyalty and insubordination – he offered his services to Weizmann to organise and command an underground force, to become the nucleus of a Jewish Defence Force. Fortunately, Weizmann was totally discreet and totally loyal to his passionate young protégé and managed to dissuade him, but this incident does illustrate the lines on which Wingate's ideas were developing. In his defence it could be argued that there was a similar situation in Transjordan, where there was an Arab force commanded by British officers.

After the publication of the Peel Report, both sides bided their time until in September 1937 Arab terrorists murdered a senior British official, and this heralded a new phase of the revolt. The British administration closed the Arab Council, deported several members, and proclaimed Martial Law. From Syria, the Arabs – led by Fawsi Kawakji – responded by stepping up their vicious raids on Jewish settlements, and by frequently ambushing the police and military as they lumbered up the roads.

At this critical moment in Wingate's life, General Wavell took over the command in Palestine. In this and in the two remaining phases of Wingate's career, Wavell was to play a decisive role. Now, when he had hardly arrived in the country, Wingate put forward plans to curb the raiding parties and arms smugglers who came into Palestine over mountain tracks from Syria. Fortunately, his views were supported by the commander of 16 Infantry Brigade, Brigadier Evetts.

Wingate followed up these proposals by writing a document entitled 'The Jewish State', in which he set out a detailed plan embracing almost every aspect of an independent Jewish State. In this plan he suggested that the first priority must be to make the Jewish settlers in the rural areas feel secure – especially in Galilee – and he used the phrase 'until a full exchange of population has been effected'. He emphasised the need for good intelligence, and for defence by local militia linked to Frontier Guards and a Jewish State Defence Force.

The basis of his whole scheme was the local militia in which every able-bodied Jew living within 10 miles of a frontier – that covered a large part of Palestine – should be taught to use a rifle, to fight as a member of a rifle section, and to be issued with a rifle and 50 rounds of ammunition. Based on the British infantry pattern, they would be organised into sections of seven, linked to platoons and companies in the larger settlements. He argued that the certainty of speedy assistance 'would give security and make everyone self-reliant and confident of their ability to defend their homes'.

Above the local militia, he planned the Jewish Frontier Guard, comprising battalions of eight companies 100-strong, armed with rifles, light machine guns, and provided with Ford trucks for mobility. The Frontier Guards would be based on carefully sited blockhouses,

built with old petrol tins filled with sand – all accomplished by voluntary labour. At the top of the defence pyramid would be the Jewish Defence Force with its HQ at Mount Carmel, which was close to Haifa, close to the threatened pipeline, and which had large caves for defence against air attack. The main purpose of all these plans was to provide a cadre ready for rapid expansion. Further plans included air defence and anti-gas provision, the encouragement of civil aviation to ensure a supply of pilots, the enrolment of women, and the establishment of a steel industry helped by experts brought from Sheffield. (Original MS Hagana Museum Tel-Aviv)

This remarkable document is the earliest indication of Wingate's ability to grasp the widest strategic concepts and at the same time to plan down to the smallest detail – like filling the petrol tins for the blockhouses. Here were the original ideas for guerrilla warfare, hammered out in a war situation, which came to fruition in his detailed plans for the two Chindit expeditions.

With the tacit approval of both Wavell and the brigade commander Evetts, in February 1938 Wingate was posted to 16 Infantry Brigade in North Palestine with a fairly open brief to investigate the way Arab infiltrators came in from Syria to attack the oil pipeline and the Jewish settlements in the area of Galilee, Jordan and the Plain of Esdraelon. At the same time he badgered the Jewish leaders and Jewish settlers to believe in him and to take a more positive and aggressive attitude to their own defence. He made his base at Tirat Tsevi, about 20 miles south of the Sea of Galilee. Here he first had the opportunity to put his ideas into practice. He spent weeks vigorously exploring the wild country along the border, and checking on paths and tracks which the terrorists might use. Arab attacks on isolated rural Jewish settlements continued and these Wingate determined to eradicate.

He proposed to Brigadier Evetts that to counter Arab terrorism he would organise patrols at night which would operate from the Jewish settlements, and would be made up of Jewish supernumerary constables with a stiffening of British officers and NCOs. This revolutionary proposal received a scathing response from the staff at GHQ. Then Wingate, with his usual sound intelligence and unorthodox methods (repeating his technique with the CIGS) ascertained the proposed time of a visit by Wavell to the north, calmly stopped his car, jumped in, and put his proposal forward. Wavell agreed, to the fury and consternation of those who disagreed.

Having surmounted this hurdle, Wingate still had a difficult struggle to obtain support on the Jewish side. Decades of suspicion could not be easily overcome, and although he had the constant support of Weizmann, and of another powerful leader Wilenski, there were many who were very strongly opposed to him. Most still supported the current Zionist policy of restraint, which sought to live in peace with their Arab neighbours. He approached the Jewish underground organisation Hagana to let him have their best trained men, but the idea of co-operating with the British army was anathema to their leaders, and they refused. This so enraged Wingate, that he went to the head of the Jewish Agency in Jerusalem, and shouted at him 'why do you flirt with your enemies and ignore your friends?'. Surprisingly, this outburst seems to have convinced them and after it Hagana agreed to help, though in many of the settlements there remained deep suspicion of this eccentric Englishman, who did not behave or dress like an officer, and who was always wandering off alone into the wild hill country along the border. They wondered if he could really be trusted.

In April 1938 Wingate went on a tour to Hanita, a settlement nearly on the border of the Lebanon, which had suffered frequent Arab attacks. He severely criticised their defence plans and proposed that, instead of allowing themselves to be cooped up inside their village, they should go out and meet their enemy in the open. He then took several of their leaders out on a patrol with him and they were deeply impressed with his toughness, bravery and resolution. While he was at Hanita, the Arabs made an attack and killed two settlers, but he took charge of the defence and drove off the attackers.

By May 1938 several significant developments had taken place. The British forces had been substantially reduced, and General Haining had replaced Wavell. Because he had fewer troops available, Haining altered the policy and instead of mounting mobile military patrols, he established standing pickets in the more populous areas. This new policy fitted in reasonably well with Wingate's ideas and in May 1938 Haining agreed to the plans for the Special Night Squads. This was an absolutely crucial decision for Wingate, and he now came under the direct command of Brigadier Evetts. He was able to devote himself entirely to organising the Special Night Squads, with the help of volunteers from the three battalions of 16 Brigade – The Royal Ulster Rifles, The Royal West Kents and The Manchester Regiment. At the same time, the Arab terrorists had started blowing up the oil pipeline to

Haifa and Wingate therefore set up his base at Ein Harod, which had a good supply of water and was fairly close to the pipeline.

Wingate's detailed, original and vivid ideas are illustrated from another document drawn from the Hagana Museum in Tel-Aviv, and entitled 'Principles Governing the Employment of Special Night Squads'. This document again shows his amazing attention to detail and his practical grasp of the principles of war, which he was later to prove to the world in the Chindit expeditions.

The squads, including the cadre of British officers and NCOs, were to be based in the Jewish settlements. The first aim of the Special Night Squads (SNS) was to train the supernumeraries, who were admirable material – fit, young, intelligent and determined. Training started with the use of rifle, bayonet and grenade, training in cross-country movement by night, and training in the role of section commanders, since in spite of the volunteers' enthusiasm they had no military experience. One British cadre was expected to give basic training to two Jewish squads of supernumeraries within a week. After training, it was hoped that in every group of colonies there would be squads capable of moving by night, able to destroy a superior force of enemy, and by observing good discipline carry out orders to the letter.

All the squads were given detailed instructions about movement: aim to mislead the enemy; any movement noted by an Arab will be passed on to the enemy – therefore use this to spread deception; movement along tracks will be noted, so cross-country movement is essential; open movement from police and military bases must be used to deceive and confuse the enemy; all squads must be trained to drop off slow moving vehicles and reassemble at an RV; after a patrol the SNS should make its presence felt and show that it upholds law and order. Kit must be kept to a minimum – light rubber-soled boots, woollen socks, and peasant clothes; every SNS must be able to cover 15 miles cross-country at night. Each man to carry rifle, bayonet and 50 rounds, but two men in each squad to carry three bombs (grenades). Firm discipline is necessary in order to kill enemy gangs in night encounters, preferably with bomb and bayonet, and not wild firing. 'Well disciplined squads must seek opportunity to assault the enemy and turn the tables on the enemy gangs.'

Wingate was extremely – and perhaps unfairly – critical of British tactics. Arab gangs often ambushed police or military patrols and, through their informers in offices and barracks, always knew when an action was planned. They usually mounted an ambush in a hilly area and the patrol would leave the road and take cover. It would then call for air support which came fairly quickly, but the terrorists could easily melt away among the hills and were hardly ever caught because the patrols rarely followed up an air strike. Perhaps Wingate's brilliant and original use of air power with the Chindits had its foundation here, when he criticised the system of air support for the army. He said 'the way air power is used has a bad effect on the initiative and gumption of the troops'. He argued that the successful round-up of an Arab gang on the ground was 10 times more effective than sporadic air action, and pointed out that police and troops never moved off the roads at night, and the police hardly ever left their barracks at all. While the Arabs through their informers always knew in advance about any action to be taken against them, the British had totally failed to use the support of the loyal Jewish population. In contrast, Wingate proposed to base the SNS in Jewish colonies, to dress as colonists, to operate secretly, to move across country at night, and to use all available intelligence.

At first, the squads operated in the area of the oil pipeline to Haifa. They gained surprise by travelling in civilian lorries, covered by tarpaulins, and all wearing blue peasant shirts. At dusk they would leave the settlement either by lorry or individually as if going out to guard their flocks or crops. They then met at an RV, moved off in silence and tried to use bayonet or bomb for any encounters. Each squad included an Arabic speaker and after an action they would visit the villages to explain that they were taking action to stop the terrorists. Many Arab villages approved of their action, and requested the help of the SNS against the terrorists. Because of the vague and unsubstantiated claims of the army against the terrorists, Wingate always insisted that the bodies of terrorists who were killed should be taken to the local police station.

In the initial training of the SNS, Wingate had the support of two young officers, King-Clark and Bredin (now Lieutenant-Colonel R. King-Clark, and Major General Bredin), who have recorded their experiences of these days on audio tapes at the Imperial War Museum. King-Clark described Wingate as a man with an iron constitution, with formidable will-power and determination, who kept going long after other men had stopped. He treated Arabs with courtesy and respect, and spoke to them in Arabic, but his sympathies were obviously all for the Zionist cause. Other officers felt uneasy in his presence because 'he was so intense, single-minded and commanding. He had our deep admiration and respect, but he did not have my liking.'

King-Clark described one of the new Jewish settlements at Afikim, where he was stationed. It resembled a wild west frontier fort, with a wooden stockade and a large main gate which was floodlit at night, and guarded by manned watchtowers. Life was communal and aimed to be self-supporting. Every morning workers went off to the fields, and children went to the crèche or to school. Everyone ate in the communal dining room, which also served as the community centre where all main issues were discussed, usually at great length. The settlers tended to keep the British officers at arm's length – concerned at the effect their presence might have – but although they could speak no English, they got on well with the English soldiers who helped enthusiastically to train the supernumeraries.

When a patrol went out, they wore khaki slacks or shorts, blue shirt, hockey boots and a bush hat. The patrol leader, who rarely used a compass, relied on maps and the position of known villages to guide him. One fairly typical patrol from these early days went out at dusk after some crops had been set alight. They did not find anyone, but visited a Bedouin camp where some shots were fired and some men ran off. The patrol searched the village and took three prisoners.

When the terrorists tried to sabotage the pipeline, they usually lit a small fire under the pipe and then punctured it with a rifle shot. Bredin, with his Royal Ulster Rifles volunteers, took a very tough line in protecting the pipeline and successfully kept the terrorists at bay. Anti-terrorist patrols were serious enough, but there were light-hearted moments. One patrol, after 20 miles of night marching without seeing any enemy activity, found a small fire by the pipeline and, with Wingate in the lead, put it out by peeing on it. After a patrol, King-Clark, who had his own car and aeroplane, would go off for lunch in the hotel and have a swim or a flight with his RAF friends. (See R. King-Clark, *Free for a Blast*, Chapter 5. Published 1988)

SNS patrols effectively got under way in June 1938 when there were six main actions, and patrols gradually gained in confidence from each success. In one of the early actions a patrol zigzagging along the pipeline came upon an Arab gang about to blow it up. The Arabs fled into a village, which was then surrounded by the SNS who killed two, wounded three, and captured six prisoners with a number of weapons. When on patrol, Wingate exacted a savage discipline, becoming furious with anyone who did not carry out an order, or who missed an RV through bad map reading. He often struck the offender, but back at base he would sit informally and chat – though he was more at ease with the Jews than the British.

By the end of June he had established an effective intelligence centre at Nazareth, and he received detailed reports from all over north Palestine. With this improved intelligence, the SNS were able to take on larger concentrations of terrorists and during July there were some serious engagements. On 5 July, Bredin with an SNS patrol came upon an enemy force of 100, and they opened fire. He divided his patrol into two and, giving each other covering fire, they advanced on the enemy who quickly ran away. This defeat of a fairly large Arab force prompted a reprisal and by 10 July several Arab groups had assembled in the area of Dabburiya – a village lying a few miles east of Nazareth towards Mount Tabor.

These events led up to the so-called battle of Dabburiyah on 10 July 1938. This clash illustrates some of the problems of giving accurate descriptions of battles. The generally accepted version, supported by Wingate's biographer of the 1950s Christopher Sykes, is roughly as follows: it was known that a fairly large Arab group had assembled in Dabburiyah and Wingate determined to attack them first. On 10 July he launched his attack, sending patrols out in different directions, and dropping them off in a circle around the village. These groups, armed with rifles, grenades, light machine guns (LMGs), and Lewis guns, moved to their allotted positions on the southern side. Wingate, with a force of about 50 –including the Royal Ulster Rifles and the Royal West Kents – prepared to attack at dawn from the north.

Some patrols lost their way, others blundered too far forward, alerted the enemy, and surprise was lost. Therefore, soon after midnight, Wingate was forced to make an immediate attack. Several more blunders were made in the ensuing chaos and several sections came under well-directed fire. Wingate's group got into the village but found themselves outnumbered and decided to withdraw. In the confusion of their withdrawal, they were fired on by one of their own patrols with a Lewis gun. There were casualties and Wingate himself was wounded. Bredin then arrived with his patrol and took command. He put in another attack and the Arabs fled. Nine enemy dead were counted and local people spoke of large numbers of wounded being spirited away in the following days. Wingate was in a state of high excitement. He checked all his patrols, and then, despite his wounds, insisted on going to his HQ in Nazareth. Eventually, Brigadier Evetts sent an ambulance and ordered Wingate to go to hospital.

This version is disputed by King-Clark, who led one of the patrols. He was about a mile from the village when he heard a fusillade of shots, including automatic fire. He therefore put his patrol into extended line and advanced towards the village. He reached the centre where he saw Wingate, seriously wounded, but sitting giving out orders in English and Hebrew. King-Clark thought 'he is the most extraordinary man'. Later he wrote, 'this action was a cock-up of the first water'. (*Free for a Blast*, p190)

The thing he had feared most in moving at night with inexperienced patrols had happened – that the SNS were firing on each other in the darkness. He added in conclusion that perhaps they frightened the Arabs more than they frightened themselves, and afterwards everyone, even the wounded, seemed pleased. He made one further comment – that a description of the battle in *Gideon Goes to War* by Leonard Mosley (an American journalist) 'is so wildly inaccurate that it can be factually discounted. (*Free for a Blast*, p191) Having described the battle, King-Clark added 'this is a marvellous job for a young officer'.

Wingate returned to the unit after two weeks in hospital, to a tumultuous reception from the settlers, and even though he was still heavily bandaged, he immediately led a large patrol on to the slopes of Mount Gilboa. He briefed the patrol carefully, explaining that Mount Gilboa was where the Philistines defeated Saul and killed three of his sons, after which Saul 'fell on his sword'. (*1st Book of Samuel*, Chapter 31) In an aside, Wingate was highly critical of Saul's tactics and use of ground! After an absolutely exhausting patrol, King-Clark and Bredin wondered just how Wingate kept going. 'Its not his legs that cope with it,' said Bala (Bredin) with his broad infectious grin on a face still scarred from its recent wounds, 'it's his mind'. (*Free for a Blast*, p195) For his outstanding bravery and leadership with the Special Night Squads, Wingate was awarded the DSO.

Through July, August and into September 1938, the SNS mounted increasingly powerful patrols and achieved significant success against the terrorists. On 4 September, at Beit Lidd, Wingate, King-Clark and Bredin led a large patrol and attacked the village at dawn. Suffering no casualties themselves, they killed 14 enemy, captured a number of prisoners, 16 rifles and an array of documents which gave the names of supporters and also future plans. After this action, King-Clark returned to his battalion which was to be posted to Singapore. He described Wingate as a man of formidable physical courage and moral integrity, who was uncomfortable and abrasive at close quarters, but 'it seemed his destiny, in truth, was to burn himself out for a cause... I consider it a high privilege to have served under Wingate's inspiring leadership.' (*Free for a Blast*, p204)

The Arabs retaliated against the success of the SNS by mining the roads in the area of Ein Harod. One day, Wingate was giving a lecture when he heard that the head of the Kibbutz at Ein Harod had been killed by a mine. With uncharacteristic impetuosity, he stopped, ordered all the squads into their lorries, and drove to the Arab village from which the terrorists operated. The squads swept through the village and shot anyone who tried to escape.

By this time, the SNS had achieved success out of all proportion to their numbers, and Wingate – still a captain – was invited to address the Royal Commission considering the Partition of Palestine. He put forward his views on internal security but then, as so often happened, he got carried away and launched into a strong criticism of the British administration. He particularly attacked the British policy on immigration, which in spite of Nazi atrocities had been reduced in 1938 from 60,000 per annum to only 12,000. He argued strongly for a transfer of population and for the establishment of a Jewish state, based on heavy industry supported by Britain, which would be an impregnable bastion for Britain in the Middle East and would be the best hope for the prosperity of the Arab world.

After several months of SNS success, GHQ agreed to an expansion of the force – rather belated recognition that Wingate and his men had achieved more in the anti-terrorist struggle than two infantry divisions. As a part of this expansion, he ran a course for Jewish sergeants at Ein Harod at the end of September 1938. In his introductory address he gave one of the clearest expositions of his views on war.

He stated: 'You have a lot to learn, a lot to forget, but I shall give you a basis for your study of the art of war. Do not take notes – just listen and digest. Great soldiers are serious, diligent and of outstanding moral character. In war personal qualities are the most important – a coarse and savage man makes a bad soldier.'

On the principles of war, he stressed surprise, economy of force, and security. To achieve surprise you need mobility, and economy of force means leading your force to the exact place so that everyone makes the fullest use of his fire power. Security means imagining you have a very clever enemy, and figuring out what he would do, and then taking all necessary steps to stop him. He also emphasised the need always to plan what to do in the event of a disaster.

He put forward the soldiers' commandments: know and love what you fight for (a quotation from Cromwell); always keep your body and your equipment in good condition; endure thirst and hardship without complaining and put the welfare of your comrades before your own. He outlined the vices of soldiers – quarrelsomeness, laziness, and indulgence are the greatest vices; 'a bad soldier is one who desires drink as soon as he is thirsty, who gets ill-tempered and stubborn when tired, and who loses self-control and restraint under physical stress'.

A series of lectures dealt with the section and platoon in attack, leadership, the role of artillery and cavalry, and the revolution in desert warfare caused by changes in motor tyres and the length of the wheel base of lorries.

Having dealt with military affairs, he widened his scope to deal with the major issues affecting Palestine. Palestine had a good climate and able people – with proper development and the use of the naval base at Akaba she could make herself secure and dominate the Persian Gulf and the Eastern Mediterranean. 'As long as we hold Palestine strongly and aggressively Germany is not winning the war (ie, stirring up the Arab revolt), and the world will recognise this. We shall lose Palestine if we continue our dreary and unimaginative policies of the past.' If these ideas for the security of Palestine were adopted, it would release the bulk of British military forces to face the German threat in North Africa. To secure an economic base, the mountains of Palestine should be made impregnable, and local industry and all resources should be developed.

Then, as we have already seen, his imagination began to run riot. He foresaw the Jewish state taking offensive action through all the desert areas of the Near East, and descending on coasts and capitals. Then American money would build up the Jewish army to 30,000 strong and 'when our troops control Africa and Spain this army will be ready to co-operate in a drive through the Balkans to end the war'. (MS, Hagana Museum) In spite of the exaggeration at the end, this was a remarkable exposition for September 1938 when Chamberlain had just announced 'Peace in our time'. Perhaps referring to Chamberlain, he had a final swipe at a country controlled by men like Dickens' Barnacle, who in every situation find reasons for doing nothing – unlike Hitler.

During August 1938 there had been a lull in the attacks on the oil pipeline, but elsewhere there were an increasing number of robberies, murders, bank robberies, and sabotage on railways and telegraph wires. In September, over 200 Jewish settlers were killed by Arab terrorists.

Throughout his colourful career, Wingate, both by chance and design, grasped remarkable opportunities to make contact with influential people. In October, he received information of a planned Arab attack on Tiberias. He telephoned Evetts to clear his plan of action, and when he got through discovered that the brigadier was in conference with Haining and General Ironside – shortly to become Commander in Chief Middle East. Ironside had been arguing that the forces in Palestine were making far too much fuss about the rather paltry Arab uprising, but in view of Wingate's phone call he decided he would go up to Tiberias the next day.

That night the Arabs massacred 19 Jews in Tiberias, including women and children – some of whom were burnt alive. What made matters worse was the presence of a new British battalion in Tiberias, which just stayed in barracks, unaware of the atrocities being perpetrated outside. The SNS were in the area but did not reach Tiberias in time and Wingate bitterly reproached himself for not protecting Tiberias more effectively. As soon as he heard of the outrage, he quickly gathered a patrol together and prepared an ambush on the road out of Tiberias. The Arab raiders had spent most of the night celebrating, and when they left in the early morning they walked straight into Wingate's ambush. Over 50 were killed. Ironside, who had been so sceptical, saw the carnage and destruction all over Galilee, and in Tiberias saw too the corpses both from the massacre and from the ambush. He sacked the CO of the battalion, but remembered Wingate as the only one 'to meet, fight, and punish the assassins' on that bloody night. (Sykes, p180)

In October, Weizmann was in London and heard alarming rumours about the findings of the Royal Commission, to which Wingate had given his views in Jerusalem. He cabled Wingate to come at once. When, in November 1938, the Woodhead Commission Report came out, it was an absolute disaster for Jewish interests. It proposed that Galilee and the Negev should be kept under British Mandate, leaving a Jewish area about 40 miles by 10, and suggested a general prohibition of all land sales to Jews except in a few designated areas.

In London, Weizmann put Wingate in touch with powerful and influential spokesmen, including Malcolm Macdonald, the Secretary of State for the Colonies. Most, even among Zionist supporters, were taken aback by his fanaticism and appalled by his ideas for a Jewish army. He had a fierce clash with Lord Beaverbrook, the owner of the *Daily Express*, and shortly afterwards it warned its readers about the dangers of Zionism and suggested that immigration to Palestine should be stopped. Most of Wingate's activities during this leave seem to have been counter-productive, but there was one encouraging moment, with perhaps some significance for the future. During a dinner party, Churchill listened intently while Wingate described the activities of the Special Night Squads.

He returned to Jerusalem in December 1938 to report to GHQ, only to discover that Bredin had been given command of the SNS and the base at Ein Harod had been closed. His time in Palestine was drawing to a close, but one further incident throws some light on his mercurial character. Before 1939 officers always received a confidential report which they had to acknowledge. Wingate's superior officer in GHQ had been Wing Commander Ritchie, and their relationship had not been easy – largely the fault of Wingate. In November 1938 Ritchie wrote a confidential report which stated 'Captain Wingate is fundamentally an individualist, he possesses an extremely strong character, which accounts for his success when working alone, but is a handicap to him when working as a member of a team... His judgement, when not obscured by preconceived notions is good... Captain Wingate is an exceptional officer who, provided he finds the correct employment, will make a name for himself.' (Wingate Papers) The average officer would have been quite pleased by such a report, but Wingate was far from average. Nonetheless, it seems surprising that he considered it so unjust and so damaging to him professionally that, as was his right, he sent off an appeal against it to the Army Council and to the Sovereign. Wingate stubbornly stuck to his complaint but, with the outbreak of war and the helpful intervention of Ironside, who had become CIGS, he eventually (in December 1939) accepted that the matter be closed.

At the end of 1938, British forces in Palestine had been substantially increased and in January 1939, 8 Division held a conference of Intelligence Officers – which Wingate did not attend. It issued a report which included these comments: 'The Conference is generally opposed to dressing up Jews as British soldiers; it was undesirable to have Jews in SNS detachments which should be entirely British; the pipeline has been unmolested since the SNS left the area; and if it is desired that we conciliate the Arabs we should not provoke him by using Jews in offensive action against him.' (Wingate Papers) If he objected to his confidential report, his reaction to this document can easily be imagined, and it is contained in a letter dated 31 January 1939 to his staunch ally Brigadier Evetts.

Wingate tried not 'to give way to the indignation which the combination of misstatement and offensive wording causes in one who in 15 engagements fought '"with Jews dressed up as British soldiers" against rebels'. He then argued that the SNS had made an unparalleled contribution to the suppression of the rebellion. This had led to the pacification of the whole of northern Palestine, while sabotage had continued in other areas – in fact while the conference was meeting the pipeline was blown up again. The SNS used those loyal to the Crown, and were led by British officers, and should not be described as 'Jews dressed up as British soldiers'. In this paper 'the facts are untrue, the conclusion is erroneous, and the terms employed are improper'.

He then gave a useful outline of the achievements of the SNS. Before they started, because the majority of the Arab population sympathised with the revolt and it had proved impossible to contain the rebels who had always been able to dictate the action. During the main period of SNS activity, 100 Jews and 40 British troops had become a well-trained unit with high morale and their methods had been adopted all over Palestine. In areas where the terrorists had been driven out, the local population was positively friendly. Because of the support of the loyal Jewish population, the SNS were fed and housed in the settlements, cost the Exchequer nothing, and were hampered only by hostile regulations. In April and May 1938, the pipeline had been blown up nearly every night. Then the SNS mounted their first action on 3 June, and from then through to October, in addition to countless patrols, there had been nearly 20 major actions, and the pipeline had not been sabotaged. This episode soured Wingate's last months in Palestine, but it does illustrate the deep gulf which existed between him and most of the military establishment, and the latent antagonism which existed between him and many of his fellow officers.

While Israel reveres him as one of the founders of the Jewish state, and particularly of the Jewish army – his name is commemorated in the names of schools, colleges, roads, and many organisations of youthful enterprise. It would be true to say that in the military establishment – both Army and RAF – from his time in Palestine, he made a few valuable friends but many dangerous enemies with long memories, and he left with a reputation as a rather dangerous and fanatical eccentric. Even King-Clark who worked closely with him, admired him, and understood his idealism, wrote later 'I think GHQ was wise to send Wingate home, and close the whole thing down – for a number of reasons including the private army angle – when it did'. (*Free for a Blast*, p178)

Relieved of his responsibility for the SNS, Wingate had time to spend with the many Jewish leaders who now nicknamed him 'The Friend'. After the adverse report of the Royal Commission, the Jewish leaders awaited the resultant White Paper with trepidation, and Wingate was subject to wildly fluctuating moods. On one occasion he offered to resign his commission and lead an underground Jewish army, on many others he begged the Zionists not to resort to violence however much they were provoked, because they would lose the goodwill of the British people.

The Wingates were in Haifa in the middle of May waiting for a troopship to take them back to England when, on 17 May, the Government published the White Paper on Palestine which rejected the proposals of the Royal Commission on the Partition of Palestine. Instead, it decided to include Jews and Arabs in the administration, and restricted immigration to 10,000 per year for the next five years, plus 25,000 refugees. After that, the Jews would form one-third of the population and no more immigration would be allowed. The difficult issue of land sales would be controlled by the British High Commission. The White Paper came out at a time when the Jewish leaders were increasingly worried by the major new problem of illegal immigrants, who in increasing numbers were being shipped out of Germany by dishonest contractors and secretly dumped on the Palestine coast.

Before he left to return to England, Wingate had a final and emotional farewell party with his friends. He was enrolled in the Golden Book of the Grand Synagogue, and took the Hebrew oath, 'If I forget thee O Jerusalem, let my right hand forget her cunning'. (Wingate Papers)

A note of farce, caused by fate or army incompetence, entered into his departure. He and Lorna left Haifa on 26 May 1939 by train, to travel to Port Said to embark on the troopship, only to find when it sailed that its first port of call was Haifa.

For his work with the Jewish Special Night Squads, and his passionate espousal of the Zionist cause, he was to become one of the founding heroes of the State of Israel. On the military side his work with the SNS had laid the foundation for his future. He alone conceived the idea of the SNS, and then planned, organised and led it – as he was to do later with the Chindits – but as war loomed he left for England and uncertain prospects in the British army.

When Wingate reached England he was posted to an Anti-Aircraft unit in Kent. Here he fumed in frustration, but he met L. S. Amery, the powerful ally of Winston Churchill, and also managed to keep contact with Jewish leaders who were arguing for a Jewish army of 10,000 men, possibly led by Wingate. When this scheme was rejected, Wingate was plunged into despair but was rescued by the good offices of Amery and Wavell.

4

The Ethiopian Campaign

Gideon Force

In September 1940, the ever-resourceful L. S. Amery contacted Wavell on Wingate's behalf and, thanks to that initiative, Wavell sent for Wingate to go out to the Middle East. He travelled by sea via the Cape and arrived in Cairo on 17 October 1940. He had complained strongly that he was going out as a supernumerary major with no specific responsibility or appointment, and he had no idea where he would be posted. He suspected another ruse by the authorities to keep him quiet.

In spite of his suspicions, his mind, as usual, was ranging energetically over the military problems of the day, and when he arrived in Cairo he submitted to GHQ a detailed scheme for an attack on Libya from the south. He proposed a base in the Tibesti mountains, which the RAF could supply by air and from which expeditions could mount attacks on the Italians and Germans, using motor transport with specially adapted wheels for desert operations. This scheme, based to some extent on his experience with the Special Night Squads and on his pre-war expedition to the Sudan, was really a forerunner of the Long Range Desert Group. It is a good illustration of the range of his ideas and the maturing development of his later thesis of Long Range Penetration. After several weeks he discovered from a friend that 'as usual GHQ turned it down'. (Shirreff, p101) Despite the relevance of his ideas to the North African campaign, Wingate's future lay not in Libya but in Ethiopia, and events progressed at a remarkable speed.

(Note: The most important source of information about the campaigns in Ethiopia – and to which I am deeply indebted – is a thesis by David Shirreff entitled *Barefoot Bandoliers*, to be published in 1995. A meticulous and scholarly survey, it is the only detailed and up to date account, and is based on British, Italian and Ethiopian sources. David Shirreff has done for Ethiopia what Louis Allen did for Burma – with many years of devoted study. References in this chapter are to Shirreff's work.)

In October 1940, because of the increasing Axis threats to the whole of the Middle East, Anthony Eden went to a conference in Khartoum which was attended by General Wavell, General Platt who was the GOC in the Sudan, General Cunningham who commanded the forces being built up in northern Kenya, and by General Smuts, the South African leader, who held a general strategic brief. Emperor Haile Selassie, whose country had been occupied and, while enjoying some modern development, had been brutally ravaged by the Italian fascists since 1935, sent a complaint about the lack of support for his Patriot forces fighting against the Italians. The conference, with some reluctance, agreed to boost supplies of men and equipment to the Patriots, and to increase the training and operation of irregular forces. Wingate was appointed GSO2 (ie, Major), with a fairly general brief in this field, and was positively welcomed by Haile Selassie. In trying to support the efforts in Ethiopia Wavell had grave problems, since he had urgent requests for help when the Italians invaded Greece in October 1940, and again when the Germans attacked in April 1941.

The historical background to the situation in Ethiopia was long and complex. The Ethiopian royal family traced its links back nearly to King Solomon, but by the 19th century it was in danger of being overthrown by rival warlords. Then some good leaders came forward, notably the Emperor Menelik, who consolidated his power and extended his boundaries –the only African ruler to benefit from the Scramble for Africa. In the Scramble, during the last quarter of the 19th century, European powers took over most parts of Africa; Italy, itself only recently united in 1870, laid claim to territory on the Red Sea coast and in the Horn of Africa. Here it came up against the growing power of Menelik who, with the help of French rifles and Russian artillery, was powerful enough to defeat an Italian army 16,000-strong at the battle of Adowa in 1896 – a defeat which Italy did not forget.

Britain, the most powerful nation in the Scramble, established its power in Egypt and after Kitchener had defeated the Khalifa at the battle of Omdurman in 1898 and avenged the death of Gordon, British control was established in the Sudan under the Anglo-Egyptian Condominium of 1899. General Sir Reginald Wingate – Orde's Cousin Rex – had fought at Omdurman and later succeeded Kitchener as Governor-General of the Anglo-Egyptian Sudan, where he remained until 1917 when he became British High Commissioner in Egypt.

In Ethiopia the powerful Emperor Menelik survived until 1913, but after his death there was a further period of disturbance among the rival contenders, until Ras Tafari re-established control and took the title Haile Selassie. Virtual ruler since 1916, Haile Selassie did much to modernise Ethiopia, establishing a parliament and founding schools and hospitals, but he still had powerful rivals, notably Ras Hailu. Thanks largely to Haile Selassie, Ethiopia was admitted as a full member of the League of Nations in 1923.

When Mussolini and the Fascists came to power in 1922, they very quickly determined to expand in North Africa and to avenge Italy's humiliating defeat at the battle of Adowa. Using Eritrea as a base, they rapidly built up their military power. In the 1930s Italy stirred up rival nobles in Ethiopia, and Mussolini was advised that with their support it would be easy to defeat Haile Selassie. During 1935 four Blackshirt Divisions were transferred to Eritrea, and Mussolini promised 10 divisions before the end of the year. All of the military equipment for this huge force – including substantial air force units and large supplies of mustard gas – were shipped through the Suez Canal which Britain, had it had the political will, could have blocked.

At this stage, Ethiopia became a pawn in the appeasement policies of Britain and France. Haile Selassie had trusted that, as a member of the League of Nations he would have great power protection, but the Conservative government of Britain was pledged to appeasement in the vain hope that they could detach Mussolini from his collaboration with Hitler. Mussolini, relying on the Conservative policy of appeasement (the Labour Party had demanded that Fascist war supplies should be prevented from using the Suez Canal), waited until the Conservatives won the 1935 election and then, with no declaration of war, invaded Ethiopia in November 1935 with a two-pronged attack from Eritrea and Somalia. Using aircraft to attack Haile Selassie's forces, often armed only with spears, and to spray villages and crops with mustard gas, the Italians rapidly overran the country and in May 1936 entered the capital Addis Ababa.

Many of the traditional Ethiopian leaders foolishly led their forces into mass actions against the invaders and were slaughtered by superior Italian fire-power, by large scale air attacks, and by the widespread use of mustard gas. Haile Selassie proved himself a good leader and encouraged his forces to wage guerrilla war, but in the end he had to

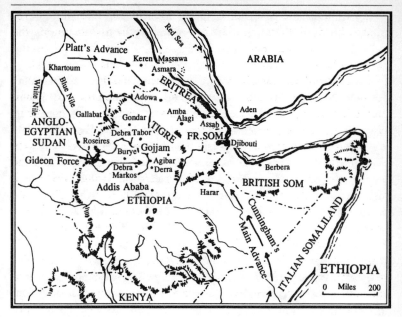

face the Italians, and in a bloody battle in March 1936 he was defeated. He fled to Britain in order to launch his appeal to the League of Nations.

He went to the Headquarters of the League at Geneva in June 1936 and made a dignified appeal, but the response was pathetic. The USA and the Soviet Union refused to recognise Italy's claim, but Britain with the appeasers still hoped to detach Italy from its alliance with Nazi Germany. Far from helping Ethiopia, the League even voted to suspend sanctions against Italy. In spite of these betrayals, Haile Selassie still seemed to trust Britain, and he went to live in Bath and sent his children to British schools.

In Ethiopia Mussolini ordered the brutal elimination of all opposition, by the indiscriminate use of mustard gas, and by the deliberate slaughter of rebels. In 1937 an assassination attempt on the Italian Viceroy, Graziani, led to 9,000 people being killed as a reprisal. Refugees flocked out of Ethiopia into British and French Somaliland, and into northern Kenya where very substantial camps were set up. Resistance to the Italian occupation continued – particularly in the province of Gojjam – and then at the end of 1937, when the policy of brutality had clearly failed, the Duke of Aosta replaced Graziani and attempted a policy of reconciliation. The Italians, rather like the Romans in Britain, tried to control the country by building roads and establishing garrisons along them at strategic points. Fighting continued into 1940.

Mussolini waited until he thought Hitler had defeated the Allies and then, bravely, he declared war on Britain and France on 10 June 1940. France signed an armistice two weeks later. At this stage Italy appeared to have overwhelming forces in the Middle East – 300,000 troops in Ethiopia with 300 aircraft, and a cruiser, destroyers and submarines at the naval base at Massawa; and in Libya another 250,000 troops. Against this huge force, Britain had about 4,000 men of the Sudan Defence Force, three British battalions (2nd West Yorks, 1st Essex, 1st Worcesters), three squadrons of Vickers Wellesley bombers and Gloster Gladiators – all commanded by General Platt from his HQ in Khartoum. In Kenya there were some battalions of the King's African Rifles and an Indian Mountain Battery. The whole area came under the control of Wavell in Cairo where there were 36,000 British troops, but these were more concerned with enemy attack in the Western Desert than in Ethiopia.

Even before the Italian declaration of war, Wavell had instructed his intelligence services to encourage rebellion among the loyal groups opposing the Italians, called the Patriots, but in the Sudan – at least until June 1940 – the attitude of the British military command was that nothing must be done to annoy the Italians, and it was dismissive towards the Patriots. Platt did not believe that Haile Selassie had the support of the majority of the people, he did not really support the idea of mobile British columns, and did not approve of supplying arms to the Patriot groups. As soon as war was declared, Wavell issued orders for immediate action against Italian East Africa. He aimed to spread revolt among the Patriots, to assist them to drive out the Italians, and to help Ethiopia to achieve freedom and independence. It was emphasised that Britain had no territorial claims over the country, but with its previous colonial record, this did not convince everyone.

Orde Wingate, with the experience from his own Sudan expedition, and from his family links to Cousin Rex, was much better briefed on the Middle East situation than most young officers arriving in Cairo in 1940. He was about to re-establish some family links which went back several decades. A Colonel Sandford had been in the Sudan at the same time as Cousin Rex before 1914, had served with distinction in the First World War, and had spent the rest of his life in Ethiopia where he had become a close friend and adviser to Haile Selassie. He also had close links with Wavell who, even before the declaration of war, put him in charge of the intelligence activities in Ethiopia. Another family link included Wilfred Thesiger, one of the most distinguished explorers and travellers of the 20th century, whose father had worked with Cousin Rex and who was to be one of Wingate's most valued leaders in Gideon Force.

Early in 1940, and before Wingate arrived, Sandford, who received little support from General Platt the British commander in the Sudan, had been appointed to lead Mission 101 which, from August 1940, had been operating successfully in Gojjam with the Patriot forces. Platt had eventually sent a letter to the Patriot chiefs saying they would be provided with arms and that Mission 101 under Colonel Sandford was co-ordinating attacks on the Italians. Sandford had also been working to bring Haile Selassie out to the Sudan in order to galvanise the Patriots and, to his delight and surprise, the Emperor arrived in July 1940. For security reasons, and because of the imminent fall of France, Haile Selassie had been rather unceremoniously bundled out of England and he received a distinctly cool reception from the military in the Sudan – for example, Platt wanted to have him sent back. He had come out imagining that there was a large force ready for him to lead victoriously against the Italians, but the reality of the situation was very different. Just after he arrived in the Sudan, a British force had been driven out of British Somaliland and evacuated through Berbera, but soon after that re-inforcements began to build up. By October 1940 two Indian brigades had reached the Sudan and, with the three British battalions already there, formed the 5 Indian Division. In northern Kenya, three brigades of the King's African Rifles, three South African brigades, and two brigades of the Royal West African Frontier Force from Nigeria and the Gold Coast (Ghana), were preparing to attack Ethiopia from the south, aiming at Addis Ababa.

The Emperor had been shocked by the cool if not hostile attitude of Platt and his senior officers, but had been impressed and heartened by the drive and enthusiasm of Wingate, and by the success of 'Operational Centres', which were small groups of officers and NCOs going into enemy held territory to instruct and co-ordinate the operations of the Patriots with Mission 101.

By coincidence, on the day Wingate arrived – 6 November 1940 – Slim, who was to be so deeply involved in Wingate's future, took part, as commander of 10th Indian Brigade, in a military debacle. His brigade had been ordered to drive out the Italians from Gallabat, a village on the border of Sudan and Ethiopia. Supported by 26 aircraft and 12 tanks, Slim launched his attack. Although the Garhwali battalion did well, a battalion of the Essex Regiment retreated in disorder, most of the aircraft were shot down, and nine of the 12 tanks were put out of action by mines. Slim's own comment 'British troops behaved even worse than the Italians', (Shirreff, p102) shows that it was a serious reverse. Soon afterwards, Slim also suffered the indignity of being wounded in the backside while taking cover from Italian fire. Later, writing *Defeat into Victory*, Slim was extremely disparaging about Wingate in Ethiopia and about the fighting qualities of the Italians, forgetting perhaps that his brigade had suffered a serious defeat at their hands, while Wingate was beginning to prove himself as a guerrilla commander.

In November 1940, when Mission 101 under Sandford had been operating for three months in Gojjam Province, Wingate was given a brief to liaise between Platt, Mission 101, and the Emperor. Wingate went to the Emperor and pledged his personal loyalty to him – again making a deep impression. One of the most unfortunate aspects of this campaign, which quickly caused deep and bitter friction between Wingate, Platt and Sandford, was the complete failure within the command structure to specify clear and definite areas of responsibility. Platt had overall command of the regular divisions preparing to attack from the northwest. He had a poor opinion of Haile Selassie, of Sandford and his Mission 101, and of Wingate, and he strongly opposed giving arms to the Patriots. With this background, and without a clear demarcation of responsibility, it is easy to see how Wingate with his vehement and passionate enthusiasms – here devoted to Haile Selassie – would almost inevitably fall foul of the other commanders with whom he had to work.

On 20 November 1940, Wingate flew into Gojjam to see Sandford and at this stage they both agreed that the Emperor should be brought into Gojjam as soon as possible in order to rally the people, an idea still not fully supported by Platt. Two days later Wingate attended a conference in Khartoum where, because he was still resentful at his continued exclusion from Palestine, his attitude was rude and aggressive.

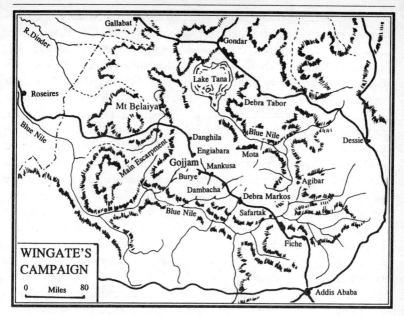

Already he was formulating his plans for the action in Ethiopia and in early December Wavell called him to a senior conference in Cairo where he put forward his proposals. Privately he recorded that his highest priority was to achieve an outstanding success which would boost his claim to raise a Jewish fighting force, and to this end he asked to have his old friend Abraham Akavia, from the Special Night Squads, and some Jewish doctors from Palestine, so that Jewish people were seen to share in the success. (Wingate Papers)

The overall plan for the campaign in Ethiopia, which was formulated by the start of 1941, was for Platt with two divisions to attack from northern Sudan into Eritrea and Tigre; Cunningham to advance with three divisions from the base in northern Kenya into southern Ethiopia and Somaliland; and Wingate's group which he had named Gideon Force, accompanied by Haile Selassie, to advance into Gojjam Province where Mission 101 was already operating. Through these weeks of planning and discussion Wingate's forceful ideas were gradually accepted, but responsibilities were still not clearly defined and this led to bitter clashes between Wingate and Sandford - much of it Wingate's fault.

He formally took command of Gideon Force on 6 February 1941. He was highly and unfairly critical of Sandford – and of Lawrence of

Arabia before him – for their method of going around dispensing arms and materials to so-called leaders, hoping they would join the revolt. He said, 'To raise a revolt you must send in a Corps d'Elite to do exploits and not just as peddlers of war material and cash... A thousand resolute and well-armed men can paralyse 10,000.' (Wingate Papers and quoted Shirreff, p134)

Gideon Force consisted of a Sudan Defence Force Frontier Battalion, and the 2nd Ethiopian Battalion, together with four 3in mortars in place of artillery. This battalion had always been organised into Patrol Companies of about 180 men – and these proved to be the forerunners of the Chindit Columns which were to be used so effectively in Burma. There was a serious shortage of mules both in the Khartoum area and in Gojjam, where the Italians had deliberately removed them, but by February 1941 Wingate had acquired over 15,000 camels to ensure that his force would be able to move forward.

His plan was for Gideon Force to make a base for Haile Selassie in the area of Mount Belaiya, and then to lead the Force up the high escarpment on to the Gojjam Plateau prior to moving towards the capital Addis Ababa. Once the action had started the contrast between Wingate and Sandford immediately became apparent. Sandford was widely respected, and through his known friendship with the Emperor he wielded great influence among the Ethiopian people and their leaders but, although he had won two DSOs in the First World War, he was not in 1941 a dynamic guerrilla leader. Mission 101 had made contact with many local leaders and had distributed arms, and although they had a number of successes to their credit – notably at Danghila – they had not actually defeated an Italian force. Wingate, having assembled, armed and trained Gideon Force, was determined that nothing should stand in his way or prevent him advancing with the Emperor towards Addis Ababa.

In January 1941, although he was not formally in command, Wingate had begun the daunting task of leading Gideon Force towards the Gojjam escarpment. He was determined to proceed because Haile Selassie had arrived and he was eager to reappear in the country and establish himself at the proposed base at Belaiya. With his usual dynamic energy and leadership, Wingate began his campaign. At first he was remarkably lucky when, after a recce patrol of the Frontier Battalion had approached an Italian strong-point on virtually the only feasible path up a daunting hill, the enemy immediately withdrew and Gideon

Force was able to reach the top. Wingate made some serious mistakes. Against all advice, he set out with a lorry convoy and a car intended for the Emperor, but the track was impassable and eventually the Emperor, accompanied by Wingate and a Coptic High Priest, arrived on horseback in Belaiya on 6 February. In a serious action the Italians were able to rescue one of their garrisons because they had good ground to air co-operation, and because they had a doctor with their column. Although he did not take part in this battle its lessons were not lost on Wingate as he began to develop and nurture his ideas on Long Range Penetration.

For the next two weeks there was great tension throughout both Mission 101 and Gideon Force because, naturally, Sandford assumed he was in overall command, and that Wingate and Gideon Force were coming to assist him. After some unseemly quarrels, Sandford and Wingate were called to Khartoum on 12 February where Platt attempted – unsuccessfully – to resolve the problem. Wingate was made an acting Colonel and confirmed in his position as commander of Gideon Force. 'Sandford was very cut up' at this decision (Shirreff, p149), but then he was called to Cairo, appointed Brigadier and congratulated all round. His role thenceforth was to liaise with Haile Selassie on the political front, while leaving Wingate to get on with the Gideon Force campaign. This decision prolonged and exacerbated an almost impossible position, because Sandford commanding Mission 101 was inevitably involved in military matters. Wingate commented that 'this could not and did not work'. (Wingate Report, Wingate Papers)

Opportunities were lost because of divided command, and because co-operation between Gideon Force and the Patriots had not been worked out. There were faults on both sides. Sometimes the Patriots did not carry out what they had promised, and sometimes Gideon units refused fully to support Patriot actions, if they were tactically unwise.

Having got Gideon Force and the Emperor up the escarpment and into Gojjam Province, where resistance to the Italians had always been strongest, Wingate completed his plans and gave his orders. Gideon Force would advance to Engiabara where their role was to fight as guerrillas, usually operating at night, and by making sudden attacks on ill-defended camps, to cause confusion among the enemy, and to create the impression of a large attacking force. He issued an Order of the Day (18 February, Wingate Papers) claiming 'a bold stroke will demand all your energies and all your devotion. Your courage and endurance will be put to the severest test in the coming weeks.' He also appealed to the Patriots 'Rouse yourselves and put an end to these bickerings which have disgraced your Ethiopian name'. There is little doubt that most of the clashes with Sandford were Wingate's fault, but an interesting comment came from one Patriot leader who said that Sandford was all wrapped up in politics, but Wingate was concerned 'only how to attack the enemy and win victory'. (Shirreff, p165) Wingate reached Engiabara on 20 February, together with the faithful Akavia, and explained to him that he saw success in Ethiopia as directly relevant to his hopes of raising a Jewish force. (Wingate Papers)

By the end of February 1941, Gideon Force, with about two battalions and four 3in mortars, had entered Gojjam Province ready to face enemy forces of about 25,000 men. In Eritrea 4 Indian Division had attacked Keren and had then been joined by 5 Indian Division, facing about 40,000 Italians. In the south, Cunningham facing enemy forces of 90,000, had built up three divisions ready for his drive towards Addis Ababa.

Facing overwhelming forces, Wingate's aim was to frighten and bluff the enemy into submission – tactics successfully illustrated in the approach to Burye and Mankusa, where the Italians had about 6,000 troops. On 23 February Wingate issued his orders for separate columns to harass Burye, but for the main force to by-pass it and make for Mankusa. This early operation brought into prominence some of the remarkable characters in Gideon Force: Thesiger an outstanding leader, Sergeant Luyt who became a famous colonial administrator, and Hugh Boustead who had a flamboyant career in the Gulf States and post-war Africa. Boustead commanded the Frontier Battalion and had many clashes with Wingate. As the Force moved off, for the first few days Thesiger and the other columns attacked outlying Italian posts while the main body under Wingate and Boustead drew near to Mankusa. One column had even been sent beyond Mankusa to Dambacha in order to alarm the enemy, but the actual attack on Mankusa on 1 and 2 March did not succeed, mainly because a Patriot group failed to put in an attack, but Wingate's overall plan began to work. Propaganda units, operating with the Patriots, had been provided with loudspeakers with which they announced the Emperor's presence, and this induced large numbers of Ethiopians to desert from the Italian forces. These tactics convinced the Italian commander at Burye that he was in real danger of being cut off by superior forces, which he realised had already reached Mankusa and Dambacha. In early March he was given permission to evacuate Burye, and to retreat past Mankusa and towards Debra Markos.

When he received this news, Wingate prepared his plans. He sent a major section of Gideon Force under Boustead to sweep around Burye, and to prepare for the expected withdrawal. At dawn on 4 March as he observed the town, Boustead saw an amazing sight: 'The road was black with troops and transport as far as the eye could see – in all over 10,000 people.' (Shirreff, p204) Facing this very large force – which had effective cavalry units in support – Boustead decided it would be too risky to attack. Thesiger criticised Boustead for not attacking the massive columns of marching men, and Wingate, furious at missing such an excellent opportunity for damaging the enemy, accused him of cowardice – for which Boustead never forgave him. In contrast, small groups of Patriots successfully attacked the retreating Italians and, clearly, Boustead missed a great opportunity when the enemy was completely vulnerable. Wingate ordered the immediate pursuit of the large column and attacked them the same night. Wingate's determination certainly drove everyone forward, but he made some serious mistakes himself, for example in handling independent columns – another useful lesson for later.

Burye became an important base for Gideon Force. Large supplies of food, weapons and vehicles had been captured there, but in spite of this the Force faced very serious supply problems. All supplies had to come from Khartoum by road or rail following the course of the Blue Nile to the road head at Roseires, after which there was very difficult terrain and the hazardous climb up the Gojjam escarpment. On 5 March, Wingate went to discuss these problems with Haile Selassie and Sandford, and they decided that Sandford would take charge of all supplies – but this proved to be another source of conflict.

Poor wireless communication, also discussed with Sandford and noted by Wingate for the future, played a part in a fierce action by the 2nd Ethiopian Battalion under Major Boyle. Boyle's unit lay astride the road from Burye to Debra Markos, but he had received no information about enemy movements except in the most general terms, he had not prepared an ambush, and on the morning of 6 March he had not stood-to. At first light, a large Italian force just blundered into Boyle's position, and a fierce fight ensued with heavy casualties on both sides. The Italians were in such large numbers that in spite of their casualties they were able to push the opposition aside and make for Debra Markos. There were bitter feelings about this action, including the comment of Sergeant Luyt about some Patriot groups who took no part in the fighting but the moment it was over descended like locusts on the bodies of friend and foe, and on the debris of battle, to loot and scavenge. 'The despicable Shifta – human vulture rats – people we are supposed to be helping.' (Quoted Shirreff, p221) Shirreff's research included another significant quote from Luyt's diary, but on a different issue. 'We have brought death, murder and evil to these pre-biblical people, and now we make them a battle ground between two European powers, and range the local people on opposite sides. What a debt we have to repay!' (Shirreff, p202)

While this major action continued, with a large group of the enemy trapped, Wingate asked for an air strike which, he claimed, could have finished off the Italian resistance in Gojjam. Shirreff in his detailed commentary rejects this claim because there was no prospect of aircraft from the Sudan giving direct air support in that way – but it does illustrate the way Wingate's ideas were developing and close air support was to become an important part of Chindit tactics.

He kept up the momentum of the advance and on 8 March he bluffed a strong Italian contingent to move out of Dambacha, and then advanced again, intending to by-pass Debra Markos and attack the Italian lines of communication towards Addis Ababa.

By this time Haile Selassie and his entourage including Sandford, had reached Burye. There was a considerable rallying to the Emperor, as had been expected, but it appears that the Patriots then tended to feel that the professionals had now arrived and they could get on with the fighting. Haile Selassie also realised that the powerful local chief Ras Hailu had openly supported the Italians and he did not wish to start a civil war. On the other hand the Operational Centres to the north of Gideon Force, with their well-trained officers and NCOs, had been operating with Mission 101 for some months and were beginning to rally some local support.

As soon as the HQ was established, a small existing airfield was taken over for bringing in supplies and flying out the wounded – a good example of Wingate learning from his experiences and using the knowledge to develop his future plans.

While Gideon Force was advancing in Gojjam Province, Platt with 4th and 5th Indian Divisions made slow progress in Eritrea, with some bitterly fought exchanges against powerful Italian forces. Soon after this a British unit from Aden recaptured Berbera and cleared the Italians out of British Somaliland, while Cunningham, with three divisions made rapid progress – his main units advancing via Mogadishu and sweeping north towards Harar. The plan of the Duke of Aosta, the Italian Commander, appeared to be to keep some fortified strong points at Gondar in the north, and at Debra Markos, in order to keep the British occupied until the Germans arrived from Libya. In the immediate area of Gideon Force, the Italian commander Maraventano took command of about 14,000 troops around Debra Markos.

Wingate planned to leave Boustead to deal with the villages on the approach to Debra Markos, while he skirted south of the town and approached Safartak where the road to Addis Ababa crossed the Blue Nile Gorge. (Wingate Papers) The Emperor, Sandford and Wingate all shared an uneasy suspicion that Britain might try to take over Ethiopia, should Cunningham's divisions from the south reach the capital first. As the advances continued this was to become a more urgent and more controversial issue, not helped by the official title Occupied Enemy Territory Administration.

In the middle of March 1941, the Gideon Force operations developed swiftly and they illustrate some of the difficult command problems associated with this type of warfare, and some aspects of Wingate's relationships with other colleagues both above and below him. Major Donald Nott (later Brigadier), kept a diary (Shirreff, p75) and from the Force HQ at Burye made shrewd comments about this. He remained close to the action right through to the Italian surrender.

On 17 March Thesiger set out with some patrols to by-pass Debra Markos and to threaten the road from there to the Nile Gorge at Safartak. In Debra Markos the new Italian commander Maraventano was resolute and aggressive, and by recapturing a number of villages he restored the morale of his troops and changed the attitude of some of the fickle local people. This caused problems for the overstretched units of Gideon Force, and at this difficult stage the ill-defined division of responsibility between Sandford and Wingate caused a dangerous rift.

Platt had suffered a serious hold-up at Keren in Eritrea, and had signalled to Wingate for him to try to prevent any enemy reinforcements being sent to the north up the road through Gondar. This order reached Sandford who tried but failed to contact Wingate. Facing a difficult situation Sandford, who had few spare troops at his disposal, despatched one of the six-man Operational Centres to reinforce the Mission 101 groups which were attacking the road to Gondar near Lake Tana. Wingate, under considerable pressure from the more resolute opposition of Maraventano, reacted furiously to Sandford's action, claiming that he had made an unacceptable intrusion into operational matters. Sandford cabled to HQ at Khartoum to have the matter sorted out, and Nott commented: 'I am utterly sick of Wingate's orders and letters. He expects the most impossible things, without considering the A and Q difficulties. He is out of touch and has no clear picture.' (Quoted Shirreff, p 260)

This explosion came after a long period of tension. During the previous week Wingate had complained that he had received 'not a mule, not a horse since he started'. (Wingate Papers) Writing to Colonel Airey at Khartoum he complained, 'Sandford has cancelled every order that I have sent back which was not in accord with his own views', and again, 'since we came up the escarpment not a man, not a weapon, not an animal has reached me from the rear.' He complained further that Sandford had issued 561 Springfield rifles to the Patriots and none to him, and that Gideon Force had suffered casualties because of Sandford's refusal to co-operate. Wingate's allegations are contradicted by Nott's diaries which give detail of the supplies which were sent forward.

The clash between Sandford and Wingate arose primarily from lack of demarcation, but also from fundamentally differing views about the campaign. Sandford supported the Emperor who had demanded a regular force of 3,000 for himself for swift and dispersed action by the Patriots, 'not the comparatively slow advance of regular forces planned by Wingate'. Sandford continued, 'present plans are paralysing Patriot activities by diverting rifles, ammunition, and pack saddles exclusively to Wingate's forces, instead of giving equal priority to Patriots. I am personally in agreement with the Emperor.' Sandford then ordered 'Rush in by air, earmarked for Patriots, 8,000 rifles and ammunition, 400 pack saddles, 2,000 sets of equipment, as Wingate unwilling to spare.' (Sandford signal to Khartoum, 1 April. Wingate Papers)

On 2 April Wingate replied in detail to this message pointing out that when arms had been issued to Patriots, except in close proximity to Gideon Forces, they were not used effectively. He complained that the view attributed to the Emperor merely reflected the detail Sandford had been feeding him all along, and was directly contrary to clear instructions on operational matters. He objected as strongly as possible to the order to rush 8,000 rifles to the Patriots. He continued, 'I do not feel justified in continuing to accept responsibility for operations which are brought to nought by interference and disobedience in my immediate rear'. (Wingate Papers) Later he returned to the question of the 8,000 rifles, saying the correct use, if they materialise, would be for them to be issued to the Emperor's regular forces, with a few kept for issue to the Patriots. (Wingate Papers)

Sandford's signal brought a reasonable rebuke to both of them from Platt but Wingate, trying to play it down, replied to Platt 'Sorry the dispute in our small company reached you. The storm in a teacup was over before it reached you.'

Serious communication problems caused this clash between Sandford and Wingate, they added to the difficulties of co-ordinating the operations of the Frontier Battalion and the 2nd Ethiopian Battalion, and they brought bitter rows between Wingate, Boustead and Boyle. When Wingate returned to the HQ on 27 March, Nott, who had been so critical, wrote 'However, his magnetic personality dominated and dispelled all disgruntled thoughts'. (Shirreff, p265)

Elsewhere, the Italians were retreating rapidly. Keren and Asmara in Eritrea fell to the 4th and 5th Indian Divisions, and Harar, 200 miles east of Addis Ababa, was captured by the 23 Nigerian Brigade from Cunningham's advancing divisions. On 2 April the South African Air Force bombed Addis Ababa and destroyed 32 Italian aircraft, and on 6 April 1941 Cunningham's forces entered the capital. Maraventano had already been contacted by Aosta and warned that, because of the critical situation in the south, Gojjam might have to be evacuated. In fact, by early April the villages which Maraventano had captured were again abandoned, and his forces concentrated at Debra Markos. Wingate too had his problems – he was seriously ill with malaria, and the 2nd Ethiopian Battalion had mutinied. In spite of his illness, Wingate acted decisively and sacked the CO after which the unit immediately rallied to his successor and performed well for the rest of the campaign.

Gideon Force now aimed at Debra Markos and undertook most of the fighting, since the Patriots appeared more interested in securing their position with the newly-returned Emperor. On 4 April, Maraventano under orders from Aosta, started the controlled withdrawal from Debra Markos of a body of 12,000 people including 4,000 women and children. They set out on a desperate journey of nearly 200 miles to Safartak, then to Agibar, and onwards to Dessie. The equivocal attitude of some of the Patriot groups at this time can be illustrated by Ras Hailu. A powerful leader, who had known Mussolini personally, he had supported the Italians for years. He helped them when they started their withdrawal from Debra Markos and then, when Boustead and Nott at the head of the Gideon Force units entered the town, he was there to receive them – in practice doing a useful job in preventing the almost inevitable looting. On 6 April, Haile Selassie entered Debra Markos and was formally welcomed by Wingate, with Gideon Force drawn up under the command of Boustead. The formalities included the presentation of Ras Hailu but he, 'an awkward old devil to the end', tried to upstage the whole occasion by keeping everyone waiting for half an hour. (Wingate Papers)

Maraventano's group struggled grimly forward and on 7 April they approached the Nile Gorge. Thesiger was in the area and had arranged with a powerful local chief, Belai Zelleka, to ambush the Italians, but – unbeknown to Thesiger – the chief had been suborned by the ever equivocal Ras Hailu, who offered him his daughter in marriage. Such was the power of Ras Hailu that this ruse worked, no attack took place, and another wonderful opportunity of destroying the Italian column was missed. Boustead was angry with Thesiger for not carrying out an ambush even without the Patriots, though for once Wingate was more philosophical.

As they slowly realised the serious problems of Maraventano's lumbering column, more Patriots started to harass them while the Gideon units kept their distance during daylight, but made sudden attacks into the sprawling camp area at night. All over Ethiopia Italian resistance started to crumble but the British too faced problems. The fall of Greece and Rommel's rapid advance in the Western Desert meant that 4 and 5 Indian Divisions and three South African brigades were urgently needed in Egypt.

While the main Gideon Force advanced to Debra Markos and beyond, Mission 101 and the various Operational Centres had been fighting effectively in the area around Lake Tana. Their main objective was to block the road from Dessie, going northwestwards through

Debra Tabor, to the main Italian garrison at Gondar. The Italians still had nearly three divisions in this area and managed to keep the support of local chiefs by the continuing offer of rank and land.

While these operations were taking place south of Lake Tana, Wingate with a large part of Gideon Force had to break off in order to support Haile Selassie when he entered Addis Ababa. This became a highly sensitive and complex military and political issue. In view of his very powerful rivals – including Ras Hailu – the Emperor wanted to move into Addis Ababa as soon as possible with a contingent of at least 3,000 troops. He was conscious that the British were getting all the credit for driving out the Italians, and he was cutting a very poor figure. This 'was galling for him now and dangerous for him in the future'. (Shirreff, p396) Wingate, who shared the Emperor's suspicion of British intentions, supported his claim, but the decision was not straightforward. Cunningham and Sir Philip Mitchell (later to become Governor of Kenya) had to consider other factors. Mitchell believed, quite correctly, that because Haile Selassie had been with Gideon Force all the time – a force of about two battalions – he was unaware of the fighting and achievements of the five British divisions which had been the main factor in eliminating the Italians. There were about 20,000 Italians in Addis Ababa, including armed troops and police, as well as vast numbers of women and children. Cunningham was seriously concerned for the safety of the women and children if ill-controlled hordes of Patriots came rushing in to greet Haile Selassie; and the very real danger, if that happened, of fighting between the Patriots and the remaining Italian troops. He therefore decided that before the Emperor's official entry could take place, the British units must disarm and intern the 12,000 armed Italians, and remove the 5,000 women and children to safety zones. He also sent a message that Haile Selassie would not be allowed into the capital until operational factors permitted. This was a reasonable decision, but the manner in which the negotiations were conducted with the Emperor was insensitive and tactless.

Cunningham also instructed Wingate that he was to ensure that Haile Selassie did not approach the capital. This put Wingate in a difficult situation and is the main reason why he withdrew a substantial part of Gideon Force from operations in order to form a suitable escort for the Emperor. After he received Cunningham's signal, he replied that the Emperor could not be persuaded to wait any longer, and he had left Debra Markos on 27 April. (Sykes, p306) Wingate and Nott set off with the escort. During the journey, Nott recorded in his diary: 'Orde and I stayed up late discussing matters and drinking innumerable brandies. Brilliant brain he has. He will be CIGS or I'm a Dutchman.' (Quoted Shirreff, p403) On a more formal occasion, Wingate defused a difficult situation by proposing a toast in which he raised the wider issues of the rights of small countries against aggressors, of liberty and freedom of conscience, and of Haile Selassie's undisputed sovereignty. (Wingate Papers)

Discussions about a suitable date for the formal entry of the Emperor into Addis Ababa continued during the laborious journey from Debra Markos, and eventually 5 May was agreed – the fifth anniversary of the capture of the city by the Italians. For the ceremonial march, Wingate had obtained a white horse for the Emperor, but he preferred the comfort of an open touring car captured from the Italians and insisted that Wingate rode the horse. This did no harm to Wingate's general image and a photograph shows him, mounted on the horse, wearing a pith helmet and shorts, leading the parade. He was followed by the faithful Akavia and Luyt, then the 2nd Ethiopian Battalion and then the Emperor in a car with General Weatherall (Cunningham's 2 i/c). The route was lined by thousands of Patriots as well as British, Kenyan, Nigerian, and South African soldiers, and was decorated with triumphal arches in green, yellow and red. General Cunningham greeted the Emperor and there was an official ceremony with toasts and speeches, attended as Wingate noted, by 'that old fox Ras Hailu'. (Wingate Papers) After his entry into the city Haile Selassie, who did not wish it to appear that an Italian administration had been replaced by a British one, expected to resume his authority at once. But he soon clashed with Wavell who pointed out that Britain was providing all the funds, and who insisted that in areas where there was still fighting the local British military commander should have authority.

Almost immediately after the ceremonial entry, Wingate returned to join up with the main section of Mission 101 – known as Safforce – which was harassing Maraventano's column. Safforce, with Nott in command, assisted by Thesiger and Major Johnson, had been operating cleverly by making frequent night attacks on the sprawling Italian camp, but the enemy were beginning to resist more stoutly. Weakened by shortages of food and ammunition, Safforce were losing their momentum and were becoming increasingly dispirited. In that situation, Wingate arrived with substantial supplies, accompanied by Ras

Kassa, the most powerful local leader. Suddenly the spirit of the whole force changed. Thesiger wrote, 'He was a man I think we all disliked, but with his arrival the situation was transformed. Now for the first time, I really appreciated his greatness. (Thesiger, *The Life of my Choice*, p334)

As the campaign of Gideon Force reached its climax at the approach to Agibar, the Duke of Aosta surrendered to 5 Indian Division and the 1st South African Brigade at Amba Alagi, about 200 miles north of Agibar. After Aosta's surrender, strong Italian forces still held out at Gondar, and also in the southwest of the country, where they were attacked by 11 and 12 African Divisions, including the 24th Gold Coast Brigade and the 22nd East African Brigade.

The Italian garrison moved off towards Agibar the night after Wingate's return and, on 16 May, he issued his detailed orders to Gideon Force for all units to attack the Italians and force their surrender. At this moment, Cunningham ordered Wingate to break off the action and to send all his subordinate commanders elsewhere. Wingate then dissembled at great length – 12 foolscap pages of Akavia's close typing – and claimed that he could not understand the message because the ciphers were corrupt. He responded in a similar vein to a second order from Cunningham, and then closed down his set and continued with the attack. (Wingate Papers)

A fairly flat tongue of land stretched for several miles south from the small fort of Agibar, and Maraventano had drawn up his forces in an arc at the southern end of the tongue. Wingate, approaching from the south, sent Thesiger with 100 troops and 300 Patriots to work around the eastern flank towards the Agibar fort, in order to cut off the enemy's retreat. After Thesiger had left, Wingate and Johnson moved off with a depleted company of the Frontier Battalion, two mortar sections, and 1,200 Patriots, and that night climbed up the escarpment on to the spur. By the morning of 18 May they could see the Italian formations on the ridge. At nightfall, Wingate attacked the Italian position from the front, while Johnson with a mixed patrol of troops and Patriots attacked the left flank, and a Patriot group attacked the right. In these actions both sides sustained heavy casualties.

The next day (19 May) attacks on the Italians resumed, but they counterattacked using artillery, machine guns and some cavalry charges. Then news came through of Aosta's surrender at Amba Alagi, and of the likely surrender of Debra Tabor to Boustead's units. Wingate used every opportunity to give the impression to the enemy that there were large forces following up. Similarly, Thesiger, by sending an old man to tell his sons that the Emperor was just coming, got a sizeable unit to abandon a fort that was blocking his advance. On 20 May, the Italians moved off northwards along the flat tongue of land towards the positions taken up by Thesiger and were involved in heavy fighting with the Patriots, who lost over 500 killed or wounded. Thesiger had sited his small force cleverly, and when the enemy attacked using artillery, although he was wounded, he was able to withdraw his men to a prepared position.

Maraventano faced a serious situation, with shortages of food, ammunition and water, shortages of all types of medical supplies for his 1,200 sick and wounded, and fear of the huge forces he imagined were surrounding him. Wingate in a letter dated 19 May, and carried by a peasant to whom he had given 100 dollars with the promise of as much again when he returned, outlined his terms to Maraventano. He told him of the very substantial forces of Sudanese troops and Patriots about to join him; he elaborated on the surrender of Aosta which would soon lead to large scale air reinforcements coming to help him; he warned that the British troops were about to withdraw and Maraventano's whole group would be left to the mercy of the Patriots; he demanded his surrender in order to save needless loss of life, and gave him 12 hours to reply. Maraventano replied the same day, saying he would never give in, 'Danger, privation, and fatigue we Italian soldiers bear for the honour and grandeur of the Motherland', but he concluded that he could not surrender except on the order of his superiors. Wingate replied again, emphasising that continued resistance would do no good to Italy, and would be cruel and inhuman to the soldiers who had fought so bravely. He set a deadline of 1500 hours on 22 May. (Wingate Papers)

Maraventano signalled to his HQ in Gondar, relaying Wingate's terms, and explaining that his troops were exhausted, that his ammunition, food and medical supplies were exhausted, and the whole region was up in arms against him. In a classic exercise of passing the buck, the HQ replied, leaving the decision to him. He then called all his officers together and, fearing their extermination if they were left to the Patriots, they agreed unanimously that further resistance was impossible.

In fact Gideon Force and the Patriots were nearly out of ammunition, and Wingate's whole approach had been pure bluff. He had played cleverly on the Italian fear of Patriot vengeance for, during the five years of war, there had been many cases of the enemy castrating Italian prisoners. This unpleasant practice had been immortalised in the British army song to the tune of the British Grenadiers:

'Now they can't participate in any form of grind,
For they're back from Ethiopia with their organs left behind.'

Wingate's bluff succeeded and at 1800 hours on 21 May he received notice of the Italian intention to surrender . He arranged a meeting next day. Major Nott carried out the negotiation and agreed that the honours of war were conceded; that for their own safety the Italians could keep their personal weapons until they reached Fiche on the way to the capital; and finally that Maraventano would have a suitable guard of honour. Nott wrote, 'As our total regular troops were a platoon or so, the joke was too good to miss'. (Shirreff, p376)

In his diary, Nott described the surrender on 23 May 1941: 'It was an amazing sight. First Colonel Maraventano and his staff arrived and were taken to Wingate and his staff. A guard of honour of 10 Hamla men did a ragged present arms. Then came the Nationals – Blackshirts, Political Officers, and one white woman. After that the Colonial troops – artillery, cavalry and infantry. They dumped their arms, MGs, LMGs, bombs, shotguns and ammunition in great piles. The Sudanese troops were used to guard the dumps. By 1700 hours they had all camped within our lines. We had a handful of Sudanese troops and Patriots and a column of 10,000 prisoners! 1,000 nationals, 5,000 Colonials, 2,000 women and children, 1,000 mule men and camp followers!' (Shirreff, p377) In Wingate's description he added 'While to receive them stood 36 Sudanese'.

Shirreff has tracked down and interviewed some of the Italian officers present at the surrender. One described how the soldierly figure of Major Nott, who had learned Latin at school, spoke to him 'in the language of Vergil'. Of Wingate he said 'He was, in short an insignificant little fellow of miserable appearance', but later, after he heard of Wingate's other exploits, he added 'The anger I felt against this man who had humiliated us and pursued us without respite for months, turned to esteem'. (Shirreff, p378) As a prisoner, he extended some sympathy to Nott, who was taken prisoner by the Germans at Tobruk and, after escaping, recaptured in Italy. (In 1993 Nott wrote 'Latin was not my best subject at Marlborough'.)

Thesiger went to receive the surrender of another village, with less than a platoon to overcome a rabble of over 2,000 local tribesmen who shot at him, when, waving the Ethiopian flag, he approached their position. He was so furious that he yelled at them until they stopped firing. He then told their commander that the next man to fire a shot would be hanged, and that he was to remove his rabble forthwith. This he did. Thesiger next had to stop the Patriots looting and he threatened to hang them as well.

Wingate's worries were far from over, for with a tiny force of professional troops and the unpredictable Patriots, who barely understood the idea of 'prisoners of war', he was responsible for moving the vast mass of prisoners with women and children all the way to Addis Ababa. They did not reach there until early June, when the Emperor demanded a parade of Italian prisoners. They protested in vain against this humiliation. Rumour has it that Ras Kassa, whose two sons had been executed by the Italians in 1936, had been behind the proposed parade, and he had even threatened to shoot all the Italian officers.

In the Ethiopian campaign over 200,000 Italian troops were defeated by the five Commonwealth divisions which operated from Eritrea and Kenya, but Wingate, with about two battalions, grabbed the limelight for his brilliant work with Gideon Force and the Patriots. So too did his espousal of the cause of Haile Selassie against the hostile views of Platt, and the relative indifference of the other military commanders. His achievements had been crowned by the Emperor's entry into Addis Ababa, followed by the surrender of Maraventano and 12,000 prisoners to Gideon Force. Once again Wingate had found a cause to which he gave his passionate support, but which he linked directly to his hopes of raising a Jewish fighting force. More significant than all of this for his development as a military leader, were the lessons he learned, and which his remarkable mind took note of and used, in order to develop his views on Long Range Penetration. All his experiences were used to formulate his plans for future operations. When, later, he set up the Chindits, his views were clear-cut on wireless communication for each column; the importance of ground to air communication; the use of airstrips both for supply and for the evacuation of wounded; the role of air power, the lessons of which he had learned from the Italian domination of the Gojjam campaign; and finally all the tactical lessons of moving columns in enemy territory.

After the surrender of Maraventano and all his forces, Haile Selassie thanked and congratulated Wingate, who then had visions of achieving his one great hope – a new Jewish command. The view of Force HQ was very different.

Although Wingate had had some contact with Platt's HQ in Khartoum, he had hardly any with Cunningham's HQ, yet as soon as he arrived in Addis Ababa after the battle of Agibar and the Italian surrender, he was summoned to HQ. General Weatherall informed him that he no longer had a command, Gideon Force was disbanded forthwith, and he would fly at once via Cunningham's HQ to Cairo. Even though Wingate was hardly known at Cunningham's HQ, it appears that he was heartily disliked, and the clear impression was that they wanted to get rid of him as soon as possible. The Staff hierarchy of the Army, even with wartime expansion, remained fairly close-knit, and for the rest of his life Wingate was to be dogged by such prejudice.

He arrived in Cairo in June 1941 in a mood of anger, frustration and bleak depression – reduced to the rank of major. He met Major Simonds, who had been taken out of one of Boustead's battles for an urgent posting to GHQ, yet he was still sitting about in Cairo with no job to do. Simonds recorded that in Cairo, Wingate seemed to count for nothing, and they were received with cold indifference at GHQ.

A hurt, sick and angry man, Wingate immediately wrote his report on the Ethiopian Campaign. (Wingate Papers) In it he returned to his general criticism that you should not try to foment rebellion by giving arms and cash to local leaders, but send in professionals to give a lead and set an example.'You must appeal to the best in human nature... Down at heel spies and pretentious levies are worse than useless.' He again used the phrase 'Long Range Penetration' in order to bring actual war and rebellion on to the enemy's lines of communication and in his back areas. He argued that such a force must be independent, with air support, and must be given a precise role.

He was highly critical of the make-up of Gideon Force and, while the Sudan Frontier Battalion was good, there were also 'a thoroughly bad lot of officers' in the other units. He levelled severe criticism at the divided command and the confusion it caused, and then gave detailed comment on the main weapons, including the 3in mortar, the Vickers machine gun, Bren guns, the 36 grenade, and the need for anti-aircraft weapons.

On the political background, he argued that their liberty should be won by the Ethiopians, and the Emperor should not have been seen to be returning on the backs of another white Imperialist power. He felt that the line taken after Platt's victory at Keren, 'Your chains have been broken by the British', was disastrous.

He protested very strongly in his report about the inadequate pay and allowances for the men of Gideon Force, and spent much of his time in Cairo badgering GHQ on their behalf – pointing out that the men in the firing line are the worst paid of all. He complained bitterly that officers should not be peremptorily removed in the middle of active operations – this had happened to Simonds, Boustead, Nott and Wingate himself. Then, coming to the disbandment of Gideon Force, he wrote 'It is astonishing and demoralising to find that the reward for success is the dissolution of the command and staff that gained the success. Increased scope is the proper answer.' (Wingate Report. p16) He then continued provocatively, 'To dissipate such a military organism after it had been created, and while the need for it still exists, or to suppose that you get equal results from the employment of equal numbers in sporadic operations, is the mark of the military ape.'

Wavell saw the report, which was completed on 18 June 1941, and in a personal interview rebuked Wingate for his intemperate language, but promised to look into the complaints he had made. Shortly afterwards, Wavell was posted as Commander in Chief India and so had no time to deal with the issues Wingate had raised, but the tenor of his report was well-known in Cairo, and it continued to fester.

In the Wingate Papers, there is a document entitled 'Narrative of Events May-November 1941'. It is undated and unsigned, but it could have been written by Akavia who was with Wingate most of the time. It is generally sympathetic to him and gives a clear outline of the distressing events which followed the production of the Report in the middle of June. Left at a loose end in Cairo, his appeals for further active service ignored, Wingate was wracked by frequent and serious bouts of cerebral malaria, which induces moods of suicidal depression. He went to a civilian doctor because he thought that if he reported sick in the Army he would be dismissed to some non-combatant role. The doctor gave him atabrin, the forerunner of mepacrine, but which had not been fully tested at the time. Wingate dosed himself heavily with atabrin, and during bouts of severe fever lay alone in his hotel room, or else, when he was able, dragged himself to GHQ, where a sympathetic colleague lent him a corner of his office. He fought urgently for the allowances due to his men, but was met by complete indifference. His anger only increased when the authorities, hoping he would call off his demands, offered him personally back-dated allowances – an offer he rejected with disgust. Near to despair, he wrote 'It is a bottomless morass... and beyond it incompetence and indifference sit and grin'.

On the afternoon of 4 July, during a particularly severe bout of cerebral malaria, he found his temperature was 104°F (40°C). He got up and staggered along the street to the door of the doctor who had treated him, but it was locked. Hardly able to walk, he returned to the hotel. He passed a waiter who noticed him trembling and sweating, and saw him go into his room. Here he took a revolver from his bag, put it to his head and pulled the trigger. It misfired. He then took a knife he had been given by an American journalist, and plunged it into his neck. Streaming blood, he crossed the room, locked the door, and then crashed to the floor. An officer in the adjoining room heard him lock the door and then heard the crash as he fell. He rushed for help, broke into the room and found Wingate unconscious. He was rushed to the military hospital where his wounds were stitched and he was given blood transfusions – 14 pints in all. For days he was delirious and hovering close to death. Once, in a break from his delirium, he found a Catholic priest by his side and asked him 'Father, am I damned?', to which the priest replied 'God will forgive you', and this appeared to comfort him. Bearing in mind his Plymouth Brethren upbringing, one can imagine the torment in his mind before he asked such a question. His attempted suicide became a cause célèbre in Cairo and beyond, and the devotion of those who supported him was matched only by the viciousness of those who opposed him. The intensity of his enemies' hatred is shown in a remark recorded at a high-level dinner party. 'We've got him now. It is either a court-martial or a lunatic asylum for him.'(Report, p9. Also quoted Sykes, p332)

Shirreff wrote of Wingate, 'He had shown courage, professional-ism and strategic ability of a high order ... instead of receiving praise he had been hustled out of Ethiopia by Cunningham as though he was a delinquent, had met with indifference in Cairo, and the rejection of his claim for allowances for his men, and his recommendations for awards. He had justifiable anger at the disgraceful way he had been treated.' (Shirreff, p420)

Wingate's convalescence was assisted by a Mrs Newall, herself a patient in the military hospital, who through her cheerful and sympathetic conversation gradually helped him back to normal. She encouraged him to talk and to read. One evening he read her nearly the whole Book of Job, and at the end said 'Isn't that magnificent', to which she replied that she couldn't really say as she had been asleep. She also introduced him to her many visitors, and this proved to be the ideal therapy. On 22 July, the senior psychological consultant, who fortunately knew about the suicidal effects of both atabrin and cerebral malaria, declared him perfectly fit and gave him a period of convalescence, followed by a passage on a troopship leaving for England in early September 1941. Wingate used the intervening period to some advantage, and managed to get Oliver Lyttleton (later Lord Chandos) to read his report. He was fascinated by it and mentioned it to Churchill.

Before the end of the voyage, in November 1941, Wingate had another medical board which declared him fit and offered him the opportunity to be regraded for active service after three months. The board concluded that his return to combat duty was most desirable from the national point of view. (Wingate Papers) When he reached England he was able to return at once to his wife and family, who supported him with warmth and affection – just what he needed. Determined to be declared fit at the earliest opportunity, he was helped by influential Zionist friends including Dr Weizmann, to obtain an appointment with Lord Horder, the King's physician. Weizmann argued that Wingate was a strange and eccentric man, but was truly a man of genius. He personally was prepared to vouch for his mental stability.

In December 1941, with the help of Cousin Rex and L. S. Amery, his report on the Ethiopian campaign was substantially revised – omitting the paragraph on the military apes – and then circulated by Amery at the highest level, including Sir Hastings Ismay, who made sure that Churchill saw it. This ready access to people at the top – which Wingate used to the full – seems to have been a major factor in causing resentment among colleagues who lacked that sort of contact.

During his leave over Christmas 1941, Wingate became involved in an unofficial campaign to ensure that Haile Selassie and his country were not sacrificed to sinister British colonial ambitions. At the same time, Sandford was in London advising a Cabinet Committee which was negotiating the Anglo-Ethiopian Agreement of December 1941. He had to fight hard to support Haile Selassie's interests, since there were some, including Sir Philip Mitchell, who wanted Ethiopia to become a British protectorate. While Wingate continued with his activities, at the back of his mind was his longing to return to Palestine, together with a suspicion that the War Office wanted to post him to some backwater where he could be silenced. This suspicion appeared to be confirmed when, as a major, he was posted to 114 Field Regiment in Dorset. Before this and unbeknown to him, Amery had contacted Wavell, to inquire if there was any chance of employing Wingate in the Far East.

Just as he was posted to Dorset, a signal arrived from Wavell requesting that he should be sent to Rangoon as soon as possible. With his experience in Ethiopia and Palestine, and with his mind bubbling over with ideas for Middle East strategy, he was far from pleased with this posting. In spite of the helpful attention of Amery, Weizmann and even Churchill, Wingate still suspected a conspiracy to muzzle him and to send him off to the Far East, in his words 'As a supernumerary major without a staff grading' – ironically, the identical words he had used when he was posted to Cairo in 1940. He wrote a lengthy memorandum, full of shrill resentment which showed him at his worst, and which later provided considerable ammunition for his critics. (Wingate Papers) During this dark period he met his old friend from Woolwich, Derek Tulloch, and after long discussions with him decided to accept his posting to the Far East. For his work in Ethiopia he received a bar to his DSO, and shortly after left for Rangoon on 27 February.

For Wingate, the two main legacies of the Ethiopian campaign were, firstly, the positive development of every aspect of his philosophy for Long Range Penetration which came to fruition when he arrived in the Far East; secondly, his clashes with authority, and his suicide attempt, had provided valuable ammunition for his detractors. By the time he arrived in India they had already been at work.

5

The First
Chindit Campaign

Wingate arrived in India in March 1942 and was appointed by Wavell as a full Colonel to organise guerrilla groups behind the Japanese lines. He quickly left for Burma and went to see the Bush Warfare School at Maymyo, run by Major Michael Calvert. Fortunately, these two strong characters got on well from the start. Wingate spent some days with Calvert and then on 6 April he flew to Chungking to see Chiang Kai Shek, to discuss the operation of guerrilla groups. By the time he returned the Japanese had rapidly advanced, so he reported back to Wavell in Delhi.

Shortly after this Wingate gave a lecture in Delhi to GHQ staff and some representatives of Chiang Kai Shek's forces, on Long Range Penetration. He outlined his initial plans for an operation in the Arakan. The army is a close knit society and while Wingate had arrived in India with a reputation for his daring guerrilla work in Palestine and Ethiopia, his reputation for being difficult, eccentric and abrasive had also preceded him. By August 1942 he had established his training centre near Gwalior in the Central Provinces about 150 miles south of Delhi, but his detractors were already at work.

Michael Calvert, whom Wingate had appointed as his second in command, and who was to become the most successful of all the Chindit leaders, attended a conference on Long Range Penetration (LRP) at GHQ in August 1942. From Maiden's Hotel he wrote to Wingate warning him that a number of the top brass thought that LRP was impracticable and Wingate was not fit to command. One general had said that 10 per cent of Wingate's ideas were brilliant, but 90 per cent were dangerous or absurd. Calvert added, 'I think "impractable" and "not fit to command" is the attitude of those few who, due to jealousy, listening to gossip, and guilt over their own previous unpreparedness and inefficiency have put themselves against you. Their minds must be small.' (Wingate Papers, letter 6 Aug 1942)

Calvert, who throughout his life has remained intensely loyal to Wingate and to his memory, was warning Wingate of the type of opposition he faced and continued to face. Wingate wrote an impassioned reply. He considered that Wavell was their only hope, since the opportunity to prepare LRP groups depended on the very people making the attacks on him. He added that in action against the enemy he had had sole command of up to 2,000 troops in 73 different actions, and in Ethiopia the establishment were saying exactly the same things before his campaign started. 'It is because I am what I am, objectionable though that appears to my critics, that I win battles.' (Wingate Papers, letter 8 Aug 1942) He believed his brigade could be ready for action by October 1942 if he was not prevented by people with a defeatist attitude, who said British troops could not do it.

A few days later, his enemies received more ammunition. There was a sudden monsoon downpour and the river through his training area rose by 30 feet. Wingate, dressed only in his topee, swam calmly past the tree tops to rally the troops, but some men were lost in the flood, and Command sent a panic telegram with no fewer than 43 copies to the vast bureaucracy at GHQ. Unperturbed, Wingate outlined his philosophy to Calvert. He believed that LRP Groups up to brigade strength could go into the jungle behind the enemy lines, and supplied by air could stay there while wreaking havoc on roads, bridges, railways and all the enemy's lines of communication. He believed that by the end of the war every Army group would have an LRP brigade. He believed British troops were better than any once they were interested and he rejected the idea of getting volunteers, because an existing infantry unit could be adapted more swiftly to guerrilla warfare. He denied that you must be exceptional to undertake this type of training, though he was concerned at the prevailing hypochondria of his men, who went sick far too readily. (Wingate Papers, letter 15 Aug 1942)

Against this background, 77 Indian Brigade started its training. Composed of the 13th King's (Liverpool) Regiment, the 3rd/2nd Gurkha Rifles, and the 2nd Battalion Burma Rifles, to which was added 142 Commando, an RAF section, a signals section and a mule transport company, this new brigade was subjected to a training schedule of savage severity. At that time many officers thought it was infra dig to actually run, but Wingate ran everywhere, and his officers soon learned. Initially, he had an uphill task: 70 per cent of the King's went sick, and the unit was reduced from 650 to 400. The Gurkha battalion was reduced from 750 to 500, but later had to be made up with untried recruits and inexperienced officers who could not speak Gurkhali – this was to have serious consequences. The Burma Rifles proved to be the most successful of all the units involved. The Gurkhas were generally hopeless at watermanship of any sort, but the Burma Rifles, in training and in action, were superb at patrolling, handling boats for river crossing, living off the country (eg, knowing which pythons or frogs to eat), and all the activities of guerrilla warfare. After several weeks of jungle training the sick rate was reduced to 3 per cent and Wingate had established the view that the platoon commander was his unit medical officer.

He organised the Brigade into eight columns, which could operate as completely independent units with their own mule transport, controlled by wireless signals, and supplied entirely by air. The Column became the key operational unit of the first Chindit expedition for which they were now actively training. The key to the success of Wingate's training was his fanatical attention to detail, and very rapidly officers and men built up their confidence, fitness and stamina.

The original aim of the first expedition was to move into the jungle, attack the Japanese lines of communication, and to destroy roads, railways, bridges and transport, in order to assist major advances by the main British forces 'so that each helped the other'. (Wingate Papers, report 22 Sept 1942) Their method would be to penetrate up to 200 miles behind the enemy lines, establish a permanent column rendezvous, and from there make major attacks either with independent columns or with several columns acting together. The overall aim remained: to attack, destroy and disrupt enemy transport and communications, and to cause enemy forces to withdraw from the front.

Wingate's leadership and attention to detail comes through all his training directives: hit the enemy at vital spots; always take the offensive view; attack with surprise; concentrate to strike and disperse for security; leave wide scope for commanders to adapt or exploit success. One theory which, ironically, did not work out was 'operate in healthy country, eg around Mandalay, and avoid the Assam border and dense jungle'.

After weeks of training, Wingate held a major exercise in which 3,000 men in eight widely separated Columns were handled effectively, and controlled by signals and ciphers. The offensive spirit was good, the sabotage squads excelled themselves, and the RAF liaison worked well. Several things did not measure up to Wingate's perfectionist standards, but Wavell was there to reassure him. Valuable lessons were learned from the mistakes: mules needed longer training and to be trained with the Columns; march discipline was uneven, and there were too many faint hearted stragglers. Signals were vital to the whole operation, and while the signals officers excelled themselves, there were too few trained signallers for the huge load of signals work in this sort of operation.

The efficient handling of intelligence was crucial to all Chindit operations and the exercise taught valuable lessons but, with no direct support from divisional or Corps HQs, 'intelligence' remained a heavy burden for 77 Brigade. Wingate had realised this and prior to the operation large supplies of maps were provided, together with complete pictures of enemy forces and dispositions. The Chindit operations room, 25 feet square, the walls covered with maps and air photographs, and the floor covered with one inch to the mile maps, operated 12 hours a day. In addition to this was Wingate's strong belief in detailed sand table exercises, so that every officer and NCO could be trained in aggressive tactical thinking. Whether in training or in action, the troops were amazed at Wingate's attention to detail, whether on Allied strategy or where you sited a Bren gun or rifle section. One officer commented that after Wingate's savage training the operation was a piece of cake. During this training period, when Wingate had the support of two educated Burmese officers, he mistook the name Chinthe – the traditional lions at the entrance to Burmese temples – and produced the name Chindit.

Towards the end of 1942, Wingate visited the HQ of 4th Corps at Imphal, and he received considerable help from General Scoones, the Corps commander, in arranging for 77 Brigade to move up to Imphal and to pass through the 4th Corps area. He was also able to carry out an air recce over the terrain between Imphal, the Chindwin and the Irrawaddy. After this successful visit, and a tough final exercise, 77 Brigade, in January 1943, moved by rail to Dimapur, and then marched the last 130 miles to Imphal. Because of the heavy volume of traffic on the tenuous road, they marched by night and slept in bivouacs by day – completing the march in eight days. Wingate chose a site for their camp eight miles from Imphal – not wanting them to be softened up by going to the camp cinema!

Wavell's plans at the start of 1943 had included an advance by 4th Corps from Imphal down to the Chindwin, an advance by Stilwell and

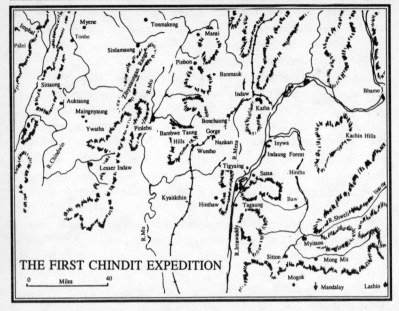

THE FIRST CHINDIT EXPEDITION

his Chinese divisions towards Myitkyina, an advance by 15th Corps in the Arakan towards Akyab, and Operation 'Longcloth' by the Chindits to disrupt Japanese communications and supplies just when they were being attacked on three fronts. On 5 February 1943, Wavell came to see Wingate in Imphal with the depressing news that none of the proposed offensives could take place. He was afraid that, because of this, 77 Brigade could well be sacrificed if it went in alone, since the Japanese would have all their forces available to destroy the Chindits at leisure.

Against this sincere expression of concern, Wingate argued strongly. The Chindits were in a high state of readiness, if the operation did not proceed it would give ammunition to his opponents and critics, the opportunity to develop his revolutionary ideas about jungle warfare would be lost, and, because of the opposition in the Indian army, might never recur. In addition, there was an urgent need to disrupt a Japanese attack on a small British garrison manned by loyal North Kachin Levies at Sumprabum in the extreme north near Fort Hertz. Wavell had to balance the inevitable losses of the Chindits – likely to be heavier because of the absence of any other advance – against the valuable lessons to be learned from LRP, and he needed to be reassured that it would not be a senseless sacrifice. After lengthy consideration, Wavell sanctioned Operation 'Longcloth', gave them a final inspection, and in a moving gesture he saluted them.

77 Brigade moved off from Imphal on 12 February 1943 and started the operation which Wingate had planned so carefully. He had received considerable help and intelligence from 4th Corps at Imphal, from 23 Division which held the territory forward from Imphal towards the Chindwin, and from small Chindit patrols led by Burma Rifles officers, which probed eastwards up to and beyond the Chindwin. Wingate's plan included a substantial element of deception and bluff. His main group – HQ together with 3, 4, 5, 7 and 8 Columns were to cross the Chindwin at Tonhe, lying almost due east of Palel. At the same time, No 1 group, consisting of 1 and 2 Columns crossed the river at Auktaung, about 50 miles south of Tonhe. This group hoped to deceive the Japanese into thinking that the main drive of the whole operation was to the south towards Mandalay.

As the Chindits moved towards the Chindwin, Wingate issued his Order of the Day. This impressive order – reproduced in the prologue – caught exactly the right note for the Chindits, who were now keyed up and confident after their vigorous training.

During the night of 13 February, unobserved and in total secrecy, 150 men of the Burma Rifles crossed the Chindwin. Next, on 14 February, the decoy group – 1 and 2 Columns numbering about 1,000 men – crossed at Auktaung, making little effort to conceal their movements. The next day they had an air drop in broad daylight and then a Wingate look-alike, complete with beard, topee and red tabs, went into villages with known pro-Japanese headmen and ordered massive supplies to be delivered in villages further south. At night on 14 February, the main force, about 2,000 strong, crossed the Chindwin at Tonhe, and rapidly moved eastwards completely undetected. The deception had succeeded completely.

During training, considerable emphasis had been given to river crossing techniques but, as Wingate later admitted, it had been hopelessly inadequate. Attempts had been made to develop a technique with long ropes and stakes driven into the river bed, but the Chindwin and the Irrawaddy could be up to a mile wide with a surging fast flowing current, and few attempts to cross them were successful. Parts of this first crossing became chaotic. There were some rubber dinghies with inadequate paddles, and these were mixed up with strings of mules, bullocks and elephants. The mules caused immediate chaos. Wingate wrote, 'Every method from kindness to brutality was employed to induce the intensely non-cooperative animals to cross quietly'. The main body were unable to get across in darkness and daylight produced a scene of bewildering shambles, with naked men swimming, pulling mules, and fighting with mules trying to return to the shore. Among the mules, heavily laden rubber dinghies were being gingerly manoeuvred by anxious Gurkhas, who were never happy or at their best on water. At this and on many subsequent occasions, the equipment provided was virtually useless and nearly every Column came to rely on local boats.

After they had crossed the Chindwin, the Columns moved off rapidly to gain the protection of the jungle. A Chindit normally carried a load of about 70lbs. He wore tropical uniform, army boots and a mosquito veil, and each man had a machete and light rubber boots for patrol work. He carried a light blanket, groundsheet, mess-tins, sterilizing kit, rifle or Bren gun, 50 rounds of .303 ammunition and, finally, six day's iron rations. One day's ration consisted of 12 wholemeal biscuits, 2 ounces of nuts or raisins, 2 ounces of cheese, 4 ounces of dates, 2 ounces of chocolate, 20 cigarettes, tea, sugar, powdered milk, salt and a vitamin C tablet. The mules carried heavier items, like the 3in mortar, extra ammunition, wireless sets, and the important battery-charger.

Calvert, commanding 3 Column led the way eastwards away from the Chindwin, and on 17 February the main group took their first supply drop at Myene. After this 3 Column again led the way and they enjoyed a fairly easy passage through attractive teak forest, but this led to a slackening of discipline, and Wingate constantly harangued his officers about noise, litter, 'abysmal ignorance', poor intelligence, and march discipline generally. Column leaders felt they needed a successful clash with the enemy and when reports came in of a Japanese garrison at Simlamaung, Calvert's Column, with 7 and 8 Columns, was ordered to attack. They made a night march through difficult country and attacked the village at dawn, but found the Japanese had just left in a hurry. An elephant and some useful documents were captured. This first attack was not a success, partly because the maps were found to be inaccurate. In another early encounter, when 3 Column suffered its first casualties, several British soldiers panicked under fire and had to be put back into their positions by kicks and threats. Even Calvert, who later became the most successful and aggressive of all the Column commanders, felt depressed at the reaction of his group and at the loss of stores and mules. One comment reveals the pressures on a commander behind enemy lines, 'During one period I became very depressed and rather useless, but my officers carried on excellently'. (Wingate Papers, 3 Column War Diary)

Wingate was undoubtedly an eccentric, and some of his eccentricities were latched on to and exaggerated by his detractors. One such incident occurred during the first weeks of this march when the Columns were traversing some difficult country. Wingate halted the Columns, called all officers together and, to their amazement, gave them not some urgent information about the Japanese but an hour's lecture in scathing terms about the defeatist attitude shown by 'the so-called miracle of Dunkirk'. These were certainly trying days before the Columns settled into a routine, and one officer said 'If I had not been an officer I would have fallen out... and told everyone to go to hell'. (Sykes, *Orde Wingate*, p397)

By 1 March, the main body of the Chindits, after a few set-backs, had reached an area of relatively safe hills to the south of Pinbon. From there, Wingate planned for 4 Column to ambush the road to the north of Pinlebu in order to prevent Japanese reinforcements coming south; 7 and 8 Columns to attack Pinlebu itself; and finally, the most important object of the whole expedition, for 3 and 5 Columns, under Calvert and Fergusson, to destroy the main railway line, bridges, viaduct and station at Nankan and Bonchaung Gorge.

Before these actions could take place, two Columns suffered serious reverses: 2 Column, which had taken part in the original feint to the south, reached the area Kyaikthin, nearly 40 miles south of Nankan. Here a strong Japanese force ambushed them as they moved out of their bivouac. In the fight, the CO changed his dispersal rendezvous, but in the noise of battle few heard him and most of the Column lost contact in the ensuing chaos. The unit lost mules, weapons, equipment and the unit cipher. In his report, Wingate was highly critical of the Column Commander who, by marching down the railway and bivouacking near the track, caused a disaster which was easily avoidable.

To the north of the main body, 4 Column, which should have ambushed the road north of Pinbon, were themselves ambushed by a stronger Japanese force. They had been patrolling in the area when the

Japanese attacked the centre of the column. Some young Gurkhas with, in Wingate's words 'a disgraceful exhibition of panic', broke their line and stampeded their mules. In the resulting pandemonium, the Column lost its wireless, ammunition supply, the reserve weapons and much equipment. The survivors of this debacle eventually made their way back to Imphal. Thus 2 and 4 Columns had ceased to be effective fighting units. Out of the original eight Columns, No 6 had

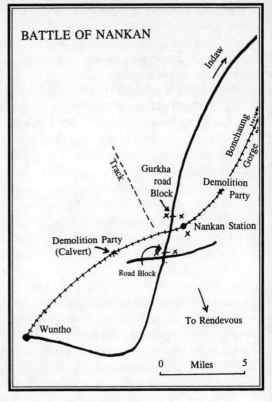

BATTLE OF NANKAN

been dispersed among the other Columns, 2 and 4 had been destroyed, and No 1 had not been in touch since it made the feint to the south. Thus Wingate was left with Columns 3, 5, 7 and 8 to carry out the attack on Nankan and the strategically important railway from Mandalay going north to Myitkyina – the main supply route for all the Japanese divisions facing Stilwell.

The loss of 2 and 4 Columns and the loss of contact with No 1 had been a serious blow to Wingate, and in a period of mounting tension he waited to see if the attack by Calvert with 3 Column on Nankan station, and by Fergusson with 5 Column on the Bonchaung Gorge, were successful.

On 4 March, Calvert and 3 Column reached the outskirts of Nankan, and in a secure bivouac he rested his men before the main attack. While the unit rested, he ordered an RAF attack on Wuntho,

84

about 10 miles south of Nankan, where there was a Japanese unit of about 60 men. Nankan was full of wrecked and rusting vehicles left from the 1942 retreat, but the area around the station seemed to be deserted. Calvert then fixed the rendezvous and divided his attack into two groups, one of which he commanded himself.

He sent a small group of Gurkhas to establish a road block just north of the station, another group to make a road block to the south, and a 'Keep in touch Party', including the intrepid Thompson (RAF Liaison Officer), with the wireless, the mules, and Flossie the elephant, to a small chaung or stream just south of the station. At 12.45pm the two demolition teams moved on to the railway, one three miles north of the station and one three miles south, and they worked along the track towards the station, laying over 70 mines as they went. Everything seemed remarkably peaceful until about 1.15pm two truck loads of Japanese, approaching on the road south from Indaw, drove unsuspectingly into the road block manned by the Gurkhas.

The Gurkhas inflicted heavy casualties on the enemy, but then Japanese reinforcements arrived and soon the Gurkhas were outnumbered. The base group sent a section to help the Gurkhas, the demolition parties sent some more, and Thompson with the wireless wisely moved into the jungle. Calvert and the demolition groups worked swiftly, mining both the spans and columns of the bridges. Another bridge close to the station was mined and blown up, in spite of intense Japanese fire. At that moment, Captain Petersen, a flamboyant Dane with a grudge against the Japanese, arrived unexpectedly near the station and went straight into action. Calvert, having completed his demolition task, quickly re-sited his 3in mortars and with the first bomb hit the Japanese truck. The Japanese fled and the Chindit Column moved off at once to their rendezvous, leaving booby-traps all round the station. A swift roll-call at the RV showed that in this model action, 3 Column which had destroyed the railway and several bridges, and had inflicted heavy casualties on the enemy, did not suffer a single casualty. It was Calvert's 30th birthday, and for his outstanding leadership he won the DSO. Sykes, the biographer of Wingate, refers to Calvert's macabre sense of humour, and added 'Calvert's widespread lethal practical jokes (illustrated best in his booby-traps) kept the enemy in chronic bewilderment'.

Fergusson's attack with 5 Column on the railway as it crossed the Bonchaung Gorge (6 March) was less successful. He sent one group south of the gorge and they clashed with the enemy in a small village. The Chindit commander thought he had driven off the Japanese, but he had overlooked a machine gun which opened fire, killing four and wounding six of the Chindits. The killed and wounded had to be left behind. Fergusson hurried on from this incident towards the gorge, where one huge explosion brought thousands of tons of rock down on to the railway, and by evening the bridge too was totally demolished, with such a loud bang that it was heard and gave fresh heart to Chindit groups scattered through the jungle up to 10 miles away.

While the main attack on Nankan and the Bonchaung Gorge went in, 7 Column had got into difficulties and shortly afterwards about 70 of them had joined Calvert's group, thus adding to the problem of food supplies. At the same time, 8 Column under Major Scott had been used to divert attention from Nankan, by mounting an assault on Pinlebu, about 30 miles west of Nankan. The enemy garrison at Pinlebu was estimated at 800 and on 4 March Scott called down a strong RAF attack which caused the Japanese to disperse widely. No 8 Column entered the town but then withdrew, leaving fires burning, and had the satisfaction of watching a heavy Japanese bombardment and attack on an empty town.

Wingate and his HQ were now located in the Bambwe Taung Hills, lying roughly between Pinlebu, where 8 Column had attacked, and Nankan. The successful attack on the Mandalay-Myitkyina railway had achieved his first objective, but now he had to make a difficult decision: should he move on eastwards and cross the Irrawaddy river, should he retreat westwards and return to India, or should he stay in the relative safety of the Bambwe Taung Hills, from where he could pose a continuing threat to the Japanese communications. This possibility – which showed he already had the nucleus of his Stronghold philosophy in his mind – would have been ideal if there had been a major British advance from Imphal, but Wingate knew that no such advance was contemplated.

For days he agonised over the decision to cross the Irrawaddy, knowing that the lives of 3,000 men depended on it. Serious danger faced the Chindits if they tried to return to the Chindwin through country where the Japanese were out in force, where they were guarding the possible river crossings, and where they had commandeered all the local boats. If he crossed the Irrawaddy, intelligence reports had suggested that the country would be much easier for rapid movement and the Kachin people would most likely be loyal and supportive. In practice, as the Chindits found to their cost, the land to the east of the Irrawaddy was dry and waterless at that time of year, and was criss-crossed by motor roads which the Japanese actively patrolled. If the whole Chindit force crossed the Irrawaddy there was an added danger that the enemy could trap them in the area between the Irrawaddy and the Shweli river, both of them formidable obstacles for large bodies of men to cross against opposition. In facing these difficulties, far from acting on any preconceived notion, Wingate consulted both Calvert and Fergusson and on 8 March signalled to them for their opinion. Both Columns then lay east of the railway and fairly close to the river. Both leaders replied emphatically that they should go east and cross the Irrawaddy; they added that in the hope of getting an unopposed crossing they would like to move as rapidly as possible. Wingate has been severely criticised for his decision to cross the Irrawaddy, as if it was his fixed purpose to do so, but it can be seen that such criticism is the reverse of the truth.

At this stage another factor emerged. No 1 Column, which had not been heard of since crossing the Chindwin on 14 February, suddenly regained contact and announced that it had already crossed the Irrawaddy at Tagaung, about 40 miles south of Wingate's HQ. The main rationale for the whole Chindit expedition had been to try out theories of LRP and even more important, to gain experience which could be used in the future. With this in mind, Wingate decided to order the whole force, including his HQ, to cross the Irrawaddy.

Fergusson and 5 Column made a rapid approach to Tigyaing and entered the town as a deliberate show of force. Just then a Japanese plane flew over dropping leaflets, which appealed to the Burmese people to report any miserable remnants of 'the pitiable Anglo-Indian soldiery'. Making the most of the situation, Fergusson went to the middle of the town and to an appreciative audience who laughed hilariously, he read out the message. The Japanese were not slow to react, and although the Column obtained a number of boats, the enemy attacked before the last men were over. Fergusson was the last to be hauled on to the boat, and he crossed the river ignominiously with his bottom in the air. He later claimed to be the first British officer to cross the Irrawaddy on all fours.

No 3 Column had also aimed at Tigyaing, but Fergusson's group had reached there first, and so Calvert led his Column five miles down

y were short of food and received an air drop on 11 March.
e the Japanese were alerted and Calvert faced the difficult
crossing a one-mile wide river while being attacked by formidable opposition. Although a few men got across to an island, when the enemy attacked the whole Column was in peril. Calvert organised the rear-guard himself and at a critical moment, when the crossing could have become a disaster, a convoy of boats came up the river. Calvert commandeered them, bundled his men aboard, destroyed equipment which could not easily be ferried across, and successfully made his escape.

He had to leave six wounded men behind and he left a note for the local Japanese commander, saying that they had been fighting for King and Country and had been wounded. He added 'I leave them confidently in your charge, knowing that with your well known tradition of Bushido (chivalry), you will look after them as if they were your own'. They were well treated and survived. (Wingate Papers)

Further south, No 1 Column near Tagaung were able to bluff a fairly large force of Aung San's so-called Burmese Independence Army and managed to cross the river unopposed.

Meanwhile, Wingate and about 1,200 men left the security of the hills and, travelling almost due east, reached the village of Inywa, about 10 miles north of Tigyaing where Fergusson had crossed. The Burma Rifles excelled themselves in this operation, but none more than Aung Thin who became Wingate's main liaison officer. At Inywa he bravely crossed the river to test the reaction of the people on the far side. They welcomed him and quickly supplied the force with food and sufficient local boats. Each crossing of the river took over an hour, and by early on 18 March the whole force was safely across. This was a high point for Wingate, who had achieved the main objective of destroying the north-south railway and roads, and with few losses had crossed the daunting obstacle of the Irrawaddy.

Once he was over the river (18 March), Wingate found the situation very different from that suggested by intelligence information. There was to be no easy marching through open jungle past friendly supportive villages. The area was dry and inhospitable and well supplied with motor roads which the Japanese, now fully alerted to the Chindit presence, used to good effect. The active enemy patrolling made air drops more difficult and all the Columns began to suffer severely from physical exhaustion, and shortages of water and food. The commander of 8 Column reported that his men were at the end of their tether.

The supply drop technique upon which the expedition had depended from the start, and which Wingate had planned in minute detail, now became essential to their very survival. The Chindits and the RAF, both in the air and on the ground, had nothing but praise for the way the system worked. When a drop was needed, the Column commander would tell his RAF liaison officer where they would be in two days time. He would then study the map, choose a suitable spot, and radio his orders to the base. At the dropping zone, fires were lit in a T or L pattern which could be seen from the air, but only for a short distance through the jungle. The usual dropping zone was a roughly cleared area measuring 600 yards by 100. Initially, drops were taken on fairly open paddy fields, but experience showed that it was easier and safer to take drops in light jungle, away from villages and from Japanese interference. Usually, Dakotas or Hudson bombers made the drops and they would circle 10 or 12 times before they dropped all their load. The essentials were, of course, rations, ammunition and replacement weapons, petrol, distilled water for the chargers and wireless batteries, and wireless sets. In addition to all of this, the care over personal provision amazed everyone: a Scot received a replacement kilt; false teeth and spectacles were dropped – the prescriptions for which had been recorded prior to the expedition; also pipes, Penguin books, snuff, papers – especially local papers from home – and most important of all, mail. Discipline had to be very tight during a drop and Fergusson threatened to shoot anyone who cheated over rations.

During long periods of privation nearly all the Chindits had fantasies, either about food or about chocolate. One man said if he could have the most glamorous blonde in the world he would swap her for a tin of bully beef. One unit ordered 400lbs of chocolate and it was dropped the following day. Fergusson recorded how his Column reached a village where they made a type of fudge, or Scottish tablet, and at once their morale shot up. One Scottish officer was disgruntled because he had ordered snuff and could not find it, and then found a group of unhappy Gurkhas who had put it in their curry.

Fantasies did much to keep men going during long hours and days of hunger, thirst and exhaustion, and there were many well-worn jokes about food. One sergeant was renowned for his act as a French waiter offering pâté de foie gras. While they were in India, many units had seen the film 'Moon over Burma' with Dorothy Lamour, and jokes and fantasies about meeting her in the jungle helped morale. A conversation would often start 'Where are you now?', and the reply would give a long description of a favourite restaurant and a special meal. Equally, men longed for water and the sound of a tap running.

Luck always plays a big part in war and some Columns seemed to be luckier than others in their air drops. Fergusson's Column was consistently unlucky, while Calvert's did very well. The biggest air drop of the whole campaign, with over 10 tons of supplies including boots, uniforms, food, books and mail was made to 3 Column on 18 March.

During the 1942 Burma retreat Calvert, as a junior sapper officer, but already with a reputation for his effective demolitions, had the frustration of waiting with the charges all ready to blow up the famous Gokteik viaduct carrying the road north from Mandalay to Lashio. No senior officer would give the order to blow it up and to his chagrin the Japanese took it over intact. (Years later he learned that the top brass hoped he would disobey orders and blow it up anyway.) Now it appeared he might get a second chance. On 17 March, Wingate issued orders for 3 and 5 Columns to move south towards Sitton and from there to move on past Mon Mit towards Gokteik.

While 3 and 5 Columns set out southwards, Wingate led the main group 30 miles southeast from Inywa and on 21 March ordered a two-day rest, and received a good supply drop. Shortage of water remained a serious problem and here again the Burma Rifles men were invaluable, as they had an unerring instinct where to dig for water. While briefly in a position of security, Wingate again had serious decisions to make. Lying close to Baw, there were many options – all of them dangerous, since with no general British advance the Japanese were able to concentrate their whole attention on wiping out the Chindits. He could have decided to lead the whole expedition northeast through the relative safety of the Kachin Hills and up the old Burma Road to China, but it was considered impossible to supply such a large force at such a distance; a route northwards past Katha and Myitkyina and on to Fort Hertz was feasible, but there were very substantial enemy forces in the area and the poor physical state of the men made this an unlikely option; the final option was to return over the Irrawaddy and retrace their steps back to the Chindwin.

At this stage, 22 March, Eastern Army and 4th Corps HQ intervened and ordered Wingate to bring the whole expedition back to India. As a result of this intervention he then ordered Calvert, unless he was very close to Gokteik, to come back north with his Column.

Just before he received this message, Calvert carried out a very clever ambush of a Japanese battalion near Sitton. For the loss of one Chindit casualty, 100 enemy were killed, many more wounded and the unit fled. On 23 March, Fergusson and 5 Column received orders to return to the Baw area. Fergusson was unhappy with this order since it brought him back into the fairly narrow confines of the loop between the Irrawaddy and Shweli rivers, and he had a damaging clash with the enemy before reaching the rendezvous. On 25 March, Wingate met Fergusson and appeared very pessimistic. He said they had made the Japanese commander look stupid and he would obviously do his best to annihilate the whole Chindit force.

The following day, 26 March, there was a conference with 5, 7 and 8 Column commanders. Fergusson argued that the whole group should stay together, keeping their mules and support weapons, and march north past Myitkyina. He later argued in his written report, 'I felt the Government of India deserved some better return for the lavish equipment entrusted to us than the tame abandonment of them and the valuable animals'. (Wingate Papers, Fergusson report)

Wingate countered this, arguing that by 27 March they had achieved most of their objectives and the most important thing was to bring home as many men as possible with their invaluable experience. He rejected Fergusson's idea because it would be impossible to supply such a large body of men by air and at such a distance. He then put forward his own plan which all, with some reluctance, accepted: the whole force would return to Inywa – where he had crossed – since the enemy would not expect them to return to the same place. Before crossing the Irrawaddy they would abandon the heaviest equipment, kill most of the mules and, once over the river, would disperse into small groups and make attacks on the enemy where possible as they returned to the Chindwin. Wingate's plan still allowed considerable flexibility to Column commanders and several groups did not follow him back across the river.

On 27 March, Wingate with his HQ, the Burma Rifles, 5, 7 and 8 Columns set off towards Inywa. The Japanese harried the group and Fergusson who was covering the rear had some severe clashes. On one occasion, breaking the Chindit rule not to enter a village at night, he approached the village of Hintha. It was held by the Japanese who immediately opened fire with LMGs firing on fixed lines, and with a hail of mortars and grenades. This had disastrous results. An officer,

Lieutenant Stibbe, who later wrote *Return via Rangoon*, was wounded, and his life was saved by a Burma Rifleman, who stayed behind with him and was subsequently killed. Because of this action, Fergusson lost contact with Wingate's group and never regained it.

No 5 Column, having lost contact with the main group, realised that they had to get back on their own. They had nine officers, 114 men and a horse. Their ill-luck over air drops continued and their rations were seriously depleted. At best their ration was four biscuits, a packet of chocolate and a packet of dates per man per day.

Almost at once they faced a crisis. Planning to travel north, they had to cross the Shweli river. They found a crossing not guarded by the Japanese and obtained two boats. Fergusson led the group and, thinking he had crossed the river, found to his dismay that he had only reached an island and there were still a hundred yards of black, sinister, fast-flowing water to cross. Then the boats were swept away and the party had to brave the water on foot. Some of the leaders got across, but some disappeared into the river and panic swept through the men left on the island. Officers returned and, time and again, ordered the men to cross. Because of the panic this had no effect, which led Fergusson to make a final warning that he would move off in 30 minutes and if they did not cross they would be left behind. Some still refused and he moved off with a party of only 46. Later it was heard that the Japanese had captured a group of more than 30 men in that area. Fergusson wrote in *Beyond the Chindwin* that the memory of the Shweli crossing haunted him for the rest of his life.

The Column then marched north through the Kachin Hills, where they were pursued by frequent and strong Japanese patrols. Still seriously short of food, they were kept going by a good supply of tea and malted milk tablets. Occasionally a village would sell them some pork or rice, but there was always the danger that the enemy were in the villages. Pursued by aggressive patrols and short of food and water, the men were in such a low state that often they just fainted while walking along, but during this grim time no-one even considered giving themselves up. There were clearly some cases of bad discipline but, for the most part, as Fergusson wrote 'The spirit, discipline, cheerfulness, courage, unselfishness and comradeship of the men were epic'. (*Beyond the Chindwin*, p194) When the group reached a safer area and the party were able to bathe in a river, Fergusson was shocked that the tough, fit and hardened men he had set off with could have become so frail. Their emaciated bodies emerged pallid and withered, arms and legs were mere spindles, their skin as brittle as paper, and with cavities instead of stomachs.

At last, having marched well to the north, they got away from their pursuers and, on 10 April, helped by a friendly village, the whole party crossed the Irrawaddy north of Katha. This brought them into the main range of the Kachin Hills where there were fewer Japanese and consequently the Kachin villagers were helpful and hospitable. The villages had a remarkable intelligence system and always knew if there were any Japanese in the vicinity. On 16 April, the Chindits received a lavish welcome in a village and were given a huge breakfast of pork, vegetables and rice. A wealthy Chinaman offered to pay anything to get to India; he proved to be a great help to the group and travelled out with them. A Scots sergeant major did not take to the Chinaman and after giving the poor man orders in a mixture of Gurkhali, Scots, Urdu and Burmese, complained to Fergusson 'He's no pullin' his weight. He'll nae do a bloody thing I tell him.'

In spite of the help of the Kachins, who continued to provide wonderful hospitality and kindness, the poor physical state of the Chindits remained a constant worry. They now suffered increasingly from lice and from mosquitoes, and the majority, who had worn through their boots, suffered as well from foot-rot. Many were so sick and weak that they could hardly stagger along, and lacked the strength to carry their pack. The grim trek continued through April until, on 24 April, they reached the Chindwin and found a British V Force group ready to help them across.

After the fierce action at Sitton on 24 March, Calvert and 3 Column received Wingate's message to return to India but left the route to Calvert's discretion. On 27 March they attempted to cross the Shweli river, but were opposed by the Japanese and here too some men were so tired, worn out and listless that they refused to cross. Even such an strong leader as Calvert wrote 'My own spirits dropped to zero'. (Wingate Papers,. Calvert Report) Facing this crisis, he discussed it with all his officers. He personally opposed splitting up into smaller groups, seeing it as 'Shelving the responsibility of a commander just when the men need a leader', but he agreed 'The morale of half the Column was such that it would not fight'. (W. P. Calvert, Report) After their discussion Calvert went along with the majority and agreed that they should disperse in small groups, but he remained worried that there were not enough leaders to take on the awesome responsibility of commanding troops 150 miles behind enemy lines, and he feared the leaders might crack up. He warned the officers that they were leaving their ship with its heavy guns, and taking to the boats.

Calvert then cabled to 4th Corps HQ: 'Am near Baw. Brigade orders to return to Chindwin. Japs have ringed Irrawaddy and mountains – and sending reinforcements from Mandalay. Column will move to Chindwin in groups of 40. Please help returning groups and warn Kachin Levies and Chinese. Regret troubling you.' He then spent a dismal night realising this was the end of Column 3.

He divided the Column into nine groups of 40 men, but conscious of the responsibilities of the group leaders, he gave them careful orders: march methodically and don't get overtired. 'Tiredness makes cowards of us all.' If you are up against it, sit down, make a cup of tea, and usually it gets solved. Do not, in trying to avoid Japs, get more casualties through drowning or lack of food and water. If you can't get boats in one place get them in another, and if all else fails make big rafts of bamboo and push off at night – it doesn't matter how far you drift down. Don't allow the hunted feeling to get to you. Make maps for all your men giving directions and distances. When you come in don't look like a defeated army as you pass the front line troops – overdo the drill and saluting. 'We have been under great strain. Let us keep our dirty washing to ourselves on our return.' (Wingate Papers, Calvert Report)

The Column then took a good air drop with food, boots and ammunition. Weapons, equipment, mortars, and machine guns were wrapped and buried, in case they returned next year. Then, using some of the rum ration, 'they drank to the health of the King, wished each other luck, and departed in various directions, 'but not very far due to the rum'. (Wingate Papers, Calvert Report)

A description of the return of 3 Column is given by one of Calvert's officers, Jeffery Lockett, and appears in Tulloch's book *Wingate in Peace and War*. Their privations were similar to those of 5 Column, but Lockett commented that his group were often kept going by benzedrine tablets, and before reaching the Chindwin he was taking up to 12 a day. He described how, on reaching the railway they had blown up on their way out, he was all for letting sleeping dogs lie. 'But not Calvert. He insisted on blowing it up again.' They were the first group to return, reaching the Chindwin on 15 April.

Wingate, with the main body of the Chindits reached Inywa, where the Shweli joins the Irrawaddy, on 28 March. He selected a large area to bivouac because the men were totally exhausted. They collected a few boats and at dawn on 29 March, 7 Column started to cross. Almost at once they came under Japanese fire but the Column, receiving covering fire from mortars and machine guns, managed to get across, take up defensive positions on the far shore, and drive the Japanese away. Then Wingate heard that there were three more Japanese companies coming as reinforcements. By 0900 he realised he did not have the fire power to take on a strongly opposed crossing and decided to abandon it. He gave orders for 7 Column to withdraw, and ordered the other Column commanders to retreat to a secure bivouac area, where supply drops would be arranged prior to breaking up into smaller dispersal groups.

The HQ had 200 men and these Wingate divided into five groups of 40. They stayed in their bivouacs for a week receiving successful air drops and preparing for their return journey. Preparations included killing large numbers of mules, so there was mule for breakfast, mule for lunch and mule for supper. During this period of enforced idleness, Wingate engaged in animated discussions with his fellow officers on a dozen different topics: the Italian Renaissance, Beethoven, Plato, Bernard Shaw, H. G. Wells, the United Nations, and most problems facing the world.

After destroying the heavy equipment and killing the last of the mules, Wingate's party set out on 7 April. They marched southwest to Tigyaing – where Fergusson had crossed on the way out – and on 10 April found a number of boats and some men ready to help. A small Japanese patrol fired some shots from the far bank but were driven off and the party crossed safely. They marched on towards Wuntho, receiving some help from the local people, but discovered that the Japanese had threatened to shoot them and burn down all their houses if they helped the Chindits. Wingate's group reached the railway some miles north of Wuntho and were extremely depressed to hear a train and discover that the railway had been reopened within four weeks. They crossed the railway safely although they were making a noisy progress through tinder-dry teak forests.

In the area west of the railway they were increasingly harassed by Japanese patrols and suffered from a severe shortage of both food and water, but they struggled grimly on, augmenting their starvation rations by eating python and lizards. After killing a buffalo they ate too much too quickly, and suffered serious stomach upsets. One officer was too ill to move, and Wingate halted for 48 hours. Still unable to walk, the officer urged them to go on, and staggered to his feet to salute Wingate as he left. Then, after many days of privation and prolonged suffering, they came to a monastery where they obtained chicken, sucking pigs, bananas, tomatoes, rice and plentiful water. This strengthened them for the next march which took them to a daunting ridge of mountains over 1,500 feet high – the Zebyutaung-daw Range. Here a strange hermit, they at first wrongly suspected of being a Japanese agent, led them by little known forest paths right through the mountains. One NCO of 13th King's who could not keep up, bravely lost himself in the jungle – giving his life for his fellows. The group plodded on, still guided by the hermit, and on 26 April came fairly close to the Chindwin. Japanese patrols appeared frequently and the tension in the group rose as everyone dreaded being caught at the very last hurdle. They could find no sign of any British activity and in fear of being discovered by the Japanese – and in the last stages of exhaustion – they had to spend seven hours cutting their way through thick elephant grass, Suddenly, to their delight, they found themselves on the river bank. They divided into two groups – one of which contained the non-swimmers. Wingate and the swimmers plunged into the fast flowing river and, going with the current reached the further shore.

Wingate, dressed only in a ragged bush shirt and his topee, with wild hair and beard, staggered up the beach, only to return with howls of agony as the heat of the sand burnt his sore feet. Quickly, he found a friendly fisherman who guided them to a Gurkha company post. The other party had more serious problems because of active enemy patrols and Captain Katju – a cousin of Nehru – bravely offered to go back over the river to help the non-swimmers, but he was killed instantly. The Gurkhas quickly gave covering fire and the rest of the group came safely over. It was 25 April. Wingate led his men 'with unrelenting ferocity; no-one was allowed to drop out of the line, even with diarrhoea, but the men's faith in him and his grim leadership saved the lives of dozens of emaciated, sick and wounded skeletons'. (Charles Rolo, *Wingate's Raiders*)

The remaining groups enjoyed varying fortunes. No 8 Column aimed to get out well to the north, but were hampered by an increasing number of sick, wounded and totally exhausted men. On one fortunate occasion, when they had ordered a supply drop, they found an unusually long stretch of paddy field and before the planes arrived for the drop, spelt out on the ground PLANE LAND HERE NOW. The pilot of the Dakota saw this, landed, and took off all the sick and wounded. The rest got out to Fort Hertz.

In such stressful conditions, things did not always go smoothly. Wingate reduced an officer to the ranks for failing to find a rendezvous. The Wingate Papers contain a report to the CO of the 13th King's of an incident when the groups were dispersing. Some men, wishing to remain with the main party, were threatened at pistol point by the Medical Officer and the Company Sergeant Major and were told that if they did not clear off they would be shot for disobeying orders. The officer who eventually led this group to safety at Fort Hertz added that 'He did not think it possible that British troops could be so badly treated by British officers'. On several occasions men were flogged – in most cases for endangering the Column by being asleep on sentry duty. That this was an offence had been clearly laid down in advance, but it did lead to one officer, after the war, being court-martialled for flogging a man, though he was acquitted because King's Regulations did not envisage the Chindit situation. To the officers, flogging did not seem too serious a punishment for it was rather like caning to which most of them were accustomed at their public schools.

No 7 Column, under Major Gilkes, divided into three: one group, which received supply drops, and reached Fort Hertz safely; the second, with the less fit which returned westwards to the Chindwin; and Gilke's party which, with the wounded Petersen who had turned up in the middle of Calvert's battle at Nankan, tried to make for China. They set off and crossed the Shweli river eastwards on 17 April, but were seriously harassed by Japanese patrols. They managed to shake off their pursuers and after a couple of days, and with the help of friendly Kachin people, took an excellent supply drop which included food, medicine, ammunition, uniforms and boots. They kept going by grim and determined marches, until on 1 May they made contact with a small unit of the Chinese Army in Yunnan. Here the people were friendly and helpful because the Japanese had burnt many villages in savage reprisals. The Chindit group was guided by the Chinese and was in relative safety, but still had several weeks of tough marching ahead.

On 26 May they reached the HQ of a Chinese division which had just defeated a Japanese brigade. With the help of ponies from a cavalry unit, the Chindits reached Paoshan on the Burma road on 4 June.

The Chinese treated them as heroes and the Army commander sent signals to Kunming, to GHQ Delhi, and to all their families. They were taken to the baths, deloused, shaved and issued with new clothes even down to their underpants. Gilkes was loaned 7,000 dollars to pay his men so that they could buy presents for their families and write home. Every day they enjoyed special meals to restore them to health, and the Chinese Army commander gave them a great banquet.

Finally, the British Military Attaché arrived from Kunming with a three-ton lorry full of clothes, soap, razors, cigarettes, boots and other essentials. Even then their good fortune did not desert them. They boarded lorries for the journey to Kunming and after some hours on the road they stopped at a small military post where an American major spoke to them. He was part of the air transport scheme which every day flew supplies over 'The Hump' for Chiang Kai Shek's forces, but often the planes flew back empty. He sent a few messages and in a couple of hours the whole group were flying back to India.

While the Chindit Columns completely confused the Japanese forces in Upper Burma, there is no evidence that Wingate or any of the Column commanders received any intelligence information about the Japanese units moving against them. In fact the Chindits had moved into the operational area of one of the best Japanese divisions – the 18th or Chrysanthemum Division – commanded by General Mutaguchi who had captured Singapore and who was shortly to command the Japanese 15th Army in its attack on Imphal and Kohima. When the first reports of the Chindit operation reached Mutaguchi, he sent Colonel Koba's 55 Regiment (the equivalent of a British brigade) to control the area between Homalin and Katha. At first Koba was sceptical of reports that 3,000 enemy were moving eastwards from the Chindwin, but when the news was confirmed, he sent two battalions to destroy the intruders. Before these could act effectively, the Chindits broke up into Columns and the Japanese were further confused. Koba then moved his HQ from Homalin to Pinlebu (25 February). From his divisional HQ in Maymyo, Mutaguchi went up to Katha and Pinlebu to assess the situation. He agreed that Koba should move from Pinlebu to Indaw, but he felt the local commanders could cope with the situation and he returned to Maymyo.

By 5 March, when 55 Regiment in a major clash with Wingate's group took 100 prisoners, the Japanese realised the seriousness of the Chindit threat and realised too that they were supplied by air. Then 15th Army HQ in Rangoon took positive action: 18 Division under Mutaguchi was fully mobilised, and 33 Division was sent in to destroy the Wingate force. When the Chindits crossed the Irrawaddy, the Japanese also brought in 56 Division to assist the other two. In putting the first Chindit operation into proper perspective, it must be remembered that they were attacked by three Japanese divisions – exactly the same number of divisions which attacked Slim's forces in Imphal and Kohima in March 1944, just one year later.

The Japanese commanders, realising the Chindits were breaking up into small groups, assumed that air supply would become more difficult, and the men would become more and more exhausted and dispirited. The main Japanese plan to catch the Chindits as they emerged from the Irrawaddy-Shweli triangle included the removal of boats, and active patrolling along the Irrawaddy, the Chindwin, and the valley of the Mu river between Pinbon and Pinlebu. In one clash at this time, the Japanese killed over 100 of Wingate's group near Inywa. Many Chindits were captured because of their pitiful physical state. Some had just collapsed in the jungle and had been left with a couple of grenades. The Japanese took a large number of prisoners and were surprised at their age – some were over 40. They were in bad shape and their captors thought the men were poor spirited compared to their officers. Some prisoners were quoted as saying 'Wingate's mad'; 'We've had enough of jungle marches'; and 'Our officers are rotten – they even have camp beds carried on horses'. (Quoted Louis Allen)

After the campaign, the Japanese admitted that the Chindits were difficult to deal with effectively and had completely disrupted their plans for the first half of 1943. On the other hand they claimed to have obtained much valuable information about Imphal from Chindit prisoners. When he was interrogated in 1945, Mutaguchi spoke of the valuable lessons the Chindits taught him – especially that troops could move from west to east or from east to west across the north-south grain of Burma's mountains and rivers. He gave his final assessment when he wrote in 1964 that Wingate's first expedition changed his whole strategic thinking and convinced him that he would have to attack Imphal before the Allies started their offensive.

When the Chindits returned to British lines, officers and men alike asked 'Has Wingate returned?'. He was nearly three weeks behind Calvert's group and many rumours of his death circulated around Imphal. When he did return, Army HQ were determined to control the Public Relations aspect of the campaign and flew Wingate straight to Delhi for a Press Conference.

At the Press Conference on 20 May Wingate, never one to be overawed by the occasion, claimed the expedition 'was a complete success', though privately he had worried whether he might be court-martialled because he had lost one-third of his brigade. The figures tell a grim story. 3,000 men marched in, and by the beginning of June 1943 2,180 shattered and emaciated men had returned – 450 had been killed in battle and 430 had been lost or were in enemy hands. Of the 13th King's Liverpool Battalion, 721 had started, 384 returned, and 71 survived imprisonment.

The Press Conference produced a dramatic effect. The news broke in a colourfully phrased Reuters cable from Delhi on 20 May 1943: 'Led by a relative of Lawrence of Arabia, a British Ghost Army made sabotage sorties from the depths of the Burmese jungle, and kept the Japanese on tenterhooks for three months. This must surely rank among the greatest guerrilla operations ever undertaken.' The report continued that Wingate's forces penetrated 150 miles into enemy territory, crossed the Irrawaddy and Shweli rivers, blew up the main railway in 70 places, blocked the Bonchaung Gorge, blew other bridges, and fought numerous engagements. Enemy numbers were useless against these superb lightly equipped troops. Wingate had said that proper training methods are the answer to the Japanese, and referred to the loyalty and support of the Burmese people who had affectionate memories of the British administration. He was full of praise for the Burma Rifles and for the RAF. Reuters concluded 'The Japanese were harassed, killed, bamboozled and bewildered through a vast area of Burma'.

Soon after, Wingate received a second bar to his DSO and the citation referred to his determination and inspiring leadership, and his men's spontaneous expressions of admiration for his courage and leadership. Later in May, the radio programme 'London Calling Europe' gave a portrait of Wingate and spoke of his hatred of racial persecution, and hence his passion for the Jews and later for the Abyssinians, 'He inspires men with the same passionate hatred of cruelty, injustice and oppression which have guided every step of his own colourful life'.

Interviewed on Delhi radio he referred to the fine achievements of the British, Indian and Burmese soldiers who had beaten the Japanese in the jungle. He thought the United Nations were fighting for liberty of conscience, for something better than the severe and macabre ideals of the Axis.

The media leapt on the success of the Chindit expedition because it contrasted so starkly with the defeats in the Arakan which took place at the same time. The Irwin Papers (Imperial War Museum) give evidence from the Arakan of 'undisciplined, untrained and gutless British soldiers' and of defeat by a numerically inferior enemy. In contrast, Wingate had infused a new spirit into the services and his first expedition 'had panache, it had glamour, it had cheek, it had everything the successive Arakan failures lacked'. (Louis Allen, p118)

As ever, Wingate had other enemies to fight. The military establishment did not rejoice in the success of his achievements, and their considered verdict appeared later in the Official History (*The War against Japan*' Vol 2). It agreed he had the vision to see what LRP might achieve and gave him the credit for the concept, organisation, planning and execution of the scheme, but added that in the circumstances 'The operation had no strategic value', and the military damage and casualties were small compared to the effort involved. It claimed that Wingate lacked flexibility 'for it is clear he intended to take his force across the Irrawaddy'; he formed a false picture of the territory east of the Irrawaddy although there was a wealth of information available; and after crossing the Irrawaddy he 'had no clear picture of his object and failed to appreciate the situation correctly'. Finally, the ultimate sin in the eyes of the establishment, 'There was a danger that his unorthodox views might be over-exploited and a form of private army would result'. (Official History Vol 2, Kirby p327)

Any knowledge of the facts shows that this criticism is not only unjust but perverse, and in some respects the reverse of the truth, but the view of the Official History reflected fairly accurately the attitude of the establishment staff at GHQ in Delhi, where Wingate had already made a number of formidable enemies. However, the next step in the saga of Wingate and the Chindits was to come from a totally unexpected direction.

6

The Quebec Conference and Axiom

When Wingate returned to India after 'Longcloth' he submitted a detailed report on the expedition, but this was blocked and censored by GHQ. He also sent a copy to his long-standing benefactor L. S. Amery, who then showed it to Churchill. This and the effect of the publicity given to the success of the Chindit operation prompted Churchill to take action. He had long been critical of the inertia, inefficiency and defeatist attitude prevalent in India, and his critical view had been reinforced by the continuing defeats in the Arakan. Wingate had at last brought some success through his own leadership and daring, and against the fairly obvious opposition of GHQ in Delhi. After Churchill received news of 'Longcloth' he wrote, 'In the welter of inefficiency and lassitude which have characterised the operations on the India front, this man of genius and audacity stands out and no question of seniority must obstruct his advance'. At the end of July, Churchill sent for Wingate who had to leave hurriedly and arrived in London on 4 August, when he reported to General Sir Alan Brooke (CIGS). Initially Churchill intended just to meet Wingate and to give him a pat on the back, but events soon took a remarkable turn. Churchill (*Second World War*, Vol 5) has described how he was going to dine alone when he heard that Wingate had arrived. He immediately invited him to dinner. 'We had not talked for half an hour before I felt myself in the presence of a man of the highest quality.' Churchill was about to leave London for Glasgow to join the *Queen Mary* to travel to the Quebec Conference. He decided to take Wingate with him. Wingate mentioned that he had hoped to see his wife while he was in England. Churchill then took another decision. Having ascertained that Lorna Wingate was on the night train from Aberdeen, he had it stopped in Edinburgh. She was taken off and driven to Glasgow where she and her husband joined Churchill's party of military leaders going to the Quadrant Conference in Quebec. (Wingate Papers)

During the voyage Wingate worked hard preparing a presentation of his plans for LRP, for the Combined Chiefs of Staff, and for

Roosevelt and Churchill. The paper illustrates Wingate's remarkable grasp of the wider strategic issues of the war in the Far East, and the role of the Chindits within it. He outlined plans for three groups of Chindit columns to operate: one to link up with the advance of Stilwell and his Chinese divisions; one to assist the advance of Chiang Kai Shek's Chinese divisions from Yunnan; and the third to concentrate on Indaw which was a road, rail and river centre for the Japanese armies facing both Stilwell in the north, and the 4thCorps front at Imphal and Kohima. Wingate predicted the Japanese assault with remarkable accuracy. The Chiefs of Staff accepted Wingate's plan, and cabled the decision to Delhi that they supported LRP on a larger scale, and that six brigades would be allotted to this scheme. After this Wingate made another presentation to Roosevelt, Churchill and Mountbatten, who had just been appointed Supreme Commander, South East Asia Command. When Churchill congratulated Wingate on his exemplary lucidity, somewhat lacking in modesty, he replied that it was his normal practice.

One of Wingate's most important achievements was to gain the support of General Marshall and General Hap Arnold, who saw him as one of the few British leaders who was eager to fight the Japanese. Hap Arnold (the nickname Hap derived from happy) also gave a new dimension to the Chindits, by providing them with the 1st Air Commando, so that they could fly in for their next operation.

The enthusiastic American backing for Wingate's plan related to their constant priority for the war in South East Asia, which was to drive back the Japanese so that a new supply route to Chiang Kai Shek could be established. This is why the road to Ledo and Fort Hertz was so important, and why Stilwell's operations in the Hukawng Valley leading down to Mogaung and Myitkyina were to become so closely, and ultimately so disastrously interwoven with the fate of the Chindits. The Americans hoped that, if an effective road could be opened to Chungking, 60 Chinese divisions could be trained and equipped ready to expel the 25 Japanese divisions from southern China. This in turn would make it possible to establish airfields for heavy bombers to attack Tokyo and mainland Japan.

Within weeks of plodding through the Burmese jungle, Wingate found himself among the most senior Allied leaders, and had to grapple with new and imponderable issues. A serious problem, that had grave implications for his future, arose even before he left Quebec.

General Auchinleck, who had succeeded Wavell when he became Viceroy of India, cabled to the Chiefs of Staff presenting the positive opposition of India Command to Wingate's proposal to raise six brigades for LRP Forces. He put forward some formidable arguments: there were not enough aircraft to support such a scheme; it would absorb troops needed elsewhere; there was no time to train these new units; the LRP units would never inflict any real damage on the enemy. He kept his strongest argument to last. The demand for six brigades would mean breaking up a tried and experienced British division – 70 Division under Major General Symes – and this was totally unacceptable. As a gesture of compromise, Auchinleck offered a brigade from 81 West African Division, or as a last resort the whole of 81 Division, rather than lose 70 Division. Wingate vigorously rejected these arguments, but they were to hound him for the rest of his days.

To his great relief, the Joint Planning Staff issued orders covering the following matters:
(1) There would be a three-pronged attack in north Burma;
— Stilwell with the Chinese 22 and 38 Divisions to advance down the Hukawng valley;
— 4thCorps to advance from Imphal while 15th Corps advanced in the Arakan.
— Chinese divisions would advance westwards from Yunnan over the Salween river.
(2) Directly affecting the Chindits, was the order that they would have the support of No 1 Air Commando under the leadership of Colonels Cochran and Alison. The Air Commando was a very large force, including 100 gliders, nearly 100 light aircraft – the famous single-engined L-1 and L-5 Stinson Sentinel recce and liaison – 30 P-51 Mustangs, 25 B-25 Mitchells, 20 C-47 Dakotas, and 12 larger transport aircraft. There were even some Sikorski helicopters, the first to be used in combat. This critical decision, made by Arnold, meant that the Chindits would be flown in for their next operation.
(3) Wingate was ordered to raise six brigades, which would include a West African brigade, but involved breaking up 70 Division – something for which the military establishment never forgave him.

After Quebec, Wingate went off to set up the Chindits on a much larger scale than he could ever have expected and Mountbatten, who had been hankering after another command at sea, had to set up South

East Asia Command (SEAC). He had been promoted over the heads of all the commanders of the three services in the Far East, some of whom were not too enthusiastic about the new arrangements.

After his exciting days in Quebec, Wingate was buoyed up by the support he had received from the Joint Chiefs of Staff and Roosevelt, and also by a personal letter from Churchill authorising him to communicate direct if there was any frustration of his plans for the Chindits. In August 1943, Wingate spent a brief time in London where he appointed his old friend Derek Tulloch as his BGS, and met Cochran and Alison who were full of enthusiasm. He visited the SOE HQ and inspected new weapons, including flame-throwers. Flown out by a devious route, he committed one of his most serious blunders. Arriving hot and tired at Castel Benito airfield and getting no service, he threw out some flowers from a vase and drank the water.

Tulloch (*Wingate in Peace and War*) has chronicled the cold and hostile reception they received in Delhi. They had arrived before Mountbatten and no accommodation had been provided. Initially, his staff had to work in corridors because no office was available – although 50 brigadiers all had offices. There was no car available and no secretary – just the car pool and the typing pool. At Quebec he had been promised his own aircraft, but at GHQ this was considered laughable. Part of the hostility arose from the genuine belief among senior officers, which was confirmed at a formal conference in January 1942, that no campaign should be launched until the war with Germany was over. Although Wingate had direct access to Churchill he was not allowed to see Auchinleck, who might have sorted out some of the problems. The climax of this unhappy first phase came at a conference dealing with supplies for the Chindits. Every officer present stated that his department could not help, so Wingate stormed out saying he would refer the matter to Churchill.

In spite of the opposition, Wingate launched a vigorous training programme for the Chindit brigades, but soon after this he became seriously ill with typhoid fever, picked up almost certainly during his flight out. Before going to hospital he insisted – against the wishes of GHQ – on meeting Mountbatten when he arrived at the airport. In hospital he lay close to death, but started to recover when the redoubtable Matron McGeary came to nurse him. The medical staff predicted that he would not be fit for duty until the end of February 1944, which would have prevented any Chindit operation in the first half of that year. Churchill sent sympathetic messages, warning him not to go back to work too soon, and Tulloch wondered if this covered the fact that the Prime Minister's strategic views had changed – he was now hankering after a combined operations attack on Sumatra.

While Wingate was ill in hospital, the training of the Chindit brigades actively continued. General Symes could have created problems, but gave outstanding leadership. The RAF strongly opposed the idea of attaching RAF pilots to the Chindit Columns, and this problem was only solved by the direct intervention of Mountbatten. With Wingate's prolonged illness, it was surprising that the 20-week training programme which he had started continued so successfully, but the Chindits were ready for action by early in the new year 1944.

After Wingate's death, he was charged, particularly by Kirby in the Official History, with being unreasonable, unco-operative, and with constantly threatening to resign. Yet, an outline of the top level strategic discussions which took place right up to the time that Operation 'Thursday' was launched, show that while Wingate held to the plans agreed at Quebec, the Chiefs of Staff and politicians frequently changed their priorities.

While Wingate was still in hospital, the Sextant Conference took place in Cairo, starting on 23 November 1943, and was attended by Churchill, Roosevelt, Chiang Kai Shek and Stilwell. It agreed:

a) Stilwell's forces to advance down the Hukawng Valley
b) The Chinese to advance towards Bhamo
c) British 4th Corps to advance from Imphal
d) Chindit Operation 'Thursday' to go ahead
e) An assault on the Andaman Islands, codename 'Buccaneer'
f) 50 Indian Parachute Brigade to occupy Indaw

Roosevelt and Churchill went on to Teheran (27 November-3 December) to confer with Stalin, who demanded a second front in Europe. This demand was accepted, but it meant that all landing craft were requisitioned for the European theatre, and the combined operation scheme 'Buccaneer' was cancelled. Chiang Kai Shek – who never really intended to attack – claimed he had been betrayed and cancelled the proposed advance by Yoke Force towards Bhamo. The conference

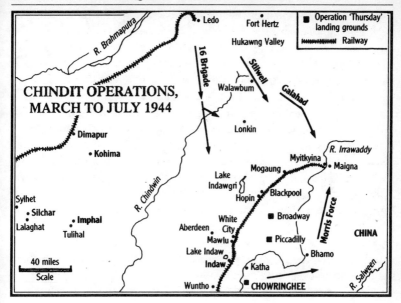

CHINDIT OPERATIONS, MARCH TO JULY 1944

resumed in Cairo (3-10 December) during which 'Buccaneer', the Chinese advance, and the parachute attack on Indaw were all cancelled. These decisions were not made public and were not passed on to Wingate.

On 1 December, against doctor's orders, Wingate returned to duty, and re-organised the big final Chindit exercise. The following day he reported to Slim at Comilla, when the plan was still for the Indian parachute brigade to capture Indaw, and for a division to fly in to hold it. To Wingate's amazement, Slim said no division was available. After this setback, Wingate spent most of December training with the Chindits and the Air Commando. On one occasion he took Calvert, Fergusson and Tulloch on a reconnaissance flight over the Indaw area, the plane piloted by Cochran and Alison. Then, prompted by Tulloch, he addressed the Special Force HQ with the usual electrifying effect.

Later in December he was again taken away from training and had to fly to Chungking to try to persuade Chiang Kai Shek to advance to Bhamo, but he failed in this quest. On this trip he also visited Stilwell who agreed to the arrangements for 16 Brigade to march from Ledo, but in return demanded an attack by 16 Brigade on Lonkin, to which Wingate agreed.

On 3 January 1944, Wingate went to see Slim and they discussed the following plan:

a) 16 Brigade to march from Ledo and attack Indaw
b) 77 Brigade to fly in to 'Broadway'
c) 111 Brigade to fly in to Chowringhee, and send two Columns to the Bhamo area, while the remainder move westwards to attack the communications of the Japanese 15 and 31 Divisions facing Imphal
d) If Special Force captured Indaw, how would it be defended?

Slim announced that only one battalion would be sent to garrison Indaw, and that 4th Corps would not be making any advances. This blow to the agreed plans was followed by what can only be called a bloody-minded memo from Giffard informing Wingate that Agartala, the main Chindit air base could no longer be used, and that their RAF close-support squadron, with which they had trained for weeks, was removed.

Wingate reacted to this double blow with a detailed and angry signal to Giffard. He pointed out that the Quebec plans had never been properly accepted by the 14th Army, that the whole idea of LRP had had no real support, and he suggested that, considering the safety of the formations for which he was responsible, Special Force should be broken up and returned to regimental duty. (Wingate Papers) Mountbatten tried to smooth over the difficulty but Wingate's mind was changed, not by persuasion but by definite news of large scale Japanese troop movements towards Imphal. He had long forecast this and now he saw that if there was a major Japanese attack on Imphal, this presented a new and better opportunity for the effective use of LRP groups to attack and destroy the enemy supplies and communications. This new situation also prompted Wingate's concept of the Stronghold and he rapidly evolved the plan to fly 77 Brigade to 'Broadway', with the aim of sending its Columns all over north Burma to attack and destroy Japanese communications and supplies.

He obtained the agreement of Mountbatten and Giffard before going to Slim at Ranchi on 19 January. Slim then accepted the plan and offered to provide garrison battalions for the Strongholds. After a hectic week of final training and travel, on 25 January Wingate had again to see Slim, who once again changed his mind and said he could not provide any garrison battalions for the proposed Strongholds. He confirmed that 4th Corps would not be advancing. Wingate had the awesome responsibility of organising an airborne operation of over 10,000 men behind the enemy lines, and the pressure on him from these constantly changing orders can be imagined. He certainly felt that Slim's sudden withdrawal of support at this critical time could put the whole operation in jeopardy. Mountbatten again tried to smooth over this clash between Slim and Wingate, and the operation went ahead. Chindit HQ received final orders on 4 February – one day before 16 Brigade started their march from Ledo.

This totally unsatisfactory situation on the ground was partly caused by the dithering and change of plan at the highest level. Even while the clashes between Slim and Wingate were going on, Mountbatten had despatched his Axiom Mission to London to clarify the operational plans for north Burma and was half expecting Operation 'Thursday' to be called off. In London, at the Chiefs of Staff meeting, there were bitter clashes between those who supported the idea of an offensive to recapture Malaya and Singapore, and those supporting a wide sweep across the Pacific supported by the Americans and Australians. Significantly, there was no mention of a major action in north Burma – illustrating how far Wingate was kept in the dark about the higher strategy in the Far East.

The Axiom Mission saw the nadir of Anglo-American relations. When the mission went on to Washington, the Americans were so alarmed at what they saw as the pusillanimous attitude of the India High Command, that Roosevelt cabled Churchill (25 February) demanding an all-out effort in Burma according to the pledges made at Quebec. Once again Wingate appeared to the Americans as the only British leader in the Far East who was ready and eager to get out and fight the Japanese. Thus the Chiefs of Staff were still arguing and dithering over the plans for the Far East when 16 Brigade were already marching from Ledo, and within two weeks of the airborne launch of 'Operation Thursday'. In a subsequent comment on this unedifying episode, Lord Ismay (Churchill's main link with the Chiefs of Staff), said 'The waffling which has gone on over our Far East strategy will be one of the black spots in the British higher direction of the war'. (Ziegler, *Mountbatten*, p277)

This disgraceful background situation illustrates all too well the pressures under which Wingate operated when he was preparing and training the Chindits for Operation 'Thursday'. During the period from December 1943 to March 1944, when the operation was launched, in spite of the set-backs, changes of policy and lack of support, he continued to give enthusiastic and inspiring leadership to all the Chindit units.

7

Operation 'Thursday' and the Chindit Campaigns

Operation 'Thursday' and the subsequent Chindit campaigns were a large and complex exercise, involving six brigades, but the main initial fighting centred on 77 Brigade under Brigadier Calvert who led the fly-in to 'Broadway', and continued fighting there and through the campaign until the victory of Mogaung. Therefore to clarify the description of the whole campaign, the operations of 77 Brigade are described first, and those of the other brigades are recounted in separate sections, with cross-references where necessary.

The real purpose of Operation 'Thursday' was to put into practice Wingate's original idea of the Stronghold. This whole concept illustrates his ability to think and act several steps ahead of the enemy, in contrast to the orthodox attitudes of many contemporary military leaders using out-of-date tactics based on linear warfare.

The concept of setting up a powerful Stronghold in the heart of enemy territory, from which marauding columns would attack the weakly held supply and communications centres, was the prime example of Wingate's imaginative and far-ranging military inventiveness. Most of the orthodox generals in India considered Operation 'Thursday' a madcap scheme, and linked their opposition to their personal antipathy to the man they considered a young upstart, foolishly backed by Churchill, Wavell and the Americans. Wingate's opponents predicted severe losses, but Operation 'Thursday' turned out to be a success.

Wingate put forward his idea of Stronghold in his typical style in a training memorandum which shows him at his best. The memorandum begins, 'Turn to the Stronghold ye Prisoners of Hope'.

Main Units involved in 'Broadway' and 'White City'
77 Brigade
1st Battalion The King's Regiment
1st Battalion The Lancashire Fusiliers
1st Battalion The South Staffordshire Regiment
3/6 Gurkhas   3/9 Gurkhas

OBJECT OF THE STRONGHOLD:

The Stronghold is a machan, overlooking a kid, tied up to entice the Japanese tiger.

The Stronghold is an asylum for the LRPG wounded.

The Stronghold is a magazine of stores.

The Stronghold is a defended airstrip.

The Stronghold is an administrative centre for local inhabitants.

The Stronghold is an orbit round which Columns of the brigade circulate.

The Stronghold is a base for light planes operating with the Columns on the main objective.

The training brief then gives precise detail on the establishment and operation of a Stronghold, which should be set up at a place sufficiently remote from main roads or railways to ensure that the enemy could not attack with tanks or heavy artillery. Therefore it had to be located in wild and difficult country, where there was a plentiful supply of water, but where there was a sufficient area of flat land for a Dakota and light plane strip. It would be a storehouse of supplies for all the LRP groups operating from it, with protected pens for the light planes, which would be used constantly to support the Columns operating out of the Stronghold, for bringing in supplies, and for flying out the wounded. As a base for a brigade, much of which would be operating outside in Columns, it would be garrisoned by a battalion, with two troops of artillery – probably 25-pounders – together with Vickers machine guns. It would be defended by earthworks, minefields, wire, and by detailed and flexible fire plans, all supported by the theme 'No Surrender'. A key part of the defence were the floater columns which would be traversing the surrounding area ready to attack or ambush any enemy units which approached the Stronghold.

While the defensive role was clearly defined, the main object of the Stronghold was aggressive – as a base for Columns to set off to destroy the enemy lines of communication and stores centres, secure in the knowledge that there was a safe haven to which they could return to replenish supplies of food, ammunition and water, and to bring back their wounded to be flown out to safety. Wingate conceived the idea of Stronghold in January 1944, when he forecast – correctly – that the Japanese would be making a major attack on Imphal and Kohima. He saw that a powerful Chindit operation of six brigades, based on Strongholds mainly in the Indaw area, would cause the maximum disruption to the enemy lines of communication, both to 18 Division fighting Stilwell in the Hukawng Valley, and to the three divisions – 15, 31 and 33 – attacking Imphal and Kohima. By March 1944, after weeks of gruelling training and meticulous planning, the Chindits were ready for the start of Operation 'Thursday'.

The launch took place from Lalaghat airfield in upper Assam on the afternoon of Sunday 5 March 1944. It produced one of the most tense and dramatic moments of the whole campaign. Against all the odds, against the positive opposition of much of the military establishment, and in spite of the dithering at the highest level illustrated by the Axiom Mission, 77 Brigade and 111 Brigade were trained, equipped and ready to embark on one of the most novel and dangerous expeditions of the war. The Chindit's clearly understood aim was to fly in by glider and land behind the Japanese lines in the area of Indaw, in order to disrupt the lines of communication to all the Japanese divisions fighting in northern Burma.

After months of rigorous training and sound staff work to provide all the special supplies and equipment, all was ready. Eighty three Dakotas from the RAF and the USAAF, and 80 gliders were lined up ready on the airfield, carefully loaded, the pilots fully briefed, and the tow ropes laid out with meticulous accuracy. The first wave consisted of 26 towing aircraft and 52 gliders all under the command of Colonels Cochran and Alison, USAAF. The difficult and complicated manoeuvre of a Dakota towing two gliders over the high mountains between Imphal and Indaw had been carefully rehearsed. Trained by Mike Calvert, whom they would have followed anywhere, 77 Brigade were to fly in as the first wave. As H-hour approached and the tense excitement rose, the Chindits realised this was a special occasion. Slim was there, with Air Marshal Sir John Baldwin, commander of the 3rd Tactical Air Force; General Stratemeyer and Brigadier Old, USAAF; and many other high ranking officers. Some had expected Mountbatten to appear, for this was the sort of occasion at which he excelled, but he went elsewhere, even though this was the biggest airborne operation ever mounted up to that time.

The landing grounds had been carefully chosen in advance, and codenamed 'Broadway', 'Piccadilly' and 'Chowringhee'. 'Piccadilly' had been used to rescue some of the Chindits from the 1943 expedition, and there had been some publicity for it in the American maga-zine *Life* (June 1943), but this was not considered a security hazard. As a final precaution, Wingate had decreed that for three weeks prior to the launch, no aircraft would go near the three sites.

The first flight was due to move off at 1700 hours and until then the men were quietly resting in the shade under the wings of the glid-ers. Thirty minutes before the start, a light aircraft of the Air Comman-do flew in and the pilot Major Russhon ran over to Cochran. He handed over photographs taken two hours earlier, which showed 'Pic-cadilly' completely blocked with teak tree trunks. Wingate reacted furi-ously and demanded to know who had disobeyed his orders. Cochran said he had ordered the flight and took full responsibility – then Wingate apologised for his outburst, because he realised that the pho-tographs had prevented a certain disaster to 77 Brigade and the first wave of gliders.

This situation put Wingate and Slim under immense pressure, because many factors had to be considered and an urgent decision had to be reached. At first, Wingate wondered if their plans had been breached in Chunking or in the Chinese forces where security was lax. His main fear was that if their plans had been betrayed to the enemy, the Chindits would fly in and find the Japanese waiting for them. Was this such a threat to all their lives that the whole operation should be called off? He had to weigh up other issues. He knew that many of the higher ranks back in India believed the whole concept was foolish and would be pleased if it was called off. He knew, too, that unless it went straight ahead, it would be cancelled altogether, and the concept of LRP finished for good.

From a more sanguine point of view, the logs on 'Piccadilly' might be part of just routine precautions against possible landings, or they might have a completely innocent explanation. Wingate was standing with Tulloch, Calvert, Cochran, Alison and Scott (Lieutenant-Colonel Scott, commanding 1st Battalion the King's Liverpool Regi-ment). After a swift discussion the issue came down to whether, under the new and more dangerous circumstances, 77 Brigade should go in. Half of the brigade had been earmarked for 'Piccadilly' and Calvert said he was prepared to take in his brigade, provided they all went to 'Broadway'. George Macdonald Fraser in his outstanding book *Quar-tered Safe out Here* discussed the question of courage in battle, and the views of the fighting soldier. He made a comment which is directly relevant to Calvert, and his universal nickname Mad Mike. Fraser wrote of his platoon: 'They belonged to a culture in which "windy" is the ultimate insult, and in which the synonym for brave is "mad", and that is all there is to be said about it.'

Calvert's agreement was quickly discussed with Wingate and Cochran, and then the proposal had to go to Slim and Baldwin for their final decision. Tulloch, who remained close to Wingate during these tense moments, has expressed his admiration for Slim, who remained imperturbable and reinforced everyone's confidence. As soon as the decision to take the whole of 77 Brigade to Broadway was made, Cochran, showing admirable leadership qualities, went to his pilots and said 'Hey, you guys, we've got a better place to fly to'. The first gliders took off an hour and fifteen minutes after the original deadline.

It is unfortunate that those two distinguished soldiers Slim and Wingate were to be so deeply and bitterly divided in their accounts of what happened at the airfield. Wingate wrote an official report (Wingate Papers) shortly afterwards, and gave a straight factual description, recording that Slim and Baldwin at the top level agreed that the operation should go ahead, cutting out 'Piccadilly', and the question of whether to use both 'Broadway' and 'Chowringhee' was left for the Special Force leaders to decide. At Calvert's insistence it was Broadway only.

Writing 10 years later in *Defeat into Victory* (published 1955) Slim described the moment when Russhon brought the photographs. Slim maintained that Wingate 'now in a very emotional state' argued for the whole operation to be called off, and Slim therefore took him on one side 'to prevent a scene in front of the Americans'. Slim continued, 'Wingate became calmer and much more in control of himself', and agreed that the ultimate decision had to be Slim's. The accuracy of Slim's account is undermined by a small but important detail – he even mistook the name of the airfield, and wrote Hailakandi instead of Lalaghat. It was of course written 10 years after the events, with the inevitable inaccuracies which that entails. Others who were present when the photographs arrived – Tulloch, Baldwin, Calvert, Scott and Sir Robert Thompson, have all written their description of the events, and every one confirms Wingate's version and refutes Slim's.

Scott described how he was standing with Wingate and Calvert when Russhon and Cochran came over with the photographs:

'General Wingate took the photographs and walked across to where General Slim and the other Allied commanders were standing. After several minutes conversation, General Wingate returned. He then turned away, with his head bent and his hands clasped behind his back, he looked a forlorn and lonely figure... After going about 30 yards, he turned and called Brigadier Calvert, and, after they talked they walked to where the Allied commanders were standing. A brief vital conference took place, after which General Wingate and Brigadier Calvert returned to me, and I received fresh orders which were so clear and concise that it was hard to realise "Piccadilly" had ever existed.'

This calm, detailed and factual account is the best and the most convincing.

Another facet of the launch of Operation 'Thursday' has often been overlooked. This glider force of 12,000 men, was launched, not into the well reconnoitred areas of Normandy, or the flat fields of Holland around Arnhem but, in the dark, tugged over mountain ranges 7,000 feet high, aiming at small jungle clearings where there was no possibility of a second run if the glider overshot the mark, and where – after the evidence of the photographs – the Japanese might well be waiting to ambush them as they left the gliders. One of Wingate's great concerns at that moment was that, in this dangerous situation, he had to ask the Chindits to go somewhere he was not going himself.

The first wave of eight gliders took off safely at 1812 hours, after which there was a 30-minute wait before the main body left. Each Dakota had a telephone link to the two gliders it was towing, and a wireless link to the control centre supervised by Tulloch. The early messages which came in were not encouraging. Some gliders had broken loose from their tow plane, three crashlanded a few minutes after they took off, and one Dakota ran out of fuel and jettisoned its gliders near 4th Corps HQ, which the Gurkhas dutifully attacked.

In the control tent, Tulloch monitored all the information, watched by Wingate, Slim, Baldwin and Old. After some of the early mishaps, more encouraging reports came from the Dakotas which had completed their mission and returned. The pilots reported that landing lights and other signals had been installed, but at a fairly early stage it was decided that because of the problems of towing two gliders, for the rest of the operation each Dakota would tow just one. Before he left, Calvert had arranged two emergency codewords with Tulloch. SOYA LINK – the most hated ingredient of army rations – meant 'trouble at "Broadway", stop further gliders being despatched'. PORK SAUSAGE meant 'all well at "Broadway", operation successful so far'.

Calvert had been the key figure in the decision to proceed with the operation and to take the whole of 77 Brigade in to Broadway. He considered all the factors, but to him the overriding issue was that 'they could never again be keyed up to such a pitch, morally, physically or materially'. He added, "We were 77 Brigade, Wingate's Brigade, and we had to do our stuff". (*Prisoners of Hope*, p23) Calvert embarked on one of the leading gliders, and soon after it took off he could see the Imphal Plain and the mountains, then the Chindwin which he had crossed three times before – once by swimming and once with the Japanese in hot pursuit – and then he looked for landmarks in case they had to make a forced landing. He looked around and saw that most of his men were fast asleep.

The hazardous nature of the operation at 'Broadway' became apparent as soon as the first gliders landed. The air photographs had failed to identify two trees on the main landing strip, and two deep ditches which ran across it. These unseen obstacles caused the first gliders to crash, and the advanced party with Calvert, Alison and Scott were unable to move them before the main party arrived. As the next wave of gliders came in, they crashed on to the wrecks of the first ones – some crashed into the jungle trees surrounding the strip, and others missed the strip altogether. With flames from the crashed gliders, flickering lights from blazing torches, the noise of men struggling to clear the strip, and the screams of the wounded trapped in the wreckage, the pressure mounted on Calvert as he surveyed the grisly scene. He feared that if another wave of gliders came in before the strip was cleared and levelled there would be a disaster. So, with morale at its lowest depths, at 0400 hours on Monday 6 March (his 31st birthday), in order to prevent any further arrivals, he signalled 'Soya Link'.

One of the gliders had brought in a small bulldozer and, overshooting the strip, it had hit trees on the edge of the jungle. The impact threw the crew clear, while the heavy bulldozer shot straight through the front of the glider. As dawn broke, Calvert was amazed to hear the noise of an engine – an American engineer, temporarily flown in by the Air Commando, calmly drove the bulldozer on to the strip.

The bulldozer had landed undamaged, its fall broken by undergrowth, and this stroke of good fortune virtually saved the whole operation. With the help of a second bulldozer and every able-bodied man on the strip, the American engineers started to clear it and fill in the ditches. They assured Calvert that by the evening the strip would be able to take Dakotas.

Back in the command tent, although Slim had left, Air Marshal Baldwin waited with Wingate and Tulloch through the tense evening hours. When the signal 'Soya Link' came through, Tulloch tried to cheer up Wingate who naturally was depressed and disturbed at the news, and suggested he got a couple of hours sleep. This he did, and then at 0630 hours they received from Calvert – who had been reassured by the American engineers – the welcome signal 'Pork Sausage'. This meant that Operation 'Thursday' could continue, although the losses of the night had been heavy: 37 gliders had landed at 'Broadway', six landed in Japanese held territory, and about 10 in Upper Assam. The majority of these groups managed to get back to British lines and soon rejoined 77 Brigade. On the strip, 30 men had been killed and 20 wounded, while from those aircraft which did not reach 'Broadway', 66 men did not return. One advantage stemmed from this confusion. With planes and gliders landing all over the Indaw area of north Burma, the Japanese were completely confused and took a long time to identify 'Broadway'.

At 'Broadway', while the American engineers worked energetically to prepare the landing strip for the Dakotas to arrive that evening, Calvert carried out a swift recce to decide the actual position of the Stronghold, and particularly where there would be an adequate supply of water for both men and mules. During the day, the Air Commando sent 12 light planes in to 'Broadway' in order to fly out the men wounded in the initial landing. The gallantry of those pilots, who flew 400 miles across enemy territory in slow unarmed aircraft, set a standard which the Air Commando kept up throughout the campaign. That night Brigadier Old USAAF, flew in and was followed by 63 Dakotas. After this, over 100 Dakotas flew in every night, bringing 12,000 men with their weapons, equipment, ammunition and food, together with over 2,000 mules.

The best description of 'Broadway' came from Air Marshal Baldwin who wrote: 'Nobody has seen a transport operation until he has stood on that jungle runway, under the light of a Burma full moon, and watched Dakotas coming in and taking off in different directions on a single strip all night long at the rate of one landing and one take off every three minutes.' The admirable work of the Air Commando under Cochran not only safeguarded and supplied 'Broadway' and the other Chindit bases which followed, but by simultaneous attacks on Japanese airfields – in which 78 aircraft were destroyed during the first two days – ensured that the fly-in and build up of 'Broadway' took place without any Japanese air attacks.

At 'Broadway', Calvert and the Chindits put into practice the concept of the Stronghold and, on 7 March, to their great delight, Wingate flew in to 'Broadway' to see them. It gave him a boost to stand in a Stronghold and to see that what he had conceived in theory was working out so well in practice. By 8 March 'Broadway' was well established, with the airstrip in constant use, garrisoned by 3/9 Gurkhas, and with two floater Columns of the King's Regiment operating outside, ready to attack any enemy unit which approached the Stronghold. Ever one to lead from the front, Calvert therefore decided to take a strong force, including the 1st South Staffords, and the 3/6 Gurkhas, to block the main road and railway at Mawlu.

This force, after eight days of cutting their way through the jungle, reached the village of Henu on 16 March. A series of low hills surrounded the village, and the South Staffs occupied one of these and started to dig in. Early next morning, an unexpected clash with an enemy patrol quickly led to a fierce battle. The Japanese attacked from Pagoda Hill with LMG, mortar fire and grenades, and the Chindits were very hard pressed when at last they received the encouraging news that Calvert and two companies of Gurkhas were coming to their relief. As soon as Calvert arrived, he sent two groups around Pagoda Hill, while he personally led the assault and bayonet charge on the Japanese position. This led to vicious hand to hand fighting. In one incident Lieutenant George Cairns of the South Staffs had his arm severed by a Japanese officer's sword, but he continued fighting and finally killed the officer. Cairns died later, but received a posthumous VC for his bravery. The Japanese were driven off Pagoda Hill but made another strong counter-attack which was also defeated. This important first victory, but in which the Chindits sustained 59 casualties, set a high standard for the whole brigade.

During this battle, two Columns of the Lancashire Fusiliers were 'floating' in the area to the north. Their commando platoon under

Hugh Patterson successfully blew up the railway, water towers, bridges, and Mawlu railway station. These actions convinced Calvert that he could now take the offensive and clear the enemy from Mawlu village. He therefore set out with the 3/6 Gurkhas and arranged for two floating Columns to prepare an ambush ready for the Japanese should they retreat southwards. Although Mawlu was only a small administrative centre, its HQ troops had prepared sound defences, as Japanese soldiers always did, and when the Gurkhas attacked they were met by sustained and effective fire which caused heavy casualties. In spite of this they pressed home their attack and reached a point from which they could use their flame-throwers. Still the defenders resisted strongly. Then Calvert called up the Mustangs of the Air Commando and, with remarkable accuracy, they hit the Japanese with bombs and cannon. Encouraged by this support, the Gurkhas charged into the smoking ruins hurling grenades and wielding their kukris, and had the satisfaction of seeing the enemy give up and run away. Unfortunately, the floater Columns were delayed in reaching their ambush positions and a good opportunity was lost, but because of Calvert's attack with the Gurkhas, the Japanese fled and did not rally until they reached Indaw, more than 10 miles away.

When Calvert set out from 'Broadway', he intended to establish a block in the Henu/Mawlu area to ensure that the road and railway leading up to Mogaung and Myitkyina would be permanently disrupted. While he was leading the attacks at Pagoda Hill and Mawlu, the rest of his group were rapidly establishing themselves at Henu. Here they set up a classic block – a more temporary base than a Stronghold – and it became known as 'White City' because of the number of parachutes which festooned the trees in the dropping zone.

Calvert had as good a tactical eye as Wingate, and he chose 'White City' because it was ideal for his purpose: low hills gave good visibility to the defenders, it had a good water supply, and it could be effectively defended. 'White City' posed a serious threat to the Japanese, and Calvert assumed correctly that they would do everything they could to destroy it. In training under his tough leadership, 77 Brigade had worked twice as hard as any other at digging trenches, but now their hard work paid off. He had also imbued the brigade with his boyish enthusiasm for mines and booby-traps, and by 19 March when Japanese troops made their first probing attacks, 'White City' was powerfully defended with excellent covered trenches, skilfully placed wire, mines, and booby-traps, with carefully co-ordinated fields of fire. Every platoon and section had stocks of ammunition, grenades, food and water, and were connected to HQ by buried telephone lines.

The defended area included a light plane strip, a main dropping zone, Brigade HQ and dressing station, and with the commando platoon nearby in reserve. In addition to the platoon infantry weapons of rifle, Bren guns, and 2in mortars, there were eight 3in mortars (one of the most successful weapons of the Burma campaign), and 11 Vickers machine guns. Behind this well co-ordinated defensive power lay the comforting assurance that the Air Commando Mustangs and RAF Vengeances could be called up at short notice. A supply drop was made each night, supplemented by the light planes coming in to evacuate the wounded. A Dakota airstrip was later built just outside the defensive perimeter and was in frequent use when the enemy were not actually attacking.

The first serious attack came on 21 March. The co-ordinated fire plan, including well directed 3in mortar fire, caused heavy casualties among the attackers, but they still advanced and established positions inside the Chindit perimeter and close to the dressing station. Close quarter fighting went on through the night and at dawn a series of counter-attacks drove out the intruders. After clearing out the enemy and restoring the perimeter, Calvert called for air strikes on their battered and retreating units. This first attack, typical of many to come, cost the Chindits over 30 killed and 40 wounded. It had been made by five companies sent down from the Japanese 18 Division. 77 Brigade's Japanese speaking Intelligence Officer gained valuable information about enemy units from his interrogation of a Japanese officer, and from captured documents and diaries.

The 'White City' garrison spent the next few days actively improving their defences, thickening their wire, and acting on the lessons they had learned during the first attack. On 24 March Wingate arrived, congratulated them on their achievements, and went around the whole block encouraging everyone and making sound practical suggestions. After a discussion about future plans, Calvert said farewell – he was never to see him again. Later, Calvert wrote 'It was the last we ever saw of him, but his dreams lived with us'. (*Prisoners of Hope*, p62)

'Broadway' was the classic example of a Stronghold and from it Calvert sent out Columns which ranged far and wide over northern Burma. Herring went off with Dah Force to raise revolt among the

Kachins; two Columns of the King's, 81 and 82, under the leadership of Colonel Scott patrolled both east and west of 'Broadway'; a Column of the Lancashire Fusiliers marched nearly 50 miles southwards to Shwegu on the Irrawaddy, and made certain that no craft went up the river to Myitkyina; another Column of the Lancashire Fusiliers marched westwards to block the road and railway near Pinwe, about 10 miles south of Mawlu. In addition, Calvert himself led the group which established the block at 'White City'. 'Broadway' met all the tactical criteria required in a Stronghold. Its only drawback – and even this is disputed by Chindits – was that it lay five day's hard marching through thick jungle and over difficult country from 'White City', where the most important action, the blocking of the road and rail link to Myitkyina, took place.

From the start of Operation 'Thursday', the defence of 'Broadway' had been in the capable hands of Colonel Claud Rome, and when Calvert went off on his aggressive forays he confidently left Rome in charge. The first attacks on 'Broadway' on 13 March came not from ground troops, but from Japanese aircraft trying to destroy a squadron of Spitfires which had been flown in. The Spitfires scrambled and, co-operating closely with the Bofors guns on the strip, achieved a spectacular defeat of the attacking Zeros and greatly heartened everyone in the garrison. A second attack a few days later caused some damage and the Spitfires were then withdrawn. Calvert commented that there were really too many light planes on the strip. He noticed that when on the ground the pilots, who calmly flew over hundreds of miles of enemy territory in unarmed planes, were quaking with fear during a ground attack, not realising that when soldiers were in the light planes 'Their bowels turned to water'. The air attacks showed that the Japanese had identified 'Broadway' and the garrison prepared for the inevitable ground attack. Information about the movements of Japanese troops came into 'Broadway' from the floater Columns, from the excellent Burma Rifles recce units, and from the local Kachin people.

Rome correctly anticipated an attack and it started on 27 March, by which time he had recalled some of the Columns ready for the battle. The Japanese attackers – a battalion from 56 Division in Yunnan – attacked at night, and had a long, noisy and bloody fight with the 3/9 Gurkhas. Spirited actions involving the Gurkhas and the King's Columns went on through the day, and then the Japanese attacked again as darkness fell. Both sides sustained heavy casualties, but the enemy failed to pierce the defences. On 31 March Rome mounted a

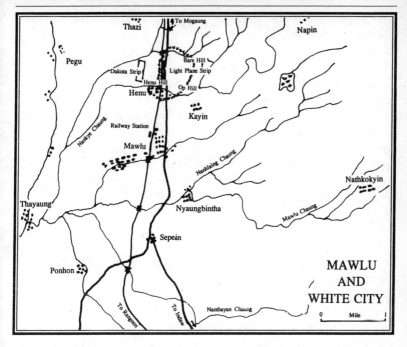

counter-attack with the Gurkhas and the King's, forcing the Japanese to retire.

Calvert has commented on the military situation of the Chindits at this time, when attacks on both 'Broadway' and 'White City' had been successfully repulsed, and road, rail and river transport to the Japanese divisions fighting in the north had been completely halted. Quoting the military doctrine of reinforcing success rather than failure, he argued that at Imphal and Kohima, where the British outnumbered the Japanese by 2:1 in battalions, and by 5:1 in guns, instead of sending more and more divisions to Imphal, one additional division should have been sent to Indaw to reinforce the success of Operation 'Thursday', and to wreak havoc on the Japanese divisions as they retreated.

In contrast, Bidwell (*The Chindit War*, p131) counters Calvert's argument by saying that at the end of March the Chindits were in disarray and 'large numbers of elite troops, imported behind the enemy lines were not engaging the enemy at all'. Bidwell, perhaps following the lead of Kirby in the Official History, did not give due emphasis to the wider strategic concept of Operation 'Thursday', which was to destroy the lines of communication of all the Japanese divisions lying north of the 24th parallel. This included 18 Division which was fighting stubbornly against the advance of Stilwell and his Chinese divisions in the Hukawng Valley; 56 Division in Yunnan facing the threat of several Chinese divisions which could have advanced if Chiang Kai Shek had given the order; and, more directly, the three Japanese divisions under General Mutaguchi – 15, 31 and 33, which had launched their attack on Imphal and Kohima on the same day as Operation 'Thursday' started. Disrupting the supplies and communications of all these enemy divisions was surely a worthwhile objective.

Death of Wingate

All the Chindits in 'Broadway' were tremendously heartened when Wingate flew in to see them on 24 March. He spent a busy day, flying on to 'White City' then to 'Aberdeen' which Fergusson had already left and, after returning to 'Broadway', he flew on to Imphal. Here he had a discussion with Air Marshal Baldwin about the problems of communication with the new Chindit HQ at Sylhet. Wingate had made his trips that day in a B-25 Mitchell bomber of the Air Commando, and at about 1700 hours, with his ADC and some war correspondents, he took off for Lalaghat. Baldwin, flying a Lockheed, followed soon afterwards. An hour later Wingate's aircraft crashed into the hills near Bishenpur and everyone on board was killed.

Baldwin, whose plane must have been very close to where the accident took place, was adamant that although there were isolated storms about, the weather between Imphal and Silchar was clear and fine and he had no problems. In contrast, a pilot of No 194 Squadron who flew out of Imphal at the same time, recorded that the weather was particularly bad with poor visibility. He recalled seeing a Mitchell which seemed to be far too low, near the Bishenpur Hills. Yet another witness maintains – contradicting Baldwin's evidence – that Wingate took off 'in pissing rain'. Many years later, Tulloch received information that while the Mitchell was at 'Broadway' the young pilots had told Colonel Rome that one engine of the Mitchell was not developing full power and they thought they should wait for a replacement, but they were in awe of Wingate and did not want to delay him. Rome passed this information to Wingate, but it is not known whether he overruled the pilots.

On 25 March a pilot of the Air Commando identified the wreckage of an aircraft and a patrol, with a chaplain, was sent out immediately. They reached the crash and found clear evidence including Wingate's well-known helmet and some of his note-books. A brief service was held and the spot identified. Some weeks later a larger group visited the site, held a memorial service and erected a cross with the names of the nine men killed. In 1947, under orders from the USAAF, and to the distress of the Wingate family, the bodies of all the dead were removed and re-interred in the Arlington Cemetery, USA.

As soon as the news of the crash was released, Tulloch issued an order of the day informing the Chindits of Wingate's death and adding that the most fitting memorial to him would be the early achievement of his purpose.

This disaster happened when Slim was deeply preoccupied with the Japanese attack on Imphal and Kohima, which was then at its height. He telephoned Tulloch and sought his advice on this difficult appointment. The most urgent need was to find a successor, who believed in Wingate's philosophy, who had the experience to lead Operation 'Thursday' to a successful conclusion, and who would defend it against the inevitable opposition of the Establishment critics in Delhi. To the amazement of virtually every Chindit, Tulloch suggested Lentaigne, who was leading 111 Brigade, and Slim appointed him.

Tulloch in his book merely says 'I recommended Lentaigne', and gives no further comment. Years later he added, 'My choice proved to be a bad one. I had completely misjudged Lentaigne.' (Memo Tulloch Papers, Rylands Library, Manchester) Tulloch's recommendation is almost incredible. He knew that there was a deep antipathy between Wingate and Lentaigne, who considered Wingate an upstart, whose ideas were unsound and unproven. Tulloch already knew that Lentaigne's leadership during the few days he had been behind the lines with 111 Brigade was seriously inadequate. Tulloch may have thought that, since Lentaigne was a Gurkha officer he would be more acceptable to Slim who, it was well known, liked to have ex-Gurkha officers commanding his units.

Lentaigne had completely failed as a commander in the field and had lost the confidence of his own officers; his inadequacy and his failure to block the railway south of Indaw contributed to the defeat of 16 Brigade, and he was so out of touch with Chindit beliefs that, even before he had taken over, he thought that 'White City' and 'Broadway' would be overrun immediately. Thompson says categorically that the appointment of Lentaigne was a mistake. (Sir Robert Thompson, *Make for the Hills*, p54) Surprisingly, although Calvert was outstandingly the most successful Chindit leader, and the very large majority of Chindits saw him as Wingate's heir, it does not appear that he was considered as a possible successor. He seems to have been thought of exclusively as a tough commander in the field, and yet he had a fine original mind, was a trained engineer, a Cambridge graduate, and he would have had the total loyalty of every Chindit.

In appointing Lentaigne, Slim unwisely overlooked the claims of General Symes who had successfully commanded 70 Division before it was broken up into Chindit Columns. With remarkable loyalty and self-control, he had accepted the role of assistant to Wingate and had shown fine leadership qualities when Wingate was ill with typhoid in the autumn of 1943. He was furious when he heard from Tulloch that he had been passed over, and went at once to Slim. Syme's diary (Quoted Louis Allen, p350) gives details of a thoroughly unsatisfactory interview with Slim, who initially said he did not know Symes was at Special Force HQ; then he said he did not know what his status was; then added that the suggestion of Lentaigne had come from Tulloch, but immediately contradicted himself. Symes, understandably, found Slim's view unacceptable and appealed to Giffard and the CIGS to be relieved of his post.

Tulloch's order of the day giving news of Wingate's death reached 77 Brigade on 27 March and prompted Calvert's prophetic comment 'Who will look after us now?'. Lentaigne, who was called in from 111 Brigade to take over, arranged a conference of Chindit brigade commanders at 'Aberdeen' in early April. The conference made an assessment of the current position of the Chindit brigades, which gives a useful summary of the situation of the Chindits at the time of Wingate's death: 77 Brigade, strongly entrenched at 'White City' and 'Broadway', was blocking the road and rail going north. 16 Brigade under Fergusson had completed its epic march from Ledo, had failed in its attack on Indaw, but had established a Stronghold at 'Aberdeen' where the conference was held.

14 Brigade, which up to that time had had no real opportunity to prove itself, and had spent much time marching and counter-marching, prompted Calvert's shrewd comment that brigades supplied by air are

almost too mobile and 'unless the commander keeps his eye very much on the ball their plans are liable to be changed at very short notice at each twist of the general situation'. (*Prisoners of Hope*, p96)

111 Brigade under Lentaigne had flown to 'Chowringhee' from Tulihal on 7 March. The flight was a success and the brigade had the clear objective of destroying the railway south of Indaw in order to prevent enemy reinforcements from the south reaching the town. A major section of 111 Brigade, Morris Force, had moved off eastwards to the Bhamo road.

The conference at 'Aberdeen' also gave the opportunity for a discussion of the Chindit role, and Lentaigne, who must have faced the conference with some trepidation, explained that he wished to hear their views.

Calvert argued strongly that 'White City' and 'Broadway' should be stoutly defended and reinforced, so that 77 Brigade could drive north and meet up with Stilwell. He vehemently opposed the suggestion of giving them up after they had been established at such great cost. He reminded Lentaigne that the decision of the Quebec Conference was for the Chindit operation to co-operate with Stilwell and with 4th Corps in driving out all Japanese north of the 24th parallel, in order to re-open the Burma road to China, and to reduce demands on The Hump airlift.

Fergusson argued that 16 Brigade should be given another chance to capture Indaw and its airfields so that a division could be flown in to hold the area. The conference then heard that the 3rd West African Brigade would be flying in for garrison duties at 'Aberdeen', 'White City' and 'Broadway', and when they were established, Calvert would lead a strong force to attack Mohnyin, 25 miles up the railway from 'White City'. These plans were soon to be disrupted by the enemy.

The next day, 4 April, Calvert flew back to 'White City' when a Chindit patrol near Sepein reported the approach of a substantial Japanese force. This proved to be the 24th Independent Mixed Brigade, consisting of six battalions, supported by mortars and batteries of medium and heavy guns. A landing strip for Dakotas lying just outside the 'White City' perimeter was on the point of being completed when the Japanese attacked. Bofors anti-aircraft guns, 25-pounders, and some small anti-tank guns were brought in, the final assignment arriving in 25 Dakotas which flew in during a brisk fire fight all round the strip. Calvert stood nonchalantly, assuring worried pilots that it was always like that, but worrying what sort of rocket he would get from air HQ if any of the Dakotas were destroyed.

The Japanese attack continued for 10 days from 6 April and included heavy bombardment from artillery and the terrifying 6in mortar which fired a projectile 5 feet long and 6 inches in diameter and, as the defenders rapidly learned, took 32 seconds to arrive. Calvert has vividly described the prolonged 'White City' battle:

'The sequence of attack was the same practically every night and only varied in intensity. The Japs would start shelling about 5pm continuing until dusk. He would then launch an attack just after last light on the east and south-east perimeter through the jungle. He would be met with a curtain of about 500 mortar shells on his forming up area. What was left would then run into our booby traps and minefields, which were regularly re-erected every day. He would then meet our outer wire, where he would be lit up by 2in mortar flares, and greeted with the continuous fire of up to 13 Vickers machine guns, coupled with a very large amount of small arms fire and grenades. He would pump discharger grenades into the block, while his 6in mortar (the coal scuttle as it was called) would also crump us. Having done his best, and all his Bangalore torpedo parties having been wiped out, the fighting would die down. Sometimes he would make a further attempt at midnight. Then between 2 and 4am the bombardment would open up again, during which time he recovered many of his wounded and dead and withdrew. At dawn, we would collect documents off the dead if they were not in too dangerous a position among our traps, evacuate our wounded, repair bunkers, sleep and direct the ever willing Mustangs on to his positions.' (*Prisoners of Hope*, p 112)

This almost casual description omits a significant aspect of the prolonged battle – the nauseating stench. As the siege wore on, over 1,000 bodies were hanging on the wire or rotting in the minefields, covered with sickening and bloated black flies, and rapidly putrefying in the damp heat. The sorely tried defenders tried to dispose of the corpses by using flame throwers, but this only made matters worse.

Opposite page, top: A Special Night Squad, including Jewish volunteers and men of the Royal Ulster Rifles and Royal West Kent Regiment, Palestine, 1938. *(Courtesy Wingate family collection)*

Above: Wingate at the funeral of a SNS colleague killed by Arab terrorists in 1938. *(Courtesy Wingate family collection)*

Left: An SNS patrol sets out towards the pipeline. Courtesy Wingate family collection.

Above: A Jewish settlement, 1938. *(Courtesy Wingate family collection)*

Below: Planting trees at the inauguration of the Wingate memorial forest in Israel 1947. *(Courtesy Wingate family collection)*

above: Haile Selassie and Wingate inspect the troops of Gideon Force at Dambacha in March 1941.

below: Wingate leads the Emperor's procession into Addis Ababa in May 1941. Haile Selassie had refused to ride the white horse and insisted that Wingate ride it instead. *(Courtesy Wingate family collection)*

Above: The Special Night Squad sets off to guard the pipeline.

Below: Brigadier Evetts, who supported Wingate and the Special Night Squads, made an unexpected visit to their camp.

Above: Wingate spent much of his military career developing wireless communications for irregular columns. Here is an early wireless set on a donkey, a forerunner of the large RAF sets carried by mules in the Chindit columns.

Below: Wingate shown in his tireless resolve to counter the malign influence of the Mufti, who supported the Arab terrorists.

Above: 'PLANE LAND HE[RE] NOW.' This dramatic message was marked on the ground by No 8 Column during the first Chindit expedition. A Dakota landed and picked up all the sick and wounded, th[en] enabling the rest to marc[h] on and reach safety at Fo[rt] Hertz. *(Courtesy Imperial War Museum)*

Left: Portrait of Wingate after the first Chindit exp[e]dition, May 1943. *(Courte[sy] Wingate family collection*

Right, top and centre: Gliders and tow-ropes laid out at Lalaghat for the launch of Operation 'Thursday' on 5 March 1944. *(Courtesy Imperial War Museum)*

Below: At Lalaghat, the moment when Russhon brought the photographs showing that Piccadilly was blocked. From right: Tulloch, Wingate, Calvert, Air Marshal Baldwin, Scott and Alison (holding map). *(Courtesy Imperial War Museum)*

Left: Wingate in a Dakot
flying to Broadway.
*(Courtesy Imperial War
Museum)*

Below left: Brigadier
Michael Calvert, the
bravest and most success-
ful of the Chindit leaders.
(Courtesy Michael Calvert)

Below right: Brigadier
Calvert at a reunion with
the First Air Commando,
1977.

Above: The Burmese jungle, typical of the terrain in which the Chindits operated. *(Courtesy Imperial War Museum)*

Right: Dropping supplies to the Chindits. *(Courtesy Imperial War Museum)*

Above: Chindits with rubber boats. These often proved inadequate to cross the Irrawaddy or Chindwin rivers, which were up to a mile wide. *(Courtesy Imperial War Museum)*

Below left: RAF wireless operator attached to a Chindit column. These sets were vital to Chindit operations but were heavy and needed several mules to carry them. *(Courtesy Imperial War Museum)*

Below right: A Canadian air-gunner mans a Vickers machine-gun inside a Dakota flyin with supplies for the Chindits. *(Courtesy Imperial War Museum)*

Right: Landing strip at Broadway, showing the bulldozer and scraper which saved the whole operation. *(Courtesy Imperial War Museum)*

Right: Mountbatten (*left*) with Wingate (*right*) and Merrill (*centre*), who led the Marauders. *(Courtesy Imperial War Museum)*

Right: Wingate (*left*) and Tulloch, convert by a Dakota. *(Courtesy Imperial War Museum)*

Above: Calvert (*left*) after his great victory at Mogaung. *(Courtesy Imperial War Museum)*

Below: Chindit casualties were heavy. Here Chindit hats lie on the crosses that mark their graves. *(Courtesy Imperial War Museum)*

Right: The airstrip at Myitkyina. *(Courtesy Imperial War Museum)*

Below: Taking supplies to the Chinese along the Burma Road. *(Courtesy Imperial War Museum)*

Below right: The Sentinel aircraft, which saved many Chindit lives. *(Courtesy Imperial War Museum)*

Above left: Major-General Woodburn Kirby, who wrote the Official History of the Burma Campaign. *(Courtesy Imperial War Museum)*

Top right and below: Orde Wingate. *(Courtesy Wingate family collection)*

The stench became so bad that the pilots of light planes coming to evacuate the wounded knew from the smell that they were approaching 'White City'.

'White City' had resisted all attacks so effectively that Lentaigne decided to put Calvert in charge of a counter-attacking force operating outside the base. On 12 April, Calvert flew out to conduct a recce for the operation, leaving Brigadier Gillmore, commanding 3 West African Brigade, defending the base with the 6th Battalion Nigerian Regiment and the South Staffs. In his attacking force Calvert took the 7th Battalion Nigerian Regiment, 3/6 Gurkhas, and Columns of the 45th Reconnaissance Regiment and the Lancashire Fusiliers, and planned to attack the main Japanese HQ in Sepein.

The attack started on 17 April, with 3/6 Gurkhas making good progress into Sepein helped by artillery support from within 'White City', but they discovered that the main Japanese position was outside the village and was protected by almost impenetrable lantain scrub. (Another good example of inadequate reconnaissance causing trouble.) After a trying day of indeterminate fighting, Calvert decided, reluctantly, to withdraw westwards and consolidate at the village of Thayaung about two miles away. In the fighting the Chindits lost 16 killed and 35 wounded.

He then changed his plan and, leaving an artillery observation officer in Ponlon to direct fire on to the Japanese in Sepein, and leaving the Nigerians in Mawlu – where they carried out a successful ambush of a large Japanese patrol – he moved off with the main body to destroy the road and railway south of Sepein. They reached Tonlon where they effectively cut the railway and blocked the road, and then prepared to squeeze the Japanese units by returning northwards towards the 'White City' perimeter.

The next day he had to change his plans again because Gillmore, after a night attack in which the Japanese penetrated the 'White City' defences, and in spite of a spirited charge by the Nigerians which drove them out, sent an urgent message to Calvert saying he doubted if he could hold out much longer. On receiving this call, Calvert felt he had to make an immediate move to relieve the pressure on 'White City'. He therefore advanced northwards with the Reconnaissance Regiment in the lead and made good progress towards the 'White City' perimeter, intending to assault the rear of the Japanese forces when they next put in an attack.

This move led to a fierce and confused battle in which the Japanese – still about 2,000 strong – found themselves attacked from the front by the Nigerians coming out of 'White City', while Calvert's force attacked them from the rear. The Japanese, with commendable discipline, rallied, and then moved strongly against Calvert's troops, coming very close to overrunning his HQ. He has described how, when he was crouching on the ground under heavy machine-gun fire, he watched with horrified fascination as the bullets ripped through the mules which were standing up.

When the battle was at its height, the Chindits called for a strike by the Air Commando Mustangs and they, diving almost vertically for greater accuracy, nearly wiped out the Japanese force as it prepared to make a new assault, but this never took place. The Mustangs had tipped the balance.

During the fighting, Ian MacPherson, a young Gurkha officer who commanded the Brigade Defence Platoon, was killed. He was Calvert's closest friend and when he heard the news he could hardly believe it, and decided to go back on to the battlefield to check for himself. His Brigade Major, realising the stress and emotional turmoil Calvert was going through, drew his revolver and threatened to shoot Calvert if he went back. This saved the situation. Later he wrote, 'The shock of what he said brought me to my senses'. (*Fighting Mad*, p196)

The Chindits regrouped at Thayaung, but they were too exhausted to prevent the enemy survivors slipping away southwards towards Indaw. In this battle the Chindits lost nearly 100 dead and as many more wounded, but the Japanese sustained nearly 3,000 casualties. (Louis Allen, p356) They never again threatened 'White City' – indeed, the 24 Independent Mixed Brigade ceased to exist as a fighting unit.

After this battle, when 'White City' and 'Broadway' had successfully fought off all Japanese attacks and had vindicated Wingate's concept of the Stronghold, with floater Columns operating outside both the Stronghold and the block, the days of the Chindits were numbered. This was the moment when the loss of Wingate and his passionate conviction proved fatal. Decisions were now being taken by commanders – notably Slim and Lentaigne – who did not seriously believe in LRP as it had evolved. Bidwell wrote of Lentaigne at this juncture, 'There is sufficient evidence that he considered Wingate a charlatan, and his military ideas nonsense' (Bidwell, p207) – and this was the man who was given the direct responsibility for the lives and destiny of all the Chindits.

By the beginning of May, the Japanese had virtually shot their bolt at Kohima and Imphal, and from the Intelligence coming into 14th Army HQ it must have been apparent that after the substantial defeat of Mutaguchi's divisions, there would shortly be a massive advance by the 14th Army. This would create an ideal situation for the proper and effective use of LRP units, but all the evidence suggests that Slim had no intention of using the Chindits in this role for which they had been armed, trained and equipped. Nor did he appear to have any conception of the use of regular airborne forces which could have been employed most effectively for the rest of the campaign. Therefore – perhaps with relief – he handed over the whole of Special Force to Stilwell, who at that stage made it quite plain that he did not want them.

Slim, in taking this action, and with the feeble connivance of Lentaigne, was virtually signing the death warrant of many Chindits. After weeks of fighting behind the enemy lines, in which they had achieved all that was asked of them, instead of being taken out, restored, re-equipped and used again in their proper role, they were left in the jungle during the monsoon and launched into an operation in support of 111 Brigade, which offended every military concept Wingate had taught. After that they were used again in an assault on a strongly defended town – Mogaung – which would have been a disaster but for the leadership of Calvert.

Thus, with the firm control of Wingate removed, 'Broadway' and 'White City' were soon to be abandoned and the Chindit brigades launched into a very different operation.

111 Brigade, in contrast to 77 Brigade with its spectacular achievements, gave considerable ammunition to Wingate's critics who claimed that a large number of highly trained and expensively equipped troops, served at great cost by its own air force, spent a lot of time milling about in the jungle without achieving very much. 77 Brigade successfully blocked the road and rail routes up to Myitkyina, but what

---

Main units of 111 Brigade and 'Blackpool'
1st Battalion King's OwnRoyal Regiment
1st Battalion The Cameronians
3/4 Gurkhas   4/9 Gurkhas

---

did 111 Brigade achieve? The answer, unfortunately, is that in spite of their appalling suffering at 'Blackpool', 111 Brigade achieved little. Having been flown in at the same time as 77 Brigade, initially they suffered neither hardship nor casualties, largely because of Lentaigne's lack of leadership and his supine attitude, which was to try to move about unseen, avoiding the enemy, with the very occasional 'tip and run' exercise; one of Lentaigne's officers added 'the emphasis on run'. When 111 Brigade did get into serious action they were tactically and mentally unprepared for it.

111 Brigade under Lentaigne started its fly-in on 6 March from Tulihal and went in to 'Chowringhee' east of the Irrawaddy. Within three days the 4/9 Gurkhas, the 3/4 Gurkhas, and Brigade HQ arrived safely with no Japanese interference. Under Wingate's directive, the 4/9 Gurkhas under Lieutenant-Colonel Morris, were detached from the brigade, and marched off eastwards to the Bhamo road. (See page 147.) While this was happening, the other two battalions of the brigade – the 2nd King's Own Royal Regiment and the 1st Cameronians – had been diverted to 'Broadway' because the fly-in arrangements there had worked so well.

On 10 March, Brigade HQ and 3/4 Gurkhas set out to join up with the King's and the Cameronians at a pre-arranged rendezvous scheduled for 24 March. To reach the rendezvous the group had to cross the Irrawaddy and this immediately caused serious problems – brought on partly by inadequate training. (Because of his illness in the autumn of 1943, Wingate had no direct involvement in the training of 111 Brigade.) At the Irrawaddy, rubber boats with outboard motors were dropped, but the mules which had been flown in refused to swim across the river. After a tense and exhausting day when the whole group felt absurdly vulnerable, Lentaigne made the decision that 40 Column (part of 3/4 Gurkhas) would stay east of the river and join up with Morris Force, while Brigade HQ and the rest of 3/4 Gurkhas would complete the crossing and march to the rendezvous. Next, an airdrop went wrong and the exhausted unit spent much of the day retrieving the stores. After about five days the group were almost completely demoralised and exhausted. With all their effort, they seemed to have marched and counter-marched and achieved nothing – except to blow up a railway track which appeared to be unused. The brigade should have demolished the main railway south of Indaw in order to prevent Japanese reinforcements from the south coming up to strengthen the town's defences, but they failed to do this, with grave consequences for Fergusson's 16 Brigade.

This brief period has been described by both Masters, who was Brigade Major, and by Rhodes-James the Cipher Officer who later wrote the book *Chindit*. They concur in their descriptions of the signs of strain in Lentaigne, who only had a tiny unit to control and was not even in contact with the enemy. One night the group stood-to and fired shots, but it was discovered that the intruders had been a couple of innocent villagers. None the less, Lentaigne drafted a signal saying that they had contacted strong Japanese patrols. Masters persuaded him not to send it and tried to find an excuse to fly out and ask Wingate to come in and decide whether Lentaigne was fit for the job. Rhodes-James wrote 'Lentaigne's exhaustion brought on a nervousness that was both obvious and acutely embarrassing' – meaning his bowels had turned to water. (Rhodes-James, *Chindit*, p77) In this worrying situation the group continued their long march to the rendezvous with the rest of the brigade and on 24 March they met the King's and the Cameronians, who had experienced a few clashes with Japanese patrols.

Masters described how the next day he settled down to sleep, but was interrupted by a message from Force HQ: 'General Wingate killed in air crash. Lentaigne to fly out immediately to assume command of Force.' A second message warned 111 Brigade to move towards Pinlebu – 45 miles north-west – and to operate against the Japanese lines of communication leading to Imphal. Masters woke Lentaigne who read the message and, apparently, turned over and went to sleep.

Next day Lentaigne asked Masters who he would suggest as Brigadier. He thought, and mentioned two of the COs in the brigade, or the 2 i/c of another Chindit brigade. Later, Lentaigne handed him a signal which appointed Morris – who was with Morris Force on the Bhamo road – as temporary Brigadier, and Masters, the Brigade Major, to command the rest of the brigade – in fact the largest part. He was promoted over the heads of more senior Colonels and became Brigade Commander, but not with the rank of Brigadier.

The background to this remarkable situation went back to 1943 when Wavell, without consulting Wingate, designated 111 Brigade to become Chindits. The Brigade Commander, Lentaigne, had never accepted Wingate's ideas or his methods. Rhodes-James said that there was 'a deep antipathy' between them. (*Chindit*, p77) In the brigade,

Lentaigne, Morris and Masters were very much three old pals together, and from the start they had been critical of, and even derisory towards Wingate, whom they saw as an upstart whose ideas were unproven. Colonel Cane, who had served in the Western Desert with the Gurkhas, was horrified at the defeatist and windy attitudes he found when he joined 111 Brigade. Others commented that, when behind the lines, Lentaigne and Morris were 'excessively timid', and totally lacked the aggressive instinct so vital for a Chindit leader. Thus soon after Wingate's death, three very important positions in the Chindits had gone to men who had openly derided him, and whose rejection of his doctrines was soon to have serious results.

Masters virtually commanded the brigade from that moment until the end of the campaign. Later he was to gain great fame as a novelist, and wrote *The Road Past Mandalay* (1961) as his description of this campaign. As a famous novelist and commander of the brigade, his description has become the touchstone for 'Blackpool', and his views have strongly influenced the general image of the campaign. Bidwell and Louis Allen have quoted extensively from him and in the 1960s, Kirby, author of the Official History, claimed that Masters' views matched his own.

More recently, with the active encouragement of the Chindit Old Comrades Association, a large number of contemporary documents, diaries and notebooks have come to light. These, mostly written at the time, give vivid descriptions of many incidents covered by Masters, but their general slant, understandably, differs substantially from that of their Brigade Commander. Just as Macdonald Fraser in *Quartered Safe Out Here*, brings alive the attitudes, feelings and language of the soldiers of a platoon of the Border Regiment, so some of the Chindit documents which have appeared recently give a very different view of the operations of 111 Brigade. Many were highly critical of the decisions made at a higher level, which condemned them to such an intensity of suffering.

These highly critical comments were strongly supported at a meeting held at Stevenage in 1991 at the request of J. Clay, the author of the biography of Masters entitled *A Regimented Life*. Officers who knew Masters well and had served with him in the Gurkhas and in 111 Brigade at 'Blackpool', were severely critical of his lack of leadership. Lieutenant Flett of the Cameronians, who commanded the rearguard and was the last to leave 'Blackpool', confirmed that the morale of the whole brigade was low, that Masters rarely appeared among the troops, and they had no confidence in his leadership or his plans. Veterans of 'Blackpool' consider the chapter in *A Regimented Life* which deals with 'Blackpool' was seriously inaccurate. Others noted that Masters had no previous battle experience, but had a conceited and amateurish attitude towards such vital chores as digging trenches with adequate head cover – an omission which cost his brigade dear.

As Lentaigne veered towards the idea of giving up 'Broadway' and 'White City' and moving all the Chindit brigades north, Calvert protested again, particularly at the proposal not to continue with more Chindit-type operations. At Force HQ, Tulloch, ever loyal to Wingate, was horrified at Lentaigne's plans for 'Blackpool' which he clearly forecast would be a disaster, and he threatened to resign over the issue. Thus, the two Chindit leaders most dedicated to Wingate's philosophy – Calvert and Tulloch – strongly opposed Lentaigne's decision, because it ignored or rejected every precept which Wingate had taught.

Calvert has admitted that his signals to Lentaigne had become increasingly insubordinate, but soldiers have to obey orders and with considerable misgivings Special Force set out on its new role. By the beginning of May 1944 the overall plan was becoming clearer. At the Quebec Conference, the Americans had given strong support to Wingate in order for him to assist Stilwell in his advance, so that a road link could be established to get supplies up to Chiang Kai Shek, and this is why Myitkyina and Mogaung became so important. In discussions at the end of April 1944, when Imphal was still under great pressure, Slim had suggested that Special Force should switch their main attack to the southwest to destroy the communications and supplies of Mutaguchi's three divisions attacking Imphal (this was virtually Wingate's Plan B). Both Calvert and Fergusson opposed Slim's suggestion, arguing that their first priority must be to block the routes going up to Stilwell's forces. After lengthy consideration, the final decision was made that the remaining Chindit brigades would move north and come under the command of Stilwell.

'Vinegar Joe' Stilwell' whom Slim called the most colourful character in SE Asia, was a very senior American general who had served several years in China during the 1930s and then, from 1942, had the unenviable task of commanding Chiang Kai Shek's divisions in Burma. He had shared with Slim the humiliation of the retreat in Burma, and then had shown determination and leadership in retraining his Chinese troops in India. From October 1943 he led them down the Hukawng Valley as the first step in driving the Japanese out of north Burma and restoring a land route to China. Stilwell had an almost impossible task. Chiang Kai Shek intrigued against him and countermanded his orders, and then when South East Asia Command was set up, Stilwell became Deputy Commander to Mountbatten. He had an abiding contempt for what he saw as the snooty upper-class British officer, and for the British in general whom he considered 'cowardly Limeys'. His colourful prejudices became a more serious issue when large numbers of Chindits came under his direct command.

On 23 April, Lentaigne gave the orders for 111 Brigade under Masters to lead the march north and to establish a block in the area of Hopin in order to continue the stranglehold on the road and railway going up to Mogaung; 14 Brigade and 3 West African Brigade were to take over 'Aberdeen' and 'White City', to organise the withdrawal from both bases as soon as all the guns and equipment had been removed, and then to march north and assist 111 Brigade; 16 Brigade under Fergusson, exhausted after their long march from Ledo and their unsuccessful attack on Indaw (see page 164), were to be flown out immediately; and 77 Brigade were ordered to move out of 'White City' and 'Broadway', to have a short respite and extra rations in the Gangaw Hills just north of 'White City', before marching north 'to assist Stilwell to hold the line Mogaung- Myitkyina'. (*Prisoners of Hope*)

The style of command quickly changed. Whereas Wingate would have been in the thick of the action, consulting and reassuring his brigade commanders, Lentaigne, although he was making substantial alterations to the operations of five brigades, did not fly in to see any of his brigade commanders, except for a very hurried trip to 'Broadway' on 8 May to reprimand Calvert for his insubordinate signals. Lentaigne did not even go in when he sacked Brigadier Gillmore from command of 3 West African Brigade, just when he had planned the withdrawal from 'White City'.

When Masters received the orders for 111 Brigade he felt that he should have asked for the orders to be reconsidered, but thought it would have made no difference, 'because the hand that pulled us away was not that of Joe (Lentaigne), but of Slim acceding to Stilwell'. (*Road Past Mandalay*, p219) This view is inaccurate, for Stilwell did not request the Chindits at that time, but the comment is significant since Masters, too, highlights the responsibility of Slim for these events. In practice, Masters did not challenge the orders and instead led 111 Brigade in two groups up the Meza Valley towards Hopin. They marched through formidable tangled jungle, crossing and recrossing the Meza river through deep dark canyons with nowhere to rest. Everyone was exhausted, and Masters found himself 'shaking with exhaustion and helpless anger'. After several days of painful, slow progress the brigade came in sight of Lake Indawgyi, 14 miles long and five miles wide.

On the march Masters had received air photographs of the area around Hopin, where he was to establish his block, and he had to decide on the exact site. He describes in some detail, and with considerable pride, how he studied the air photographs and then went forward to the vicinity of Mokso Sakan where he carried out a more thorough recce disguised as a Burmese villager. He records how he checked for observation, fields of fire, reverse slope positions, water supply etc. In considering these factors, he commented, 'my block would not be in the enemy lines of communication proper, but in an area under the control of his forward commanders. His reaction would be faster and more violent.' (Masters, p226) This description makes it plain that he followed the normal army drill for assessing a situation. It also shows that he either rejected or totally ignored the basic principles which Wingate taught – first, that LRP groups should attack communications some way behind the line, and not in the area of the forward commanders who would have immediate access to front line troops; secondly, a Stronghold should be established in rough country where the enemy cannot bring artillery or tanks to bear. By ignoring or rejecting these precepts – and in his detailed description of how he made his decision, he does not mention them – Masters bears the responsibility for the damage and carnage that was soon to engulf his brigade. The point was obvious to all the Chindits, since the Japanese artillery started to pound them even before the block was set up. It is true Masters suffered with his men, and afterwards his descriptive ability told their story to the world, but at no stage did he admit that his decision where to site 'Blackpool' was a blunder.

On this point, there were at the time those who were able to see the danger of this decision. At the top, suffering extreme frustration, Tulloch did his best to prevent the establishment of 'Blackpool' which broke every rule Wingate had taught, but his wise and experienced counsel was rejected by Lentaigne, who almost seemed to be saying 'We

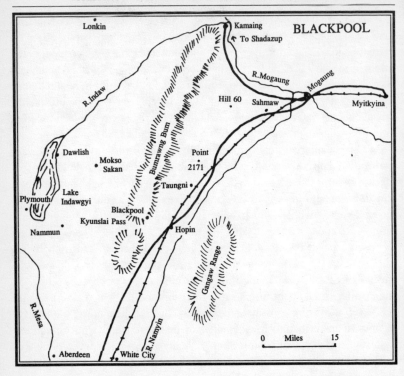

will show you Wingate was not always right'. (Tulloch Papers, Rylands) On the ground at 'Blackpool' there were men trained in the Chindit doctrines, who saw at once that the siting of 'Blackpool' was a blunder. Mr J. Milner, CBE who served in the King's Liverpool Battalion, was in one of the Columns which left 77 Brigade and was sent up to join 111 Brigade at 'Blackpool'. He survived the battle and returned to the battlefield some months afterwards with a graves registration unit, when he made notes – so his recall of the detail is as immediate as that of Masters or Rhodes-James. In a manuscript, as yet unpublished, he commented that 'Blackpool' was poorly sited and weakly defended. The northern perimeter was in deep forest – ideal cover for enemy attackers to form up. Milner's unit had operated as floater columns during the whole 'White City' operation in the classic Chindit role, and he viewed the situation at 'Blackpool' with trepidation. Having enjoyed the leadership of 'The great, gentle, humane Scottie' (Colonel Walter Scott), Milner was highly critical of the system in 111 Brigade.

In early May, as the main body of 111 Brigade moved towards 'Blackpool' in a grueliing march, there was a remarkable interlude when they took a mid-day break and swam in Lake Indawgyi. That night they reached Mokso Sakan and, by 8 May, Masters with the King's and the Cameronians took up their positions at 'Blackpool'. For 36 hours every man worked frantically to dig, set up wire, lay cable, collect stores and ammunition, and to level the strips. Masters' idea of identifying places in the perimeter by using cricket field positions – like square leg – was useful, but did not amuse everyone. There was a dangerous bump in the middle of the pitch – the airstrip – where several gliders were wrecked as they flew in. Two Dakotas were damaged and two destroyed, but in spite of the constant Japanese fire, the American pilots disregarded all danger and even managed to bring in four 25-pounder guns.

Milner recorded that Scottie's Column had received daily briefings, but at 'Blackpool' they had none. There were no floater Columns, and 'Blackpool' lacked all the essentials for a Stronghold. The proud and experienced Column of King'smen felt that there was no leadership and that they were used as general dogsbodies. Both King's and Cameronians criticised Masters for staying in his command trench and not visiting the forward positions. Most of the men grumbled that 'Blackpool' did not equate with any of Wingate's ideas which had been instilled into them, and there was just a feeling of overcast weariness, uncertainty and doom. They wondered, 'Had the Chindit doctrines been buried with their creator?' Underlying all their anger and fury was the conviction that if Wingate had been alive they would not have been at 'Blackpool' at all. (Milner, p426) In addition, having marched up to 'Blackpool', they knew and had seen places where a fully effective Stronghold could have been sited. Having been at 'Broadway' and 'White City', they had certainly absorbed the Chindit doctrine about avoiding enemy artillery, yet as they reached 'Blackpool' they were immediately bombarded by Japanese 105s, and shells were falling even as the gliders began to come in, followed by the Dakotas.

While 111 Brigade suffered so severely from the continuous Japanese assault, Masters was extremely critical of the enemy's unimaginative approach. Their main bombardment started regularly at 1700 hours, and after that they launched their ground attacks on the same place every night. He thought they were 'incredible fools' for not shelling the airstrip. At the same time – as is fairly normal in battle – he vehemently cursed the other units which should have been helping him and, incidentally, showed his equivocal attitude towards the Chindit ethos. He grumbled that 111 Brigade were worked into the ground, 'While 20 battalions, 40 flaming Columns of Chindit bullshit sat on their arses and drank tea and wondered how we were getting on'. (Masters, p243) Similarly, as he waited for 14 Brigade which should have come as his floater Column, 'Surely those bloody nitwits could cover 120 miles in 13 days'.

The relentless Japanese pressure of ground attacks, artillery shelling, and the terrifying 6in mortar, together with the equally relentless monsoon rain which had developed in its full fury as they marched north, gradually wore down the defenders, and resulted in an alarming casualty rate both from wounds and sickness. 'The rain now fell steadily. The deep sector looked like Paschendaele – blasted trees, feet and twisted hands sticking up out of the earth, bloody shirts... and over all the heavy sweet stench of death, from our own bodies and entrails lying unknown in the shattered ground, from Japanese corpses on the wire, or fastened dead and rotting in the trees.' (Masters, p245)

Every day the Japanese attackers from their 53 Division inched closer to the wire perimeter and then, in order to push them back, and at considerable risk to the King's Own men in the front trenches, Masters brought down a remarkably successful and accurate Mustang attack within yards of the front line. Mortars and all available machine guns joined in this effective reprisal and drove the enemy back for 200 yards, but even this only provided a brief respite from the grinding pressure.

On 17 May, the Japanese retaliated with a terrifying artillery bombardment (as Louis Allen said, 'Reinforcing Wingate's views on Stronghold'), and an absolute fury of shells fell on to the King's Own. They reported that all their machine gun posts had been hit, their crews killed, and they were sure they could not hold an attack. Masters immediately ordered the Cameronians to replace them, and then, as the changeover took place, when no attack could have been held, there was – inexplicably – an hour's lull, and when the attack did come in the Cameronians were able to drive it back.

The garrison asked with increasing anger and urgency 'Where are 14 and 77 Brigade?'. In fact, 77 Brigade were not too far away, but in spite of desperate efforts by the whole brigade, the Namyin river, which 111 Brigade had crossed a few days earlier, was now so swollen by the monsoon rains into a raging torrent that it defied every attempt at crossing. Some help did arrive at 'Blackpool', but not in sufficient strength to defeat the Japanese. The 3/9 Gurkhas, who had been blooded in action around 'Broadway', but were fit and at full strength, arrived on 20 May and were quickly positioned on the perimeter.

By 22 May there was a short lull and Masters still felt that the Japanese could be defeated if only 14 Brigade would arrive, but then there was a new and sinister development. The Dakotas coming in for a daylight drop were met by anti-aircraft fire and flew off. Another flight of Dakotas came in, but suffered severely with only half of the aircraft returning to base. At the same time, the Japanese had pushed in another part of the perimeter and from that position their fire could effectively prevent night drops. Thus day drops and night drops were impossible and for days on end incessant rain prevented any drops at all. While ammunition ran dangerously low, it also meant that the wounded could not be evacuated, and their number drastically increased. Lieutenant-Colonel Whyte RAMC – Doc Whyte to everyone – an intrepid Ulsterman, kept the main dressing station going through indescribable conditions. On two occasions it received direct hits from shell-fire, and the wounded bodies lying on the stretchers were blown limb from limb.

Japanese artillery launched another heavy bombardment on 24 May, followed by a strong ground attack which drove back the perimeter held by the 3/9 Gurkhas. Under this sort of pressure the feelings of the men towards their commanders deteriorated dangerously. Lentaigne, back at Force HQ, showing no quality of leadership and completely lacking any personal contact with 'Blackpool', had no idea of the situation or the conditions to which he was committing his forces, no idea of the terrain, and no idea of the morale either of his commanders or their troops. He never even sent a staff officer to 'Blackpool'. He became an object of thinly veiled contempt, in contrast to the constant refrains 'Wingate would have come in', or 'Had Wingate lived this would never have happened'.

When the 3/9 Gurkhas had to withdraw from their section of the perimeter, the whole position rapidly became untenable, and Masters sought permission to abandon 'Blackpool'. When no reply came to his request, he wrote 'Unless Slim and Stilwell have gone mad the discretionary order must be on its way'. On 25 May, agreement or not, Masters decided to withdraw. Then the remains of his brigade, men who had reached the limit of hunger, and physical and nervous exhaustion, began a slow and painful withdrawal from 'Blackpool' towards Mokso Sakan which they had left just 17 days before.

Masters has described the most distressing incident in this whole bloody debacle. The retreat had started when a doctor called him over to look at the 19 stretcher cases. 'The first man was quite naked and a shell had removed the entire contents of his stomach. Between his chest and pelvis there was a bloody hollow, and behind it his spine. Another had no legs and no hips, his trunk ending just below the waist. A third had no left arm, shoulder or breast, all torn away in one piece. A fourth had no face and a whitish liquid was trickling out of his head.' The doctor virtually had to say that if the very seriously wounded, for whom there was no hope, and for whom there was no morphine left, were shot, 30 others who were less seriously wounded might be saved. No one was prepared to leave them to the Japanese. Masters, with the safety of 2,000 others on his mind, agreed, and walked away, the single shots ringing through his head. (Masters, p259)

The withdrawal to Mokso Sakan has been described as an orderly and well-planned operation – a description based largely on Masters' own report. A very different version is given by Milner, a member of the King's Column, who wrote that it was 'a chaotic rout of exhausted troops without any clear orders or known destination'. This view is also confirmed by the Cameronian rearguard. Milner also considered that the siting of 'Blackpool' by Masters was a serious blunder, and argues strongly that an effective block could have been established at Hopin, which had none of the disadvantages of 'Blackpool', and where 77 Brigade, 14 Brigade and 3 West African Brigade could have come to the assistance of 111. He reiterates that this is not hindsight, but adds 'During the "Blackpool" siege men constantly voiced these beliefs'. (Milner, letter to the author, August 1990)

As the exhausted survivors of the brigade reached the lakeside marshes around Mokso Sakan, some help was at hand. A jetty was built and two Sunderland flying-boats, taken off duties in the Bay of Bengal, flew into Lake Indawgyi and were able to take off 40 wounded at a time. The first operation took out 240 men, and the pilots of the L-5 light planes flew other wounded to the HQ at Shadazup, from where they were flown to India by Dakota. In all 600 sick and wounded were rescued. Doc Whyte informed Masters that the majority of the brigade were on the threshold of death from exhaustion, undernourishment, exposure and strain. Men just died from a cold, a cut finger, or from the least physical exertion.

Early in June a new order came from Lentaigne – who still did not leave his safe HQ to visit the brigade – that while 77 Brigade attacked Mogaung, 111, 14 and 3rd West African Brigades would operate west of the town. So, after a brief lull, Masters led the way north. He had infuriated the NCOs when he addressed them and tried to shift the blame for the choice of 'Blackpool'. 'Any Tommy could see "Blackpool" was doomed from the start by its proximity to the Japanese front line reserves, and its artillery.' (Milner, p509) These views were echoed by many, including Jack Lindo, another King's man, and together they recall that there was such strong feeling among the men at this time that if Stilwell or Lentaigne or even Slim had appeared 'They would not have lived to see the dawn'. (Milner, p520)

Lentaigne had ordered that 111 Brigade would capture Point 2171, overlooking the Mogaung river, and firmly held by the Japanese. The prolonged struggle to capture and hold Point 2171 – from 20 June to 5 July – was considered by the survivors to be greater suffering than 'Blackpool'. Taking part were the 3/4 Gurkhas, 3/9 Gurkhas, the King's, the Cameronians and the 7th Leicesters from 14 Brigade. Every unit was weakened by battle casualties and sickness. They were told 'Just a couple of days, and its our last show', but 'Two days turned into two weeks and then into an endless nightmare'. The two Gurkha battalions and the King's led the advance – days of crushing toil up precipitous slopes, through mud and slime up to their knees, and through enemy fire and showers of grenades. They captured a ridge from where they could actually see Point 2171. Against a murderous fire the 3/9 Gurkhas went forward. Major Blaker, who had been outstanding during the whole campaign, led the final assault and was mown down by bullets, but such was his leadership that his death roused his Gurkhas to a wild unstoppable charge which drove the Japanese off the peak. Major Blaker won a posthumous VC. The Gurkhas and the King's quickly consolidated and kept the enemy at bay. Again, this was worse than 'Blackpool', since airdrops were impossible, the constant monsoon rain turned paths into dangerous quagmires, all food and ammunition had to be hauled up the slopes by man and mule, and at the top the soil was so shallow that no proper trenches could be dug. The defenders were so totally exhausted that they could not bury their dead or even mark their graves. It was the worst time – more than flesh and blood could bear, and several men just dropped dead.

Then for no obvious tactical reason the order came to pull out, giving rise to the bitter question 'What was the point of attacking the hill in the first place?'. The exhausted survivors silently, at night, slithered back down the hill that had cost them so dear. The gallant Doc Whyte kept going night and day, saving men's lives with his skill, his medicines and his example, treating malaria, dysentery, typhoid, footrot, typhus, meningitis, and every type of wound. Masters, with the strong support of every unit commander recommended him for the VC, but he received the DSO – having saved over 200 lives.

After the withdrawal from Point 2171, Masters demanded a medical inspection for all his men, which was only granted when he threatened to resign; just over 100 men out of the whole brigade were found to be fit for duty. Stilwell, still paranoid about 'Lily-livered Limeys', remained bloody-minded to the end. Eventually, the survivors were ordered to go to Mogaung and they marched slowly off. On the way they passed Lentaigne, and he did not even say 'Well done'. Their feelings about him smouldered for years, while Scottie – who had been through it all with them – they cheered to the skies. (Milner, p467) On 1 August 1944, in Mogaung, they boarded a train to Myitkyina and from there they flew to India.

111 Brigade sustained heavy casualties and suffered atrocious conditions, but although they inflicted heavy casualties on a Japanese regiment from 53 Division, they had no obvious achievement to their credit. Critics of LRP have said, unjustly, that 111, 14 and 3 West African Brigades achieved no striking success. Such criticism does not invalidate Wingate's conception of LRP: rather, it highlights the disasters caused to a large number of highly trained and brave men because, at the top, Slim did not support the idea of LRP and condemned the Chindits to be used as normal infantry under the control of Stilwell. At the next level, Lentaigne, who openly derided Wingate's ideas but had nothing to put in their place, weakly went along with Slim's arrangements. Finally, Masters condemned his brigade to suffering and slaughter because he too had rejected the basic principles of the Stronghold, and because of that, made the disastrous decision to establish 'Blackpool'.

8

The Final Chindit Campaigns

Morris Force and Dah Force, which had flown into 'Chowringhee' with 111 Brigade starting on 6 March, operated along the Bhamo-Myitkyina road which, after the successful blocking of the Indaw-Myitkyina road and rail route by 77 Brigade, became the most crucial supply route for the Japanese divisions fighting Stilwell in the north. The members of Morris Force and Dah Force to some extent felt that the great battles of 77 Brigade under Mike Calvert at 'Broadway' and 'White City' had relegated them to the sidelines, but the operations they conducted against the Japanese on the Bhamo-Myitkyina road were extremely important both in themselves and because they illustrated Wingate's remarkable strategic grasp of the whole Burma theatre. The basic concept of LRP was to destroy the enemy lines of communication, and this coloured all Wingate's plans.

The successful actions at 'Broadway' and 'White City' affected particularly the Japanese 18 Division fighting Stilwell, and their 31 Division making for Kohima. But it also highlighted the importance of the Bhamo road as the supply route for 18 Division, as well as 36 Division fighting against Chiang Kai Shek's forces along the Salween river.

Wingate realised in advance how significant the Bhamo-Myitkyina road would become, and he therefore detached from 111 Brigade one whole battalion – 4/9 Gurkha Rifles – under Lieutenant-Colonel Morris, and ordered it to operate against the road with two Columns, 94 and 49. In addition, a small force under Lieutenant-Colonel Herring and known as Dah Force, was sent in to encourage the loyal Kachin people to rise in rebellion against the Japanese, and to help Morris Force to block the road up to Myitkyina permanently. For long stretches through Kachin country, the road passed below hillsides which were

---

Main Units of Morris Force and Dah Force,
March to July 1944
3/4 Gurkhas
4/9 Gurkhas

---

ideal for a guerrilla force intent on ambush and on the destruction of the road. Peter Cane, the leader of 94 Column said, 'It was truly a guerrilla's dream'.

Unfortunately, two factors militated against the success of Morris Force. Because of the urgent priority given to supplies to 77 Brigade, and the very substantial distances from Morris Force back to base, their demands for supplies, for explosives and for air-strikes were time and again left unanswered. A second adverse factor in the operations of Morris Force lay in the poor quality of leadership, which became apparent very soon after the operation started. Lentaigne and Morris – old pre-war pals – had never fully accepted Wingate's philosophy, or his example of leading from the front. The training of 111 Brigade was inadequate and, significantly, when 77 Brigade flew in to 'Broadway', the Brigadier and the CO (Calvert and Scott) were in the leading gliders, while in contrast, when Morris Force flew in to 'Chowringhee', Morris arrived later by Dakota when all was captured and a landing strip prepared, and Lentaigne came in even later than that.

Morris Force and Dah Force illustrate both the possibilities and the problems of Chindit-style operations. They had their successes and their failures and then, like most of the Chindits, they ended up in the Myitkyina-Mogaung area under the murderous influence of Stilwell and Boatner, neither of whom had any idea how best to use the lightly armed Chindits in their proper role.

The 4/9 Gurkhas formed the main element of Morris Force. After service on the North West Frontier, where they had sustained some casualties in actions against 'Hostiles', in March 1943 they went for Chindit training in the Central Provinces in Lentaigne's 111 Brigade. They suffered a high incidence of malaria – with 150 off sick at one stage – but continued with training in swimming, river crossing, building air-strips, and organising air-drops. During this period, 300 reinforcements had to be absorbed into the unit, and 80 officers and men had to be returned to their units. In January 1944 they moved to Silchar, the Chindit base near Imphal, and on 21 February Wingate gave them their detailed orders for their attacks on the Bhamo-Myitkyina road, and for their liaison with Dah Force. On 6 March, they flew in to 'Chowringhee', their dropping base east of the Irrawaddy. 'Chowringhee' was far from ideal – the ground was very uneven and there was no water – but by 8 March a strip was ready for landings by Dakota, and the HQ of 111 Brigade together with 3/4

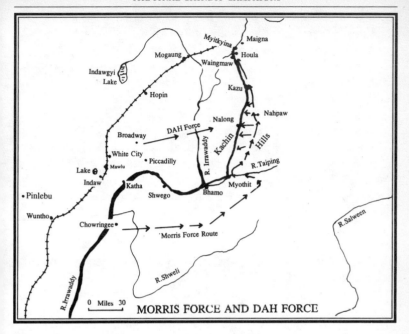

MORRIS FORCE AND DAH FORCE

Gurkhas who were to make up 30 and 40 Columns, were able to fly in. By that time the fly-in at 'Broadway' had gone so well that the Cameronians and the King's Own – the other battalions of 111 Brigade – flew in there.

From 'Chowringhee', 111 Brigade HQ under Lentaigne, and 3/4 Gurkhas, were to cross the Irrawaddy and join up with the rest of the brigade which had flown in to 'Broadway', while 49 and 94 Columns crossed the Shweli river and made for Bhamo. Several significant issues emerged almost at once. The training of 111 Brigade under Lentaigne had been lackadaisical compared to 77 Brigade under Calvert, and this quickly showed up. Soon the characters of the commanders were tested. 111 Brigade suffered frustration and fiasco because of the excessive timidity of Lentaigne, while Morris, commanding 4/9 Gurkhas, seemed from the start to be frantically anxious to avoid contact with the enemy and appeared 'peppery, authoritarian, obstinate and impetuous'. (O'Brien, *Out of the Blue*, p35) Morris made an unfortunate start by ordering 94 Column under Peter Cane to guard his HQ, which resulted in the Column missing an air-drop and being on short rations for the next eight days.

By mid-March the columns had settled down and were making good progress through the Kachin Hills with their friendly villages. In one village the son of the Thugyi (headman) enlisted, and mentioned that there were two strangers in the village. These were quickly apprehended and found to be Japanese spies. They were later killed when they tried to escape from the Column, but it had been a useful warning. Subsequently many such spies were taken in and most were executed in order to prevent the certain Japanese retribution on the village if they got away. Other problems emerged because of the inaccuracy of their maps. Although the Force were aware that Burmese villages often moved when their fields were exhausted, they now found that clearly marked roads appeared to have moved, but at least most of the rivers stayed in the same place. 94 Column found that their most useful information came from a pre-war *Motorist's Guide to Burma*, which helped them to make many roads unmotorable. (*Chinese Chindits*, a factual account of the operations of 4/9 Gurkhas, made by their officers after the war)

The inaccurate maps also hindered the effectiveness of the supply-drops, which initially did not work well, and the 22 wireless set which had been effective in open flat country, now proved quite useless. Wireless communication was a matter of life and death for a Column, and after the failure of his 22 set, Peter Cane demanded a replacement. He received a rather off-hand reply, telling him 'to experiment with the length, direction and position of your aerial'. He answered, 'I have experimented with the aerial in every position except one, and that I leave to you' – a pointed and effective riposte, since a replacement came with the next air-drop.

In spite of these drawbacks Morris Force made good progress towards their objective of the Bhamo-Myitkyina road. They found the Kachin villages very short of food but generously hospitable. The supply drops at first were 'appallingly inaccurate' and the pilots seemed to have had no training or experience in that specialised technique – indeed some supplies landed more than five miles from the dropping zone. The Columns became seriously short of petrol for their battery-chargers and this could have threatened the whole operation. In this situation Morris again antagonised most of his force. After one drop, they had just discovered a parachute in a tree with 140 K Ration packs and were just about to cut it down when Morris, obsessed with fear of discovery, ordered them to leave it and move off at once.

Terence O'Brien, who served as the RAF officer with 49 Column, and subsequently wrote *Out of the Blue*, compared the two Columns. 94 was positive and aggressive because it ignored regulations which were patently ill-founded or ineffectual, whereas Morris, who had virtually taken over the direction of 49 Column from the unfortunate CO (Russel) was obsessed by following every regulation to the letter, and appeared to have a paranoid fear of Wingate. (O'Brien, p139) O'Brien maintained that the significant difference between the Columns was that Peter Cane did not believe the Japanese were massing around every corner, and after a supply drop would collect every parachute load, and if there was interference from the Japanese, he would have welcomed the chance to get at them. In contrast, Morris seemed paralysed with fear and caused chaos by constantly changing planned dropping zones. 49 Column, virtually controlled by Morris, 'always seemed to be withdrawing into the wings, whereas 94 were always rushing into action led by the energetic and spirited Peter Cane'. (O'Brien, p150)

From March through to May, thanks largely to the work of 94 Column, they effectively blocked the Bhamo-Myitkyina road in a whole series of successful actions in destroying bridges and roads and ambushing convoys. During this time they took some successful supply-drops in superb open rolling country, and they also came upon two British soldiers who had been left behind by Gilkes' group in 1943, and who had lived safely in the Kachin village ever since.

94 Column blew up one iron framed bridge which was never repaired, and the Force also discovered that the Japanese thought they were Chinese guerrillas – a view they encouraged.

On 26 March they heard the news of Wingate's death, which affected them deeply. In *Chinese Chindits* they record their thoughts and feelings at the time of that dire news.

'Wingate as a soldier was superb. Magnificently unorthodox... he inspired all with the desire to achieve what the normal man would consider impossible. He personally led his command through any dangerous period and it was a wonderful privilege and experience to have met and served under him. As a man, too, he must be numbered among the greatest. He was utterly indifferent to his own personal success and was prepared to make any personal sacrifice for the good of his cause. It was this that caused him to make so many enemies; for he expected everyone else to do the same, and so he, by his uncompromising disgust at the selfish and the self-seekers, became their enemy.' (*Chinese Chindits*, p21)

A good illustration of the contrasting leadership of the Columns is given by the attack on Myothit, 24 miles along the road from Bhamo, where there was a motor bridge over the raging Taiping river. On 9 April 1944, after an energetic march, 94 Column attacked at 0400 hours, destroyed the bridge and a rice mill which was a main supplier for the Japanese forces, and left after setting a large number of booby traps. Morris and 49 Column should have blocked the other side of the town, but Morris had again changed his mind, had moved off, and had not even informed the other Column. There were many in the force who felt that this was a cowardly action.

The small town of Nalong, about halfway between Bhamo and Myitkyina, was a permanent staging post and maintenance centre for all the supplies going to the Japanese 18 Division facing Stilwell in the north. 94 Column found a perfect observation post in the hills above Nalong, from which they could monitor the traffic along the road and in the town. On 22 April they took a supply drop ready for an attack. They moved in to the town, destroyed the motor bridge over the river and then, with a signal to the Air Commando, had the town bombed and strafed with remarkable accuracy. Cane kept up the pressure and found an ideal spot for a demolition on a mountain road five miles south of Nalong, which would have blocked the road for good. He asked Morris to bring up 40 and 49 Columns to make a combined attack, but to the men's amazement Morris ordered the other two Columns to go with him off into the hills, ostensibly to make contact with Dah Force. This move ruined the chance of a significant success against the Japanese and again called into question Morris's determination.

94 Column continued their action with more demolitions, and on the night of 27 April had trapped 318 lorries loaded with over 1,000 tons of supplies in the centre of Nalong. An urgent signal was sent for an air attack. The weather was clear and an attack would have destroyed transport, supplies and ammunition for the whole of 18 Division, with considerable consequences for the battles at Mogaung and Myitkyina. Morris, now a Brigadier, was not even there to lift the priority of the message and 94 Column, having set up the perfect target, was forced to wait in mounting frustration as, hour after hour, no

air attack came. Even then, with the other two Columns they could have launched a ground attack, but both were off in the hills protecting Morris's HQ. O'Brien commented 'Peter Cane was justifiably bitter at the apathy of his superiors... Many thought Morris was evading real action.' (O'Brien, p168) 94 Column went in, carried out more demolitions, destroyed many vehicles, and had heavy clashes with the Japanese, but Morris himself had ruined the best opportunity his force ever had.

At the end of March, the Chindit Columns made contact with Dah Force under Lieutenant-Colonel Herring whose objective – slightly different from the main Columns – was to stir up the Kachin people in rebellion against the Japanese. There were many ex-soldiers in the villages and it was hoped that when rifles, Bren guns and mortars were supplied, former NCOs would form the nucleus of leadership for an uprising. All of this seemed very promising and the Kachins certainly hated the Japanese, but the type of leadership needed to cause a large scale rebellion was totally missing. It was unfortunate that Wingate had neither the time nor the opportunity to shape the aims, training and leadership of Dah Force according to the precepts he had established in Ethiopia. 'Fish' Herring was certainly not a Garibaldi and his report, which admits his system was a failure, shows the whole direction of Dah Force bogged down in administrative detail and lacking the fire-in-the-belly type of leadership which a successful uprising requires, and which Wingate had provided in Gideon Force.

It rapidly became clear that simply to arm groups of Kachins and expect them to train, organise and direct their own forces was hopelessly unrealistic. Herring did his best, but faced big problems. He found it difficult to control his subordinates effectively – notably Major Shan Lone of the SOE who was nominally his second in command – and there is no doubt that somewhere at a fairly high level in his command there was a traitor. The Japanese seemed to be aware in advance of every move that Dah Force made, yet the Chindit Columns were never attacked in the same way. Herring had been ordered to lead both Kachin and Chinese guerrillas, but they nurtured a fierce mutual hatred and after the Chinese looted some local Kachin villages, they had to be sent back to Yunnan, heavy with Herring's silver dollars, which did not prevent them looting more villages on the way.

Herring organised one big stand of Dah Force at Nahpaw Fort near the Yunnan border, which he manned by Kachins, British and

Chinese, but the Japanese swiftly overran it and caused heavy casualties. Dah Force carried out a few ambushes and occupied some Japanese bases, but in general they were ineffective and did not achieve their aim. They would have proved more effective if small groups had been attached to the Chindit Columns as guides and intelligence gatherers. Herring's next problem was that Shan Lone and many of the Kachin supporters appeared to think – just as the Gojjam Patriots had – that the Chindits had come to protect them.

The basic concept of Dah Force, and its attempt to raise the Kachins in rebellion, was the assurance that the British, Americans and Chinese would clear the Japanese out of north Burma down to the 24th parallel and would not allow them to return. Such promises carried little weight where top level strategic decisions were made and, after Wingate's death, there was no effective spokesman at that level to fight for the cause either of Dah Force or the Chindits. The Kachins were soon to be betrayed and abandoned, followed in a few weeks by the Chindits themselves. Herring was instructed to carry out the odious task of informing his followers that Dah Force was being ordered out and the area abandoned, though they themselves would be able to enlist in the Burma Rifles or in Special Force. Nothing was said about the inevitable Japanese retribution on the Kachin villages after they pulled out.

There could have been much more effective co-operation between Dah Force and the Chindits but, after a number of discussions, Herring had found that Morris kept changing his mind and antagonised everyone, and there the co-operation finished. (Herring Report) For their part, the Chindits often felt that they rarely had a clear run because of the complications of Dah Force.

O'Brien, who later in the war led a squadron which serviced the agents of various clandestine organisations – SOE, OSS, Force 36 etc – throughout South East Asia, is highly critical of the rivalry between these forces. For example, from Morris Force he was sent on a reconnaissance into Yunnan, when a British SOE agent was already there and who could have radioed back the necessary information. O'Brien concluded, 'There was far too much jealousy and amour propre in these organisations'. (O'Brien, p186)

Throughout the campaign Morris, like many of the Chindits, suffered periodic bouts of malaria, but by the middle of May he was clearly ill and isolated himself more and more. He remained paranoid about giving away his position and on one occasion, in a steady downpour and miles away from the road, he forbade all fires, while less than a mile away 94 Column was cheerfully brewing up. Morris caused days of chaos by petulant and impetuous orders, which he almost immediately countermanded. He ordered 94 Column to give up a promising demolition and march 20 miles to join 40 Column, and then ordered them to return next day, having done nothing. (*Chinese Chindits*, p34)

Most of the Chindits wondered what would happen to them after Wingate's death, because they were aware of the antagonisms he had aroused. So far, Morris Force, in spite of the inadequacies of Morris himself, had successfully carried out classic Chindit operations. They had successfully blocked the Bhamo-Myitkyina road for many weeks but now, in the middle of May 1944, they were about to be put under the command of Stilwell. They were already approaching the 90-day deadline considered as a maximum for troops on basic rations and under the stress of fighting behind the enemy lines. Many were in a pitiful physical condition and on one occasion, after three days of plunging through thick steep jungle under orders and counter-orders from Morris, one officer just dropped dead.

Those who had served in 111 Brigade and had witnessed the shambles at 'Chowringhee', realised that Lentaigne was indecisive, and they had been surprised at his appointment to succeed Wingate. Now they were to suffer the real effects of that appointment. Lentaigne was too weak to fight his corner against Slim or Stilwell. From Morris's HQ O'Brien recorded his feelings: 'The enticing solution, one that got rid of us and might also placate the vitriolic Stilwell, was to hand over the Chindits to him completely and let him give them orders direct, rather than keep snapping at high command with his savage criticism'. (O'Brien, p217) O'Brien paints an interesting picture of the leaders of Morris Force as Lentaigne's weakness accentuated Morris's dithering. 94 Column was under Peter Cane, 'a dashing ebullient leader with limitless energy and always eager for action, whose major trial was the maddening frustration of having to watch opportunity after opportunity fade away as his commander ignored targets he had created'. In contrast, Monteith, who commanded 40 Column, liked everything carefully and completely organised, and was driven to fury when the Brigadier always seemed to change his mind at the last moment. Finally, Russel, a good commander, was never allowed to command his Column because Morris took it over and constantly dithered. (O'Brien, p219)

On 18 May Morris Force received a startling signal from Force HQ: 'Stilwell has captured Myitkyina'. The message had an electric effect and everyone assumed that the campaign would now be over and they would be flown out to India immediately, to be retrained for the next Chindit operation. In fact Stilwell had only captured the airfield some miles outside Myitkyina, and the Chindits' elation lasted less than 24 hours until the next signal, which ordered them brusquely to move at once to Kazu, about 20 miles from Myitkyina.

Under the added pressure of Stilwell's orders, Morris deteriorated still further. The Force had just had three gruelling days caused by his frequent change of mind, and he had just ordered two days rest when the signal from Stilwell arrived. He immediately instructed the whole Force to leave within half an hour, and just when they were ready and loaded up, he changed his mind again.

The considered opinion of the Gurkha Columns (*Chinese Chindits*, p37) was 'The attack on Myitkyina (by Stilwell and his Chinese divisions) must have been one of the worst managed operations of the war, and we had the misfortune to be squandered in its inefficiency. So, too Merrill's Marauders were spent uselessly.' As the first step, Morris, always ready to obey orders from above, ordered an immediate attack on Kazu with no time for preparation or reconnaissance. This caused near insurrection among the officers and when Cane arrived he refused to lead his Column into such an ill-conceived enterprise. Operating behind the enemy lines highlights all the normal problems of command in battle and, at Kazu, many wondered if Morris should not be removed before he created a disaster for them all. After the altercation with his officers, Morris climbed down and agreed to a detailed reconnaissance. This found that the previous night 1,500 Japanese had moved out from a powerful well-sited position. If the Chindits had attacked when Morris originally ordered, they would have been slaughtered.

Kazu still presented serious dangers. As 94 Column went in (21 May) the Force heard that there could be no air support, and they suffered a second disadvantage when a Gurkha patrol shot up some Japanese and gave away their position. After an hour's delay, Morris ordered an immediate attack while, on horseback, he quickly led his HQ away from the fighting and up into the hills into a safe harbour. The attack went in and discovered that the Japanese had withdrawn leaving supplies of weapons, ammunition and food. Later that day, the Chindits suffered further problems when the rising river swept the bridge away and trapped the main fighting element on one side of the river, while a large Japanese unit, alerted by the fighting, approached the place where the support body and the mules had been left. Fortunately, an excellent Gurkha havildar fought them off until the support party got away, and then retreated without loss.

Stilwell's claim that his Chinese troops had captured Myitkyina was false. In fact, Merrill's Marauders, by a swift march had, on 17 May, captured Myitkyina airfield which lay two miles west of the town. The town, garrisoned by Japanese troops, well prepared and well dug-in, was not captured for another 11 weeks, while the Chindits and Merrill's Marauders, both physically at the end of their tether, were slaughtered in a series of ill-prepared, uncoordinated and senseless attacks.

Boatner, Stilwell's Chief of Staff, who seemed to reflect all the worst traits of Stilwell himself, on 30 May took over the command for the assault on Myitkyina, and with his Chinese troops had a numerical superiority of 15:1. The town, on the west bank of the Irrawaddy, together with the villages of Maigna and Waingmaw on the east bank, formed part of the usual excellent Japanese defensive system. Instead of using his huge numerical advantage, Boatner scattered his forces all round the area – he had no plan, no method, no concentration of force, and no co-ordination, but every few days merely called for another all-out attack, which the Chinese divisions encouraged by Chiang Kai Shek, usually ignored. On 31 May, 49 and 40 Columns were ordered into an attack without any chance of reconnaissance, and fortunately sustained fewer casualties than expected. Further futile attacks followed in which all the Columns suffered casualties in killed and wounded. Then the monsoon started in earnest and the men's physical state deteriorated rapidly. Morris went to Boatner to demand artillery support before attacking prepared positions, and was told all that the Chindits lacked was courage. 'This monstrous outlook caused great indignation.' (*Chinese Chindits*, p39)

After several days of sudden ill-prepared attacks on Boatner's impetuous orders, Morris Force was moved to a village called Houla, near to Maigna. Here they found an elderly ex-Gurkha, who gave them valuable information about Japanese movements. The two Columns 49 and 94, after a sound recce and careful planning, put in a successful joint attack. A few days later they failed when Boatner ordered an immediate ill-prepared attack – a failure compounded by 'the criminal idleness and cowardice of a junior British officer'. (*Chinese Chindits*, p43) After this setback, Morris ordered 94 Column to recapture Houla on 10 June – again allowing no time for a detailed recce. They found the Japanese there in strength and in the actions that day they lost 22 men killed including Colonel Monteith, who the previous day had said 'Boatner will kill us all off before he is finished'. (O'Brien, p256)

For the rest of the campaign, Morris Force stayed near Maigna and on 19 June put in an attack with three Columns. The Japanese were, as usual, well dug-in with powerful defences and a hard-fought battle went on throughout the day with casualties on both sides but, lacking tanks or artillery, the Chindits had not the power to make a breakthrough. The next day, Morris came down from his safe harbour up in the hills and ordered all units to pull back. Thereafter the Gurkhas kept harassing the defences with active fighting patrols, though the physical state of the men was causing serious concern.

While the Japanese lines remained fairly static, bitter clashes continued between Morris Force and Boatner's HQ. Boatner sent an American liaison officer to stay in Force HQ and, after seeing the physical state of the men, he strongly supported their views. Throughout the campaign, Stilwell had been obsessed with the capture of Myitkyina, and after the capture of the airfield he became paranoid about capturing the town. There was to be one final Chindit attack which had the promise of some air support. The bombers did not arrive on time and their bombs did not go off. Next, some Mustangs arrived and shot up the Chindits as they were forming up. Finally, an urgent message arrived, 'Do not enter the town'. It had been discovered that all the bombs dropped on the town had been fitted with delayed fuses and they continued to explode for the next 12 hours.

The siege of Myitkyina continued with sporadic patrolling through into July, and then after a visit by Lentaigne on 13 July, Morris Force handed over on 17 July to The Royal Sussex in 72 Brigade (36 Division). They flew out from Myitkyina airfield to Dehra Dun where, along with 77 Brigade and the rest of 111 Brigade, they were given intensive anti-malarial treatment and rehabilitation. During August a number of awards were made, including the MC for Peter Cane. In *Chinese Chindits*, it was recorded with some bitterness, 'A little later came the DSO for Jumbo Morris'.

After a long leave, the 4/9 Gurkhas restarted training with gusto, their enthusiasm based on the confidence they had gained from their prolonged blocking of the Bhamo-Myitkyina road. In spite of their sufferings when they came under Stilwell's command and were not used in their proper role, they had great confidence that when employed according to Wingate's precepts, they could repeat their successes behind enemy lines as the 14th Army advanced southwards driving back the Japanese. A rapidly advancing army was, after all, the ideal situation for the employment of LRP Groups.

Their hopes were soon to be disappointed. On 1 February 1945 all battalion commanders were called to an important meeting with General Oliver Leese. They attended with some excitement, expecting details of their next operation, only to be told that the Chindits were to be broken up and their battalions dispersed all over South East Asia Command.

16 Brigade and Indaw

Bernard Fergusson, a Column Commander in 1943, was chosen to lead 16 Brigade in their march from Ledo which started the main Chindit operation of 1944. The brigade was made up of two infantry regiments – the Queen's and the Leicesters – and two regiments transferred from their own specialist roles of reconnaissance and artillery, to be used not only as infantry but as Chindits. The brigade assembled in January 1944 and were visited by Mountbatten, Auchinleck and Wingate, whose address they found 'sizzling and invigorating'.

Wingate took Fergusson to meet Stilwell, whose forces were to assist at the start of the 16 Brigade march. Stilwell, who commented on Fergusson, 'He looks a dude but I think he is a soldier', made a bargain. In return for his help, he wanted a part of the brigade to turn off and capture Lonkin, which was a Japanese post 20 miles west of

---

Main Units of 16 Brigade – Ledo to Indaw
2nd Queen's Royal Regiment   2nd Leicestershire Regiment
45th Reconnaissance Regiment (as infantry)
51st Field Regiment Royal Artillery (as infantry)
54th Field Company Royal Engineers (support)

Notes: The campaign of 16 Brigade is better known than some of the other brigades because of Fergusson's description of it in *The Wild Green Earth* (Collins 1946). There is also a good account of the actions of the Royal Artillery Columns (51 and 69) written by Captain R. Needham (Imperial War Museum).

Kamaing, towards which Stilwell's Chinese divisions were advancing. This was agreed – too easily – for the lack of the two Columns which went to Lonkin contributed to the failure of the attack on Indaw. As they waited for the start, the Chindits felt their security was complete, until the Japanese broadcast a threat to Fergusson by name, and claimed they knew what he was up to.

The epic march from Ledo to Indaw started on 10 February and, after being taken some way down the Ledo road in American trucks, the leading columns set off into some of the most difficult and hostile country in the world, but morale was high and humour abundant. The Royal Engineers had hacked out an initial path, but almost at once the Columns had to cross precipitous cliffs, hills and ravines, often climbing thousands of feet at gradients of one in two or even steeper, only to descend as sharply. Many hills were so steep that loaded mules fell headlong, their hooves kicking wildly. Every day was a torment and hell to the men's wretched pain-wracked bodies, but their comradeship kept them going. After several days came the first supply-drop, which boosted morale, and then they reached the first Naga village whose loyal helpers took the seriously sick safely back to Ledo. Gradually, the men discarded every superfluous item – even blankets, a gesture which benefited the local Naga villages where a man could buy another wife for four blankets. With so much discarded, books were still preciously conserved – Dickens, Galsworthy and Charles Reade among them. Some men wilted and then the doctor had to decide if his pack could be put on a mule, although the mules too were stretched to the limit.

After 19 days of gruelling progress, sometimes wading through water up to their waist, the first Columns reached the Chindwin. Here, instead of the dangerous and daunting challenge they had expected, everything went smoothly. There was no Japanese opposition, the Dakotas of No 117 Squadron RAF specially requested by Wingate, dropped rubber dinghies and outboard motors with pin-point accuracy – as they were to do throughout the campaign – and the first Column, the Queen's, crossed in less than two hours. Later Columns crossed in about 30 minutes. Wingate flew in to see the crossing and Fergusson, knowing that 'bathing was his delight', offered him the chance of a swim. Before he left, Wingate gave them all a pat on the back, which was as Fergusson said 'more precious than a peerage'.

As the brigade continued the march south to set up the Stronghold, codenamed 'Aberdeen', Fergusson pondered on the concept, taken from Wingate's biblical quotation 'Turn to the stronghold ye prisoners of hope'. Later he wrote, 'Orde was the supreme Prisoner of Hope of all time' and, he added, 'He was sometimes wrong in small things but never in big'. (*The Wild Green Earth*, p74) As the main body pressed on, the two gunner Columns prepared to veer off on their long trek to Lonkin. After the first mountainous part of their march, Wingate had sent them a cryptic message, 'Hannibal eclipsed', and they went on their way cheered and confident – heartened, too, by a gift of cigarettes, beer and soap from an American unit they had passed on the Ledo road. Soon, the gruelling march began to take its toll. Two men, found asleep on duty, were sentenced to be flogged, since they could have jeopardised the whole Column, and the sentence was carried out by a large Sergeant Major nicknamed 'Captain Bligh'.

On 10 March, 51 and 69 Columns began the march to Lonkin in earnest. As they approached the town they expected serious trouble, since a Japanese prisoner they captured had managed to escape. Then, as they formed up for the attack, a terrifying storm of thunder, lightning and rain burst over them. 'A Wagnerian prelude, and we hated

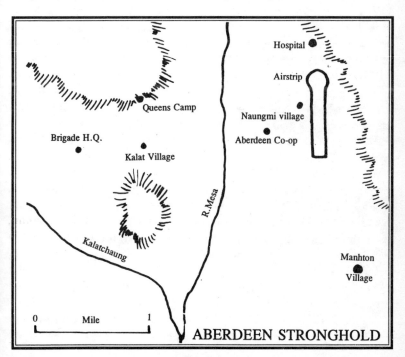

ABERDEEN STRONGHOLD

Wagner.' (Needham, p15) After the storm, they pressed home their attack against sporadic opposition, though they suffered some casualties. Near the centre of the town they used their flame-throwers with devastating effect, after which the Japanese disappeared fairly rapidly. It appeared that the escaped prisoner had warned of a very large force approaching and the majority of what had been a substantial garrison had then withdrawn. Lonkin was a big centre with a maze of trenches up to 20 feet deep, and with supplies of food, equipment and valuable documents, all of which were taken over. Both Wingate and Stilwell signalled their congratulations, but in practice the diversion to Lonkin was to cost 16 Brigade dear. It seriously weakened the attack on Indaw and had little effect on the Chinese advance to Kamaing.

Some of the problems of a Column commander were illustrated after the capture of Lonkin, when some badly wounded men needed to be flown out, but all wireless contact was lost. After hours of agonising – whether to stay until a plane could be brought in, or to go on and leave the wounded to the mercy of the Japanese – the signallers, having tried desperately to get through, at last made contact. The message was sent, a plane arrived, the wounded were loaded on, and the Column moved smartly off, making their own way towards Indaw. The two Columns do not appear to have made undue haste to catch up with the brigade, and they record having been ordered to show the flag in the Kachin Hills, and they enjoyed 'four blessed days of rest' just north of Lake Indawgyi. They eventually reached 'Aberdeen' on 10 April. The diversion to Lonkin made it impossible for them to take part in the attack on Indaw, though Fergusson had certainly hoped that they would arrive in time.

The main part of the brigade had reached 'Aberdeen' by 20 March and the Stronghold was well established by the Queen's and the Leicesters. The two Reconnaissance Columns were still two days march behind and the gunners had just left Lonkin. Wingate flew in on 20 March and gave new orders: in particular, that the brigade should move on at once and attack Indaw; and secondly that 14 Brigade would come in as soon as 'Aberdeen' was ready to take Dakotas on the landing strip. Fergusson argued for his men to be given some rest, but accepted Wingate's decision. It took two more days to assemble all the Columns and in this time 'Aberdeen' was built up into an impressive Stronghold based on three villages Manhton, Kalat and Naungmi, with the large airstrip, separate camps for the different Columns, and a shop to which the local people were welcomed – aptly named the Aberdeen and District Co-operative Society. Some slight hitches occurred: the Nigerians spread their biscuits with jam, which turned out to be the total supply of blood plasma, but 'Aberdeen' quickly became a powerful Stronghold from which Fergusson dispensed elegant hospitality to visitors who were welcome, but bundled off 'parasitic staff officers'. (*The Wild Green Earth*, p93)

During Wingate's last visit, Fergusson had the impression that 14 Brigade were going to fly in and assist with the attack on Indaw, though there is no documentary evidence in war diaries or orders to support this assertion. This is the issue which Kirby uses in the Official History to make a major attack on both Wingate's competence and his integrity. Certainly, at one stage Fergusson, who lost contact with Force HQ for a few crucial days, grumbled about 14 Brigade but when he learned about Wingate's death, he accepted that 'Wingate had died and his plan with him'. Louis Allen dismisses Kirby's argument, as does Bidwell who commented 'neither Wingate nor Fergusson can be blamed for a misunderstanding which did not in fact alter the course of events'. (Bidwell, p142)

After Wingate's insistence on an immediate attack on Indaw, the leading Columns of the brigade set off on 23 March, the day before Wingate was killed. On the same day the first groups of 14 Brigade started to arrive, but this was after Fergusson had left. There was no discussion of any joint action and, anyway, 14 Brigade did not arrive in time to take part in the attack on Indaw.

Before he started off, Fergusson discovered from local intelligence that the Japanese, having learnt of the Chindit presence, had reinforced Thetkegyin. He also learnt that except for two small rivers (chaungs), there was no water at all on his proposed route to Indaw. He was told, too, of the unfortunate ploy of 111 Brigade, which contributed substantially to the failure of 16 Brigade. The prime objective of 111 Brigade had been to block the main road and railway south of Indaw to prevent supplies and reinforcements coming up to the town from the south. This they failed to do. They also deliberately spread the false information that they were going to attack Indaw. Because of the danger of security behind the enemy lines, as little information as possible was given to the different groups and Wingate has been criticised for this. But, clearly, 111 Brigade would not have tried falsely to alert the Japanese to an attack on Indaw if they had known that 16 Brigade was going to attack. As a result of 111 Brigade's activities, the Japanese were better prepared for an attack on Indaw than they would otherwise have been.

Fergusson led the brigade out of 'Aberdeen' on 24 March, aiming to assemble at the village of Auktaw. 45 Column (Reconnaissance Regiment) led the way and as it approached Auktaw found it was garrisoned by units of the Burma National Army, strengthened by some Japanese troops. There was some confused fighting which continued until the Leicesters Column under Colonel Wilkinson arrived and drove out the enemy force.

From the area of Auktaw, 22 Column (Queen's) went off to the west to block the road from Banmauk, and to ambush any Japanese convoys bringing reinforcements to the help of Indaw. The other Queen's Column (21) moved off well to the west of the Indaw lake and aimed to come in from the west to attack Indaw east airfield.

After this, Fergusson changed his plan and sent 45 and 54 Columns (Recce) to Thetkegyin, because of the paramount need for water for both men and mules. This seems a strange decision, since he already knew that the Japanese had reinforced Thetkegyin, yet as the Columns approached the village they did not appear to expect any stiff resistance. They did not carry out a proper reconnaissance and discovered too late that the village was strongly held. The Japanese appeared to realise that the Columns had an urgent need for water and were determined to stop them. A fierce battle ensued which lasted for two days (26 and 27 March). Japanese mortar fire hit the mules carrying the flame-throwers and their fuel, and this resulted in a prolonged inferno of flames and exploding ammunition, covered by the stench of roasting mule. Prolonged hand-to-hand fighting was made more extreme by the ravages of thirst. At one stage in the confusion, the mules sensed the proximity of water and charged off out of control, followed by some of the men. Both were mown down by Japanese machine gun fire. Both the Recce Columns sustained heavy casualties in this clash and shortly after were amalgamated in a single Column, which took no further part in the actual attack on Indaw.

22 Column (Queen's) had veered off towards the Banmauk road before the other fighting started. It successfully blocked the road, ambushed some enemy convoys, and inflicted considerable damage and casualties without serious loss. The other Queen's Column (21), moving well to the west of the lake, bivouacked for the night. They had

inadvertently stopped on the edge of a road which was not marked on their maps and suddenly a Japanese convoy drove straight into their camp. Here too there was a sudden, chaotic and violent fight, with showers of grenades hurled from both sides. During the mêlée, the mules once again came under fire and they bolted off with much of the heavy equipment, though the wireless was saved. The Column had to disperse.

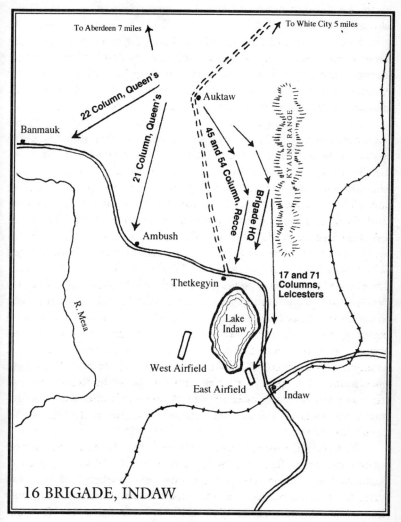

16 BRIGADE, INDAW

The start of the attack on Indaw could hardly have been more unfortunate, and then matters became even worse. Fergusson lost contact with all the Columns and also with Force HQ, which had needed to move out of Imphal to Sylhet, and was completely cut off for two days. Fergusson had clearly forgotten Wingate's dictum 'Concentrate, concentrate, concentrate'. Here, at the approach to Indaw, two of his Columns were still on the way from Lonkin, two were bogged down in Thetkegyin, and the two Queen's Columns were miles away on a flank and took no part in the Indaw attack. This left the Leicesters under Wilkinson, who had already been wounded in the clash at Auktaw. The Leicesters were an excellent county regiment, and Wilkinson was a fine leader. He organised his Columns in his own way with the support group and transport separate, and then brought together virtually all the firepower of the whole battalion, including Vickers machine guns and 3in mortars. The Leicesters had advanced rapidly down the east side of the Indaw lake where they found a clean flowing stream in close proximity to the edge of the airfield. Here they quickly dug in and established a very strong defensive position. This excellent battalion, with firm fire discipline, repulsed constant Japanese attacks, causing very heavy casualties for the loss of 11 killed and six wounded. Because of their well-sited position they also had close support from the Air Commando.

The Leicesters were still successfully repelling all Japanese attacks when Fergusson, who had re-established contact with the other Columns and realised that none of them could reach the Leicesters, decided that all Columns should withdraw to 'Aberdeen'. Here again, under the inspired leadership of Wilkinson, the Leicesters carried out the difficult manoeuvre of breaking off contact with a determined enemy. This action by the Leicesters shows how very close 16 Brigade came to capturing Indaw. If Fergusson had concentrated his forces or even kept control of them, Indaw could have fallen. He wrote later, that if he had kept to Wingate's plan, which was to advance down the range of hills called the Kyaung Range, which ran due south towards Indaw, 'we might have pulled it off'.

In *The Wild Green Earth,* Fergusson admits to making three mistakes at Indaw: that he did not insist on resting his men before the attack; that he did not assess the Japanese reaction to the known presence of the Chindits; and he lost touch with his Columns. He could have added that he failed to carry out proper reconnaissance, and that his forces were so scattered that out of eight Columns only two carried out the attack on Indaw airfield.

During the time he was cut off from Force HQ and from his own Columns, Fergusson suffered agonies of doubt, made worse by the false rumour that 'Aberdeen' had been overwhelmed. When communication was restored he learned that 'Aberdeen' had not been attacked, the Columns moved back fairly rapidly to the Stronghold, the wounded were flown out, and morale restored. 'Aberdeen' flourished as a Stronghold and the brigade established close co-operation with 77 Brigade in 'White City'. During April, active patrolling took place throughout the whole area bounded by 'Aberdeen', 'White City' and Auktaw.

Excellent intelligence came in from the local people, and this was used effectively. When a report came in of a large convoy, or a large supply dump, or a big concentration of troops, a swift recce was made by light plane to confirm it, then a message went to the Air Commando who came in and bombed the target. This technique led to a major success when a very large supply base for two of the Japanese divisions attacking Imphal and Kohima were completely destroyed by the Air Commando.

Towards the end of April, 16 Brigade made another attack on Indaw and the Queen's column took the airfield without a shot being fired but, because of the Japanese attack on Imphal no reinforcements were available, so after holding the airfield for a couple of days the force withdrew. Soon after this, the whole direction of the Chindit operation changed. 16 Brigade flew out and when 'White City', 'Aberdeen' and 'Broadway' were abandoned, the rest of the Chindit Force started their march north.

14 Brigade: Aberdeen to Lake Indawgyi

14 Brigade under Brigadier Brodie and made up of first class battalions from British county regiments, has rarely been given the credit it

---

Main Units of 14 Brigade, Aberdeen to Lake Indawgyi
1st Bedfordshire & Hertfordshire Regiment
(To the chagrin of its members usually abbreviated to Beds and Herts)
7th Leicesters   2nd Black Watch
2nd Yorks & Lancs

Note: A valuable source for this section is a long memorandum of Colonel Robertson RE, and his article in the *Royal Engineers Journal* of September 1948.

---

deserves. Taken from 70 Division in September 1943 and switched to Chindit training, it was not at first totally dedicated to Wingate's ideas, but Brodie gave it calm and balanced leadership. With the Black Watch in the lead, the brigade started to fly in to 'Aberdeen' on 23 March 1944 – the day before Wingate died – and were fully installed by 4 April.

From the 'Aberdeen' Stronghold, the brigade carried out classic Chindit tactics with the Black Watch successfully ambushing the road going northwest from Indaw, and destroying substantial stores and ammunition earmarked for Sato's 31 Division attacking Kohima. The stores destroyed included large supplies of ammunition and petrol and a million doses of quinine. At the same time Brigade HQ set out with two Columns of the Yorks & Lancs for Bonchaung Gorge, about 20 miles south of Indaw. Here, against some enemy opposition, the sappers of 54 Field Company under Colonel Robertson demolished the railway bridge. This wooden structure had been painstakingly reconstructed in place of the original bridge destroyed by Calvert in the first Chindit operation. After the explosives went off 'the whole structure came tumbling down in complete ruin'. (Memorandum, Colonel K. Robertson, Imperial War Museum)

The Columns withdrew after the demolition, but before they could regroup properly they were attacked. In a confused fight it appears that Brigade HQ were fired on by one of the Columns – subsequently proved when the Column doctor retrieved a British .303 bullet from the foot of a sapper. Brodie had also to deal with a tricky problem, when during the action some of the Defence Platoon left their position for a more secure spot. They were rather 'the odds and sods' of different units, drafted in late and not given the full Chindit training, so their morale was never good – in contrast to Calvert's Defence Platoon which was the cream fighting unit of the whole brigade. Brodie handled the situation well, imposing certain sanctions on the group, but not using the draconian powers which Wingate had laid down.

While these operations were proceeding, Columns of the Leicesters and the Beds & Herts advanced south past Indaw and carried out ambushes and raids on Japanese road and rail communications. They destroyed store dumps over a wide area, thus effectively sabotaging supplies going to those Japanese divisions attacking Imphal and Kohima, as well as those forces coming up to attack 'White City'. These actions accorded absolutely with Wingate's tactical and strategic concepts for LRP Columns. After these forays, Brodie called the Columns back to act as floater Columns around 'White City'. Both the Black Watch and the Beds & Herts fought major engagements near Mawlu.

By this time, Lentaigne had decided that 'Broadway' and 'White City' should be abandoned and, on the night of 10/11 May 1944, Columns of 14 Brigade were deployed outside the perimeter while the total evacuation of 'White City' took place.

Then came the long march north to Lake Indawgyi under increasingly trying conditions as the monsoon intensified. For most Columns it was just a wearisome and depressing slog, but it was not entirely unopposed, and 47 Column of the Leicesters were surprised by an enemy patrol and lost nine killed, including two officers and the CSM, with 20 wounded. As they were reaching the end of their march, Brigade HQ were moving in close proximity to the Leicesters. The HQ stopped for a midday break, but the Leicesters decided to go on and take their break when they reached the Kyunsalai Pass. They arrived there, and with only minutes to spare, fought off a strong Japanese patrol which had been about to occupy the pass.

The Leicesters, with help from other Columns including the Nigerians from 3 West African Brigade, held the Kyunsalai Pass until 21 June. Although it was an important strategic point, no effective advance was made from it and 111 Brigade abandoned 'Blackpool' (25 May) before any Columns from 14 Brigade or the Nigerians could give them support.

Under the onslaught of the monsoon, the conditions for all the brigades in the area – 111, 14 and 3 West African – became worse and worse. Because of the incessant rain, the airstrips were almost all unusable, and the pitiful state of the wounded from 'Blackpool', and the condition of the growing number of men suffering from malaria, dysentery and scrub-typhus deteriorated dangerously. At this low point, some inspired improvisation came to the rescue. Two Sunderland flying-boats – nicknamed 'Gert' and 'Daisy' after the comedians Elsie and Doris Waters – were diverted from their normal operations and flew into Lake Indawgyi to rescue the sick and wounded.

Faced with an urgent and daunting challenge, Robertson withdrew all the sappers of 54 Field Company from the Columns, and undertook the rapid construction of both rafts and boats – rafts to ferry the casualties out to the flying-boats, and the larger craft to take the sick and wounded along the lake and down the Indaw river to Kamaing – a precarious journey of nearly 50 miles. This operation illustrates the dogged way in which the Royal Engineers supported the forward divisions of the British Army in every theatre of war, and overcame totally unforeseen obstacles.

A massive supply drop provided Ranger rubber boats and 22hp outboard motors, together with technicians dropped in by parachute – after the shortest parachute training known in the war. The sappers built the larger boats by lashing together five Ranger boats, powered by two outboard motors. On the deck they built a bamboo superstructure draped with tarpaulins to give shade from either sun or rain. Each boat, measuring 37 feet by 12 feet, and with a draught of about 15 inches, with a crew of five, could take up to 40 casualties. The boats, named after famous naval ships, for example *Ark Royal*, had wireless contact with the two bases, at 'Plymouth' on the west side of the lake, and 'Dawlish' on the east side. The cumbersome craft were unarmed except for the crew's rifles and Bren guns.

On 3 June the first Sunderlands flew in and rafts ferried out the casualties. It proved difficult to get the stretcher cases up into the four hatches of the Sunderlands, but ingenuity improved the system, and before the end, the turn-round for loading 40 casualties and unloading a ton of supplies was reduced to 18 minutes. After some days, and after a sudden squall on the Brahmaputra had wrecked one of the Sunderlands, they were taken away.

Because of this Robertson had to reorganise. 'Plymouth' was shut down, 14 Brigade moved to 'Dawlish', and from there undertook all the transportation of casualties down the Indaw river to Kamaing. This trip usually went smoothly, but on one occasion the *Ark Royal* stuck for 24 hours in a mass of weed and debris washed down by the monsoon floods, until it was rescued by the help of the 'Vindictive' and a group of Nigerians with their machetes. The rather top heavy craft were difficult to manoeuvre, and had problems when, as frequently happened, sudden intense squalls whipped up five foot waves on the lake. The lake and river operations continued as long as necessary and took out over 300 men without loss. Every available skill was utilised – including a Burmese forestry officer with some elephants, and a former naval officer on the boats.

They continued their mission into July and then, in the final stages of the campaign, 14 Brigade really showed their mettle in clashes

"BARHAM"

"ARK ROYAL"

"REVENGE"

with the Japanese forces of 18 and 53 Divisions after they had retreated from Mogaung and Kamaing. The Japanese dug-in in the area of Sahmaw and Taungni, and this accounted for the fierce battles around Point 2171 and Hill 60. 14 Brigade put in, as Bidwell said, 'a burst of sustained offensive action unrecorded and unsung'. During this offensive, the 7th Leicesters captured Taungni on 11 August, the Beds & Herts captured Point 2171 on 12 August, the Black Watch and the Yorks & Lancs carried out other successful attacks, and finally the brigade handed over to the newly arrived 36 Division.

Masters bitterly criticised 14 Brigade for failing to help at 'Blackpool', and this criticism raises several questions about the role of the Chindits, and the attitude of the different brigades towards Wingate. At the two extremes, 77 Brigade under Calvert were devoted to Wingate and his ideas, while 111 Brigade under Lentaigne and Masters were strongly anti-Wingate, as for example when Calvert invited Masters to fly in to 'White City' to see the set-up. Lentaigne forbade Masters to go in, saying that 111 Brigade would show that they were better than Wingate's favourite brigade. Somewhere between the two extremes lay 14 Brigade under Brodie, a highly professional regular soldier who, like most of 70 Division, accepted his new role as a Chindit. He was a commander careful of his men's lives and reluctant to embark on any ill-thought-out scheme. He was certainly criticised over his apparent inactivity at the Kyunsalai Pass, but 14 Brigade's successful actions towards the end of the campaign show him as an effective commander in battle. He was to reinforce this reputation much later when, as commander of 29 Infantry Brigade in Korea in 1951, he fought an excellent action on the Imjin river in which his brigade frustrated the Chinese spring offensive and saved the whole United Nations position – an action for which he was awarded the DSO and American Silver Star.

14 Brigade under Brodie performed all its actions effectively. If there has been criticism that it marched about aimlessly this criticism should be directed, not at Brodie, but at Lentaigne for his remote and ineffective direction of 14 Brigade, and indeed of all the other brigades in that part of the final Chindit campaign.

3rd West African Brigade

By 1943 two full divisions of West African soldiers – the 81st and 82nd – members of The Royal West African Frontier Force, had been raised and trained in Nigeria, the Gold Coast (Ghana), Sierra Leone and the

Main units of the 3rd West African Brigade, 'White City' to Mogaung
6th Battalion The Nigeria Regiment
7th Battalion The Nigeria Regiment
12th Battalion The Nigeria Regiment

Note: The best specific sources for this part of the campaign are:
a) Charles Carfrae, *Chindit Column* (Kimber 1985)
b) James Shaw, *The March Out* (1953)
c) Peter Vaughan, *Diary of the Operations of 7th Battalion
The Nigeria Regiment* (Imperial War Museum)

Gambia, taken by ship via Cape Town and landed in Bombay. In India they trained in the Central Provinces, and the larger part of the two divisions took part in a successful campaign in the Arakan where they proved themselves doughty fighters. It has been assumed – incorrectly – that West African soldiers were familiar with the jungle and would find it easier than European troops to operate in Burma, but most of the fighting troops of the Nigerian and Gold Coast Regiments were recruited from the northern areas of the country which were almost desert. However, they adapted remarkably well under the firm leadership of their European officers and NCOs. They proved themselves reliable and effective in action, and the Japanese who fought against them considered the West Africans to be the best jungle fighters they faced.

The 3 West African Brigade, consisting of the 6th, 7th, and 12th Battalions of the Nigeria Regiment, were chosen to be trained as Chindits and they were flown in to 'Aberdeen' and 'White City' early in April 1944. They were relatively untested and had therefore been designated to form the garrison battalions in 'Broadway', 'White City' and 'Aberdeen', but immediate tactical issues caused these plans to be changed. The 12th Battalion became the 'White City' garrison, while the 7th under Colonel Peter Vaughan, flew in to 'Aberdeen' and had to march to 'White City'. Here, on 11 April, they 'harboured' as Chindit training required, and Calvert, complete with red tabs and riding a pony, came out to welcome them. Colonel Carfrae who led the Nigerian 29 Column, said of Calvert 'As a commander he had no peer. His praise was music.' (*Chindit Column*, p101) The 6th Battalion, which had to march to 'Aberdeen', was less fortunate and was ambushed by the Japanese before they really found their feet. Their CO was sent out and Gordon Upjohn, the Brigade Major, took over the unit and led it for the rest of the campaign.

The Nigerian Columns operated on the same basis as other Chindit Columns, and consisted of four strong infantry platoons; a Reconnaissance Platoon containing half Burma Rifles – ie, Burmese men who moved ahead of the Columns to sound out villages and collect information; a Support Platoon which provided the 3in mortars and Vickers machine guns; the Commando Platoon containing the demolition experts, mostly Royal Engineers; the Animal Transport Platoon which had 65 mules and six riding ponies, which carried all the heavier materials including the mortars and their ammunition, and when necessary the wounded; finally the Defence Platoon and the Command Group including the RAF Liaison Officer, the Signals Officer, the Intelligence Officer, the Cipher Officer, the doctor and padre. The key to the Columns' survival was the 1082 or RAF wireless set, highly efficient but bulky and needing four mules to carry it.

When the Nigerian Brigade arrived, Calvert handed over command in 'White City' to Brigadier Gillmore, and moved out to command an aggressive striking force to attack the Japanese in the area. The 7th Nigerian Battalion under Vaughan and Carfrae joined this group and attacked Thayaung, the base from which the Japanese were assaulting 'White City'. This was occupied without serious opposition and then used by the Nigerians for the next few days during which, under Calvert's direction, they mounted a sustained attack on Mawlu and also carried out several successful ambushes. These actions, interspersed with hard marching and occasional rest days in harbour, helped the unit to knit together into an effective fighting force. They were encouraged by the positive support of the local Kachin villages, in several of which the local people were already wearing clothes made of parachute silk. At the end of April there was an unpleasant incident when both Gurkhas and Nigerians were found pilfering food – one of the unforgivable crimes in a Column. Calvert was furious, and Vaughan punished the Nigerian culprits with '24 for arse' – facilitated by the bamboo growing everywhere. The unit felt that the Gurkhas were let off too lightly by their officers. The two Nigerian Columns – 35 and 29 – soon redeemed themselves with a successful attack on Ywathit.

Soon after this Calvert came to see the Nigerian units, to thank and congratulate them for what they had done, and to give them advanced notice that after 'White City' was evacuated they would all march north. The 12th Nigerian Battalion played a key role in the evacuation, which was completed by 11 May. It was a model of efficient organisation, even though Lentaigne removed Gillmore, who had planned the whole thing, just as the operation was starting. He was replaced by Brigadier Ricketts. The last days in 'White City' were used to stock up with food, ammunition, equipment, weapons and clothes from the massive surpluses. Vaughan observed that Calvert always held the initiative, but on the march north under Jeffery Lockett, confusion arose, and the initiative passed to the Japanese. Carfrae also made an interesting comment, that fear had to be kept on a leash but it 'could reduce officers to a state of pitiable ineptitude'. (*Chindit Column*, p101) The monsoon started during the march north and became the more consistent and relentless enemy, making life both trying and miserable. The Nigerian units reached Nammun, a fair sized town near the Kyunsalai Pass, on 21 May, just after the Leicesters under Lockett seized the pass.

The Japanese made several attempts to retake the pass but were successfully driven off by 74 Column of the Leicesters, helped by the 7th Nigerians. 14 Brigade under Brigadier Brodie now reached Nammun, and Vaughan tried in vain to get Brodie to climb up the pass to see the favourable strategic position. Vaughan remarked that he feared the effect 'of Brodie's prolonged marking time with the rest of his brigade in Nammun' (Diary, p28) – this at a time when 111 Brigade in Blackpool were in desperate need of help. This situation may illustrate a lack of fire in Brodie at that time but, more important, it highlights the lack of control by Lentaigne who stayed at Force HQ, never came to see the ground where his brigades were operating, and gave them no effective directions. A feeling of hopeless despondency fell on all the units, who could not understand what was happening, and received orders from Force HQ with increasing cynicism.

The monsoon now came to dominate every activity, with men soaked through and shivering as they struggled through the mud to carry their packs – now doubled in weight with the wet. The rain made the jungle tracks almost impassable, and one unit after three days of struggling through thick mud, sometimes crawling on hands and knees, and getting more and more exhausted and depressed, found themselves back where they had started. During this grim time, the brigade was buoyed up by the cheerful resilience of the African soldiers, and their willingness to head-load stores which even the mules could not cope with. To add to the horror and anguish, there was a serious outbreak of scrub-typhus which killed both European and

African alike, and those who survived suffered from such acute depression that several committed suicide.

On 26 May the news came that 111 Brigade had hurriedly evacuated 'Blackpool' after sustaining heavy casualties. This directly affected both the Nigerians and 14 Brigade, who were now clearly too late to help at 'Blackpool', and therefore reassembled at Nammun to await 'the hapless 111 Brigade'. There followed two weeks which were used to refit and stock up after good supply drops, but during which 'there was increasing annoyance at this passive inactivity'. (Vaughan Diary, p32) Lentaigne should have rushed both brigades to Mogaung to help 77 Brigade which urgently needed support. Some of the tensions in the units is illustrated when Vaughan and Carfrae objected to Rickett's suggestion that the brigade should stay in Nammun through the monsoon. They thought he had taken leave of his senses.

It became increasingly difficult to sustain morale because of the appalling conditions, the feeling of futility at what they were doing, and the conviction that there was no control or direction from Force HQ. Clearly, some of the frustration and suffering took place because of Stilwell's bloody-minded intransigence, but far more because Lentaigne was too weak to counter him, and so lacking in confidence that throughout the whole time he never visited his brigades in the field, even though they were only a very short distance from his new HQ at Shadazup. Had he gone in to Nammun when 14 Brigade and the Nigerians arrived and shown some positive leadership, there is little doubt that the two brigades could have reached 'Blackpool', and even after that they could have pressed forward and reached Mogaung to give support to Calvert and 77 Brigade.

During June the fury of the monsoon continued, as did the feelings of hopelessness and futility. Things improved a little when early in the month the first Sunderland flying-boat was able to take out the initial batch of sick and wounded, including the increasing number of scrub-typhus cases. There were frequent minor clashes with the enemy, in one of which Vaughan was seriously wounded in the arm, but he bravely continued with the Columns. Again he commented, 'On 12 June after inexcusable waste of time and undertaking no active operation, we moved'. This inactivity, when two brigades were less than 40 miles from Mogaung, where the dangerously depleted 77 Brigade were in urgent need of support, is another indictment of Lentaigne's leadership.

The Nigerian Columns complained strongly about the delay and frustration caused by inadequate and piecemeal supply drops, which in enemy-infested areas had to be carefully prepared. It often took a whole day to prepare for the drop, a day to collect it, and if the drop only provided one day's rations there was little gain. The Africans sometimes were able to supplement their rations, by climbing trees and cutting down parachute loads which other Columns had left.

At the end of June, while waiting for a supply drop, and resting his wounded arm, Vaughan described his Column: 'The signallers were hard at work, to the roar of the engines recharging the batteries; animal transport staff worked on the awful sores on the mules; the doctors tended the sick and wounded; the G Staff studied the situation and intelligence reports, while the rifle platoons strengthened the perimeter and kept up the patrolling – occasionally looking up to see if a Dakota might arrive.' (Diary, p42)

Early in July, after they had been encouraged by the news of Calvert's victory at Mogaung, the Nigerian Brigade advanced for an attack on a very well prepared Japanese position, nicknamed Hill 60. This prolonged action continued until 16 July and caused a number of casualties. The Nigerian attackers were to find – as the British and Indians at the battles of Kohima and Imphal had done – that Japanese troops who were sick and starving will defend their bunkers until every single man is dead. In spite of their efforts, the Nigerians did not capture Hill 60, which was finally overcome by the newly arrived 36 Division. Charles Carfrae, who made a number of honest and percipient comments on battlefield psychology wrote, 'Privation, physical exhaustion, and the erosion of nervous stress, combined with an eye to deliverance, had between them extinguished that spark that makes fresh well-trained soldiers eager for battle to prove ability and manhood'. (*Chindit Column*, p177)

Because the Nigerians had advanced closer to Mogaung, it was now possible to evacuate the wounded by light plane, and even by motor ambulance up the road to Kamaing, and from there to Shadazup. On 16 July, Vaughan, having seen his battalion safely into harbour with the rest of the Nigerian Brigade, allowed himself to be flown out sick – 35 days after being wounded. His diary concludes with a Japanese comment on the West African soldier: 'They are not afraid to die, so even if their comrades have fallen, they keep on advancing as if nothing had happened. They have an excellent physique and are very brave, so fighting against these soldiers is very troublesome.' Vaughan added, 'What more unbiased appreciation could be found for the loyal, courteous, brave and loveable West African soldier?'.

23 Brigade: The Kohima Flank

Although 23 Brigade is sometimes ignored in descriptions of the Chindit campaigns, it took part in what could have been one of the most crucial operations of the Burma war. The brigade had been trained as Chindits, it operated in Columns, and it was supplied by air and supported by air-strikes when necessary. It had expected to fly in to the Indaw area with the other Chindit brigades in March 1944 but when Mutaguchi attacked Imphal and Kohima with 15, 31 and 33 Divisions, Slim took 23 Brigade away from Wingate's control and, instead, deployed it in the Naga Hills north of Kohima. Here its main purpose was to prepare defensive positions along a line approximately from Wokha to Mokokchaung, in order to stop the Japanese advancing towards the great stores base at Dimapur, and the railway which ran through it and continued up to Ledo. The whole of Stilwell's divisions in north Burma and the American air operations over The Hump depended on this line.

A key element in Mutaguchi's attack on Imphal and Kohima was his plan for Sato and 31 Division to advance as rapidly as possible to Kohima, and then to drive forward to seize the great prize of Dimapur, a railhead with a supply depot 11 miles long, a mile wide, and virtually undefended. It is rarely realised just how close Mutaguchi came to his goal. He had sent off these divisions with three weeks rations and it

---

Main units of 23 Brigade, the Kohima Flank
Brigadier Perowne
2nd Duke of Wellington's Regiment
4th Border Regiment   1st Essex Regiment
60th Field Regiment Royal Artillery (as infantry)

Note: There are very few clear descriptions of
the actions of 23 Brigade, but the following are useful:
a) W. A. Wilcox, *Chindit Column 76* (Longmans 1945)
A personal story of the RAF Liaison Officer with a Column
of the Duke of Wellington's Regiment;
b) *The Chindits* (Frank Owen, Calcutta 1945);
c) A long article in the *Cumberland News*, September 1944,
entitled 'The Border Regiment's Historic March';
d) Captain H. W. W. Good, *Some Medical Aspects of Long Range
Penetration* An excellent short pamphlet.

was intended that after three weeks they could continue with the supplies they would capture at Kohima and Dimapur.

Sato and 31 Division made excellent progress towards Kohima, but the first hold-up came when the leading regiment under General Miyazaki – a very successful and aggressive commander – reached Ukhrul, about 10 miles north of Sangshak. Here, largely for reasons of personal glory, he decided that, instead of making straight for Kohima, he would turn aside and sweep 50 Indian Parachute Brigade out of Sangshak. There is little doubt that if Miyazaki had not turned south to attack Sangshak, the Japanese would have captured Kohima and almost certainly Dimapur as well, before the British could organise enough troops to defend them. The brave and stubborn defenders of Sangshak held up Miyazaki for six crucial days from 19 to 26 March, during which he lost half of his leading regiment. This delay gave the British time to rush the Royal West Kents back into Kohima. Here, against all the odds, they held out against the whole of 31 Division from 6 to 18 April. Had the Japanese attacked Kohima six days earlier, there would have been virtually no defence. Similarly, if Sato's leading troops had advanced straight to Dimapur instead of turning off to Sangshak on 19 March, the whole of the gigantic supply complex would have been at its mercy. Even when the Japanese reached a point 20 miles away, the Indian staff manning the stores – perhaps with vivid memories of the 1942 retreat – all fled. The British 2 Division, which was to play a central role in the battles for Kohima, did not arrive in Dimapur until 1 April, and this would have been too late to save it.

After this, other factors favoured the British defence and influenced the fortunes of 23 Brigade. There was bitter rivalry between the senior Japanese commanders. Sato, commanding 31 Division, strongly opposed what he considered the crazily ambitious scheme of Mutaguchi for 'The March on Delhi', for which the immediate capture of Dimapur was essential, and he was not prepared to sacrifice the lives of his soldiers in such a cause. In fact, when Mutaguchi ordered Sato and 31 Division to advance on Dimapur, the order was reversed by Mutaguchi's superior officer General Kawabe at the Japanese Burma Area Army HQ.

Meanwhile, 23 Brigade reached its designated position north of Kohima at Mokokchaung on 6 April, the very day that the siege of Kohima started. Had the Japanese not been held up at Sangshak, Kohima would almost certainly have fallen, and 23 Brigade would have been the only British force between the Japanese advance and Dimapur. As it was, a Column of The Essex Regiment made first contact with the enemy at Phekekruma, a strongly held town less than 20 miles from Dimapur – illustrating just how close they came to their goal. Neither 23 Brigade nor the Japanese facing them realised the significance of their positions, and soon the Japanese plans were to change.

Throughout April all the Columns of 23 Brigade fought actions against Japanese strong points and Japanese patrols. As they trudged or fought their way through the precipitous jungle covered hills they received welcome support from the local Naga people, who not only provided accurate intelligence about enemy movements, but willingly helped to build air-strips – one at 4,000 feet – and to move supplies. Information brought by the Nagas enabled effective attacks to be made on Japanese-held villages which, surprisingly, were often carelessly guarded. Because the Naga people were so completely loyal, the Columns were frequently able to take supply drops on a flat place near the village, instead of hacking out a strip in the jungle.

As the campaign continued, most of the Columns suffered increasingly from dysentery, malaria, and from boils and abscesses, which when added to the constant onslaught of the monsoon, gravely weakened their resistance. The role of the doctor in a Chindit Column is well illustrated in the pamphlet by Harry Good, who was doctor to a Column of the Border Regiment. His pamphlet, a minor classic in its way, shows what a positive part the doctor could play, not only during the operations, but in preparing both officers and men physically and psychologically for LRP work. He stressed strict discipline especially over water sterilization, over the taking of mepacrine to combat malaria, and all aspects of latrine discipline. He trained all officers to study sick reports during training, so that when things got tough they would know whether a man needed to be encouraged or driven. Significantly, his Border Column lost only 12 men from sickness during the whole campaign. When a man was so sick that he had to be evacuated, the help of the Naga people was outstanding. A sick man, tortured by abscesses and agonising stomach pains was often carried on a makeshift stretcher for several days by teams of Nagas who moved at a trot, and then changed bearers in the next village.

When a Column reached a village, usually exhausted and drenched to the skin, they were warmly welcomed, huge fires were built up, and their clothes and equipment hung up to dry. Many semi-formal wel-

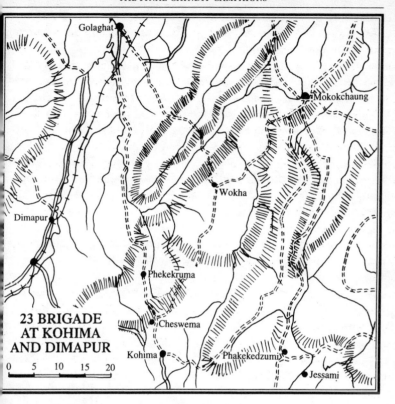

23 BRIGADE
AT KOHIMA
AND DIMAPUR

omes took place with the Chindits in their underpants. The main
drawback to the generous hospitality was that many dry Naga huts
were infested with fleas, prompting the comment 'A sense of humour
s the finest weapon a poor soldier ever had against the hell he
ndures'. (Wilcox, p107)

Gradually, 23 Brigade, operating along a front from Jessami,
through Wokha and up to Mokochaung, pushed back the Japanese to a
ew larger centres, and here fierce clashes took place with no quarter
given. One Essex Column was surprised by the enemy who forced
hem back and took 10 prisoners. Later, when the place was recaptured
ll 10 were found tied to trees, their bodies mangled by bayonet stabs.
The Columns ranged actively over the area north and east of Kohima,
nd the gunner Columns fought a successful action at Jessami where
hey captured large quantities of material and equipment. The remark-

ably efficient air support which dropped supplies, took out the sick and wounded and provided close support bombing and strafing, continued throughout the campaign. One officer who won an immediate MC received the ribbon with the next supply drop. As late as 5 June, the Border Columns had the support of Hawker Hurricanes in an attack on Phakekedzumi, and so their domination of the area continued.

Future action by 23 Brigade was decided, not by their own progress, but by the events unfolding in Kohima, where the battles continued from 4 April to 13 May. During this time, the Columns of 23 Brigade were often close enough to hear the sound of gun fire from the battle in Kohima, which was the turning point in the Burma war. Initially, The Royal West Kents, supported by The Assam Regiment and The Assam Rifles held out against the full weight of 31 Division. Then on 18 April the forces of 2 British Division fought through to them and raised the siege. From that moment the scene changed. The momentum of the whole Japanese advance had been held, stopped and bloodily repulsed. 2 Division continued their attack, while the troops of Sato's 31 Division started a dour defensive campaign. They had often proved unimaginative in attack, but their defensive fighting was exemplary. Every position, often supported by underground tunnels and heavily protected trenches, were held until the last survivor was killed. From the day the siege of Kohima was raised on 18 April, a fiercely fought battle continued night and day until 13 May, when the Japanese were finally forced out of Kohima. Even then they continued their struggle in the surrounding villages and hills, forcing 2 Division to fight every yard of the way in a bloody and costly advance.

As the Japanese were slowly driven from the surroundings of Kohima, 23 Brigade, too, was able to go over to the offensive, and they made rapid progress south eastwards where they joined up with other units of 2 Division. Together they harried and destroyed the now defeated remnants of the once proud 31 Division. The suffering of the starving and emaciated Japanese troops continued as they tried desperately to retreat back to the Chindwin and beyond. On the road leading south from Kohima to Imphal the British forces moved more rapidly and on 22 June, the Durham Light Infantry, the leading battalion of the division, made contact with units of 5 Indian Division which had fought its way north from Imphal. The road to Imphal was opened at last and one of the most dramatic sieges in history was raised.

Merrill's Marauders

The Allied Conferences of early 1943 – Casablanca (January), Trident (May), and Quebec (August), gave serious consideration to the situation in the Far East. At Quebec, with the remarkable intervention of Wingate, the Chiefs of Staff, under the influence of General Hap Arnold decided to set up South East Asia Command (SEAC) and to support Wingate's plans for Long Range Penetration. For the Americans, the Chindit operations appeared to be the best and quickest way of opening up the land route to China, and reducing the inordinate demands in money, aircraft, equipment and pilots, needed to keep up the air traffic over The Hump. Convinced that The Hump supplies were keeping China in the war, against the 37 Japanese divisions deployed in south China, this view remained the Americans' top priority in South East Asia and influenced all their decisions about the Chindits, about Stilwell and his divisions in north Burma, and about Chiang Kai Shek.

After the Chiefs of Staff approved the concept of Long Range Penetration, a call for volunteers went out to all American army units. The new volunteer group, ineptly named 5307 Composite Unit (Provisional), drew its members, initially 3,000-strong, from the Pacific theatre and from home-based units. After some initial training in America it eventually reached the central Provinces of India and trained along the same lines as the Chindits. They did some exercises with the Chindits, but were not under British discipline or control. Colonel Hunter, an able and experienced regular soldier, quickly moulded them into an effective fighting force, though to the British they appeared as a wild undisciplined crowd who caused serious problems by shooting cows and local Indian peasants.

Stilwell, who became Mountbatten's deputy at SEAC when it was set up, was already Chief of Staff to Chiang Kai Shek and commander of those Chinese divisions in north Burma, which had been trained and equipped with British help in India. Stilwell, who came

---

Merrill's Marauders, Stilwell and Myitkyina
Note: Detailed descriptions of Merrill's Marauders appear in:
a) Romanus and Sunderland's *Stilwell's Command Problems*;
b) Barbara Tuchman's *Sand against the Wind*;
c) David Rooney's *Stilwell* (Ballantine);
d) Alan Baker's *Merrill's Marauders* (Ballantine).

to be loathed by the Chindits for the way he treated them in the final stages of their campaign, insisted that the American Chindit unit should come under his command. He appointed his son-in-law, Brigadier Merrill, to command the unit, and it was soon rescued from its cumbersome title when a journalist dubbed it Merrill's Marauders.

Stilwell devoted himself in his cantankerous, irascible, and aggressive way to the prosecution of the war against Japan, and he did suffer from very serious frustrations. The greatest of these was the duplicity of Chiang Kai Shek who, while giving Stilwell overall command of the Chinese divisions, communicated secretly with the divisional commanders. He often ordered them to disobey Stilwell when necessary, in order to preserve themselves and their valuable American equipment for their future struggle with the Chinese communists. Because of his intense frustration with the Chinese, Stilwell began to ask more and more from Merrill's Marauders, the one American unit under his command. In the end, when they were close to total collapse, they came to hate him just as much as the Chindits did. One Marauder said, 'To think that I once had that bastard in my sights and did not pull the trigger'.

In January 1944, the Allies planned for Stilwell to advance down the Hukawng Valley with his Chinese divisions; the 14th Army to advance from Imphal; a Chinese army to advance from Yunnan towards Bhamo; and the Chindit operation to fly in to Indaw and to disrupt the Japanese supply lines and communications to all these theatres of war. Stilwell, leading the Chinese 22 and 38 Divisions, had been advancing slowly down the Hukawng Valley since October 1943, but had been held up by the shrewd tactics of the very experienced General Tanaka commanding the Japanese 18 Division. Several parts of the Allied plans failed to materialise – the 14th Army did not advance and Chiang Kai Shek reneged on all his promises, but Stilwell still hoped that his dogged advance would enable him to capture Myitkyina and Mogaung, clear the Japanese from north Burma, and reopen a road up to Kunming and Chungking.

The Marauders under Hunter had been organised along Chindit lines, but with different names. Their Columns, of about 500 men, were called Combat Teams, and designated by different colours. Each Team contained an Intelligence and Reconnaissance Platoon, and also a Pioneer and Demolition Platoon. With similar arms and equipment to the Chindits, and a generous provision of mules, they were supplied and supported by a section of the Air Commando based near Ledo. The Marauders had one great advantage over the Chindits: they had a fairly large number of Japanese speaking soldiers – called Nisei – integrated into the Combat Teams, and these did some valuable work. The American Organisation of Strategic Services (OSS) had been active in north Burma, and the Marauders frequently enjoyed the help of Kachin irregulars under the command of OSS officers. Having come under Stilwell's command in January 1944, by mid-February the Marauders found themselves in the Hukawng Valley alongside their Chinese allies.

Tanaka, who used 18 Division to delay Stilwell as much as possible, operated with two regiments forward and one in the rear as garrison at Myitkyina. After the successful operation of 77 Brigade under Calvert at 'White City', 18 Division had to rely for its supplies and reinforcements entirely on the road from Bhamo to Myitkyina which was frequently sabotaged by Morris Force. Facing the Japanese, Stilwell aimed to advance towards Walawbum with the Chinese 22 and 38 Divisions supported by a tank group, while the Marauders made a swift flank march to the northeast of the road, and came round to cut off the enemy from the rear. This sound tactic – similar to the Japanese'

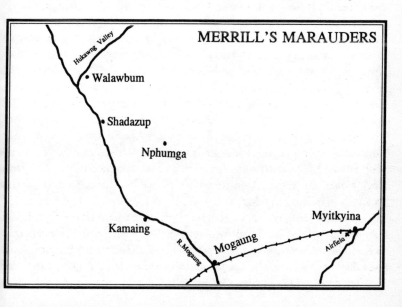

MERRILL'S MARAUDERS

Hukawng Valley

• Walawbum

• Shadazup

• Nphumga

Kamaing

R. Mogaung

Mogaung

Myitkyina

Airfield

own method in their 1942 attacks – was short range penetration rather than Long Range Penetration, but it proved effective.

By 5 March 1944, the Chinese divisions were approaching Walawbum and the Marauders were closing in from the flank. Under considerable pressure from the Chinese attacks which included tanks and artillery, and harassed from the flanks and rear by the Marauders, Tanaka decided to withdraw from Walawbum. He had carefully prepared an escape route and, because of the slow pace of the Chinese advance, he was able to extricate his forces from the trap Stilwell had set. The Americans enjoyed one great advantage – they had tapped the main Japanese telephone line and were able to hear all the orders that Tanaka issued. Stilwell's HQ was notorious for its inefficient staff work and at this stage he was so badly briefed about the action taking place at Walawbum, that he was still hoping to destroy 18 Division, when Tanaka had already escaped, and Merrill's Marauders had withdrawn in order to regroup.

After the capture of Walawbum, Stilwell mounted a similar operation on 6 March, with the main body of the Chinese advancing down the road towards Kamaing, while the Marauders carried out another flank march attempting to cut off 18 Division near Shadazup. During this advance, Kachin guerrilla units under their OSS leaders played an active role and they took part in a joint action in which Shadazup was captured on 29 March.

In spite of the loss of Shadazup, Tanaka was still in a powerful position and at the end of March he mounted a strong counter-attack with artillery and mortars, and was able to besiege the 2nd Battalion of the Marauders in Nhpumga for 10 days. These were 10 days of constant, vicious and intense fighting, in which the Marauders suffered severe shortages of food, ammunition and even of water. During the siege Merrill had a heart attack and was evacuated. Once again the Marauders were helped considerably by their Nisei comrades, who went forward to listen to the Japanese and were often able to give the exact time and place of the next attack. In one incident, because of the advanced warning, the Marauders beat off a Japanese attack without loss and inflicted 50 casualties. The bitter and prolonged fight at Nphum Ga, finished on 9 April when the 3rd Battalion of the Marauders broke through and raised the siege. The Marauders and the Chinese had caused the Japanese very heavy casualties, but had themselves lost 60 killed and 300 wounded.

Although the Marauders' tactics had worked well, Tanaka had always managed to avoid their traps and to counter-attack successfully. This added to Stilwell's frustration and he now developed a fixation that his forces must capture Mytikyina forthwith. At the beginning of May he outlined his strategic plans for SEAC HQ and the Joint Chiefs of Staff. The capture of Myitkyina and Mogaung was his highest priority, followed by the construction of all-weather airfields to assist air traffic over The Hump, and finally the opening of a road and pipeline from Myitkyina, down to Bhamo and from there to join up with the old Burma road to Kunming and Chungking. This should have been a feasible project, for Stilwell had five Chinese divisions against Tanaka who had just one division, the 18th, and the support of a few units extricated from 56 Division facing the Chinese in Yunnan.

Having set the strategic scene, Stilwell, in great secrecy, made out his tactical plan. The main Chinese force would advance as swiftly as possible down the Mogaung Valley and capture Kamaing. At the same time, the Marauders, with two Chinese regiments and some Kachin irregulars – called the Myitkyina Task Force – made a wide flank march to capture Myitkyina airfield. Tanaka had realised the urgency of things for Stilwell and determined to delay his progress as much as possible. The Marauders, already exhausted by the prolonged 10-day battle at Nphum Ga, were promised by Stilwell that they would be taken out of the campaign if they made a supreme final effort and captured Myitkyina airfield.

The Task Force set out and almost at once came in to very difficult country, with precipitous slopes, made worse by heavy monsoon rain. Many mules and their loads were lost when they just slid over the edge of the cliffs. Under Hunter's skilled leadership they progressed rapidly and swept away a few isolated pockets of Japanese resistance. Japanese intelligence was poor and the defenders of Myitkyina do not appear to have been informed of the approach of the Marauders. Nearer to Myitkyina the terrain improved and the Task Force covered 30 miles in three days. Hunter had a series of codewords to signify his progress as he approached the airfield, and Stilwell at his HQ listened in mounting excitement as the codewords came in: 'Strawberry Sundae' meaning 24 hours to go, and 'in the ring' when the attack was going in.

Hunter organised the final attack with a Chinese battalion in the lead and, in the mid-afternoon of 17 May, he signalled that the airfield was captured and aircraft could start flying in. This proved to be the most critical moment of Stilwell's whole campaign. In Myitkyina town, less than two miles from the airfield, there were two seriously depleted Japanese battalions and a few labour units – a total of less than 700 men. Hunter intended to capture it at once and sent off two Marauder units. Stilwell was justifiably exultant, but could not resist another dig at the hated Limeys. He recorded in his diary, in block capitals 'WILL THIS BURN UP THE LIMEYS'. (Quoted David Rooney, *Stilwell*, p119)

From this high point everything began to go wrong. Air HQ overruled Stilwell's priority, and insisted on sending in engineer and anti-aircraft units, when urgent priority should have been given to bringing in fresh infantry units in order to grab Myitkyina town. The Marauders' strike towards the airfield had taken place in such secrecy that other units knew nothing about it. It appears that Stilwell had made no firm plans for a follow-up assault on the town when the airfield was captured. In practice one disaster followed another. In the first real assault on the town, commands were muddled and two Chinese units fought a pitched battle with each other. They withdrew at the end of the day and then, almost unbelievably, did almost exactly the same thing the next day. Had these attacks been properly controlled, the Chinese could have captured the town on 19 May. They did attack again on 20 May, but the Japanese build-up had been swifter and more efficient than the Marauders', and the Chinese were repulsed.

Within two weeks of the capture of the airfield, the Japanese had increased the number of defenders from the miserable initial garrison of 700 to over 2,500. This later increased to 4,000, complete with artillery support – the majority drawn from 56 Division on the Salween front. The Japanese always excelled at defensive warfare and, having rushed that number of troops into Myitkyina, there was little likelihood of it being swiftly overrun. They were ordered to hold the town for three months and this they did. The Marauders and Chinese made a further attack on 21 May which failed and then, on 26 May, the Japanese were strong enough to drive them out of the western section of the town.

The initial failure to take the town was due to incompetence on the ground, but there is no doubt that after 24 May other factors influenced Stilwell's decisions. Because the Marauders were exhausted there was an urgent need for a well-trained infantry fighting force to come in, and the proximity of the airfield would have made this possible. The British 36 Division was available and ready, but Stilwell refused to have them and, instead, scoured all available American units in order to assemble a scratch force. He was not going to have the Limeys capture his great prize. Considering the cost in human lives and suffering, this was a disgraceful decision. Had Myitkyina been captured as soon as the airfield fell – as it so easily could have been – many of the traumas and sufferings of 77 Brigade, 111 Brigade and Morris Force would have been prevented.

At the same time, the physical state of the Marauders caused grave concern. They, like the Chindits elsewhere, had been ravaged by scrub typhus, and at one stage were losing 100 men a day through sickness. One Colonel with a temperature of 103°F was still commanding his unit. Men were not allowed to report sick unless they had had a temperature of 102°F for three days. Some even fell asleep in the middle of a battle. Merrill himself, who had returned to duty, had another heart attack and was evacuated. In these dreadful conditions the Marauders were reduced to 300 fit men.

By the end of May, when Stilwell began to realise that there would be no quick victory at Myitkyina, he showed himself at his worst. His intense frustration soured both his judgement and his relations with the Marauders, the Chinese and the Chindits. He had substantially increased his own difficulties by announcing to the world on 17 May that Myitkyina had fallen, when in fact only the airfield had been taken. He was to be haunted by this lie for the next three months. His black mood and his indiscreet anger were vastly increased when he heard that Masters, on his own initiative, had abandoned 'Blackpool' on 25 May, thus releasing a large number of Japanese troops to support the defenders of Mogaung and Myitkyina. At about the same time, virtually the whole of the 2nd Battalion of the Marauders had to be flown out because of sickness, fever and total exhaustion. Hunter wrote a savage condemnation of the way the Marauders had been treated, but Stilwell ignored this and ordered all remaining Marauders back into action. (Later, Hunter was shabbily treated because of his critical report.)

Stilwell's paranoia and his attitude were spread more widely by the sycophantic and inadequate Boatner who, having no battle experience himself, issued increasingly foolish orders to both the Marauders and the Morris Force Chindits lying to the east of Myitkyina. Each place mentioned had 'to be attacked at once' and 'taken at all costs'. Stilwell's obsession overcame all reason, and the Marauders and Chindits paid a heavy price for it.

Both commanders and men became increasingly furious at the orders they were given, and at the inadequacy of Stilwell's staff. Some units came close to anarchy. In a makeshift rest camp just behind the lines, the Marauders, fortified by a local brew which probably contained marijuana, ran wild and were almost completely out of control. Many of the scratch units hurriedly brought in were ill-trained; one group were instructed in the use of the rifle as they flew in. Boatner himself said that most of his men were terrified of the Japanese. Stilwell, who recorded his thoughts each day in his diary, after visiting the airfield where for days the rain had prevented any flights, wrote 'This is one of those terrible worry days when you wish you were dead'. (Quoted Rooney, *Stilwell*, p125)

During June, the situation deteriorated still further, partly because of Boatner's ineffective leadership, and also because of his failure to study the ground with commanders of the advanced units in contact with the enemy. His incompetence was noted equally by the Marauders, the Chindits and the Chinese. In contrast to the stalemate at Myitkyina, the Chinese divisions continued to advance down the Mogaung Valley and on 16 June they captured Kamaing. They continued to advance southwards against Tanaka's now depleted forces and linked up with the Chindits when 77 Brigade won its great victory at Mogaung on 27 June.

The Chinese continued to play the major role in the attacks on Myitkyina and General Wessels, an able and professional commander who in June replaced Boatner, organised an attack by the Chinese 50 Division which succeeded in capturing the town on 3 August.

The parallel between the Marauders and the Chindits is remarkably close. The Marauders were disbanded on 10 August 1944, but they were awarded a Distinguished Unit Citation and, considerably later, were reconstituted as the 75th Infantry Regiment with the battle honour Myitkyina. The Chindits were not disbanded quite so swiftly, but neither did they gain the subsequent official recognition accorded to Merrill's Marauders.

The victories at Myitkyina and Mogaung, achieved by the Marauders and the Chindits, broke the hold of the Japanese on northern Burma and achieved what had been the original plan drawn up at

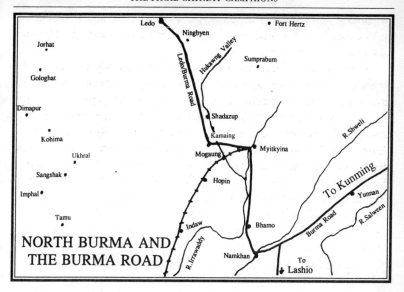

NORTH BURMA AND
THE BURMA ROAD

Quebec to re-establish a major supply route to the Chinese. With the opening of Myitkyina airfield, the monthly tonnage over The Hump trebled to 39,000 tons in November 1944.

It was a superb achievement of the American engineers, who closely followed the advancing infantry to build a road from Ledo down the Hukawng and Mogaung Valleys, past Kamaing to Myitkyina. When Myitkyina fell, the engineers went forward and rapidly repaired the road from there going south to Bhamo, which had been blown up so frequently and so successfully by Peter Cane and his Column of Morris Force. A more direct route from Myitkyina up to China was impossible because of the huge mountain mass lying directly to the east, nicknamed The Hump, over which the supply aircraft had had to fly. Therefore, from Bhamo the road ran southeast as far as Namkhan, where it crossed the Shweli river. Then it turned northeast to join the old Burma road going up to Yungling, Kunming and, after 600 miles, Chungking. The strategic thinking about the road is illustrated by an incident when Cane and his Column planned to blow up the bridge over the Shweli river at Namkhan, and were not allowed to because it would be needed later.

Thus after many months of fighting and suffering by Stilwell's Chinese divisions, the Chindits and Merrill's Marauders, the road to

China was reopened and the main aim of the Quebec Conference was achieved.

Mogaung – Calvert's triumph

On 4 May 1944, Lentaigne sent orders for 77 Brigade to move north 'to assist Stilwell to capture and hold the line Mogaung-Myitkyina'. At the same time, the 3 West African Brigade and 14 Brigade were actively preparing for the withdrawal from 'White City' and 'Broadway'. These orders reflect a fundamental departure from Wingate's strategy. Calvert wrote later:

> 'Slim's total misunderstanding of the Chindit role influenced Lentaigne who later said he also would have preferred to remain in the Indaw area, rather than to be caught on the hop near 18 Division rear echelon ... Slim's misinterpretation of the Special Forces role was a blind spot in one whom many people believe to be the greatest general bar Wavell that Britain produced in the war.' ('Chindits', p115)

When 77 Brigade was relieved at Broadway, Calvert led his men northwards into the Gangaw Hills where they enjoyed a brief respite. Here in pleasant hilly country, away from the stench of 'White City' and its rotting corpses, and with unchallenged airdrops, they were able to build up their strength and restore their morale. Then, after a few days, and with considerable misgivings, they left the relative peace of their haven in the hills and marched north. When they were approaching 'Blackpool', in increasingly heavy monsoon rain, Lentaigne sent Calvert further orders. He was to make a detailed recce of Mogaung and, if possible, assist Masters in 'Blackpool'. Calvert therefore divided his brigade, sending one part on the recce to Mogaung, and the other to drive forward towards 'Blackpool'. Strong patrols of 3/6 Gurkhas and the South Staffs set off for 'Blackpool' but the Namying river was completely impassable. The patrols had to turn back and the men suffered so badly from leeches that they needed blood transfusions. On 21 May, the main patrol which had approached Mogaung reported that there appeared to be about 4,000 Japanese troops holding the town. Then the whole of the brigade again tried desperately, but in vain, to cross the river and come to the help of 'Blackpool', which was now very close to surrender.

    The confusing situation for the Chindits at this stage arose largely from events elsewhere in Stilwell's command. The general situation had changed when Stilwell's forces captured Myitkyina airfield on 17 May. From then onwards, Stilwell was less concerned about blocking the road and rail links from the south and instead wanted the Chindit brigades to attack and capture Mogaung. Very soon after hearing the news of the Marauder's success, he heard that 111 Brigade had withdrawn from 'Blackpool' without his authority. This inflamed all his old prejudices that the Limeys disobeyed his orders and would not fight. In practical terms, the abandonment of 'Blackpool' meant the release of several thousand Japanese troops, with all their artillery, to speed north to Mogaung or Myitkyina. Lentaigne had just moved the Special Force

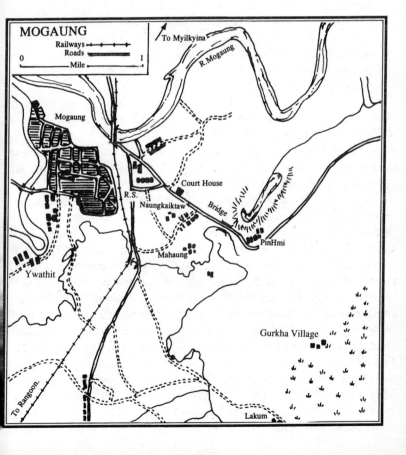

HQ to Shadazup to be nearer to Stilwell's main HQ, and he came in for the full force of Stilwell's vitriolic ire. Under that unpleasant pressure, and suffering very serious communication problems in his new HQ, Lentaigne appeared a weak and beaten man. He was hopelessly out of touch with the reality of the situation in any of the Chindit brigades and kept on sending out signals that were, in the end, absurd, and had a disastrous effect on both the commanders and men in the field.

In this deplorable situation in the aftermath of Master's withdrawal from 'Blackpool', on 27 May Lentaigne sent Calvert the peremptory order 'You will take Mogaung'. Having studied the detailed recce report, Calvert made his plans and calculated that he could reach the environs of Mogaung by 1 June, and could mount a major attack by 5 June. He realised that he would be facing units of 18 Division as well as 53 Division, now released from 'Blackpool'.

By 2 June, 77 Brigade were moving along a range of hills lying to the east of Mogaung and they captured Lakum village. From there they could see that Mogaung, about two miles away, was covered on the north side by the wide and swift flowing Mogaung river, and that the railway to Myitkyina from Mogaung crossed the river on a substantial bridge north-east of the town. Calvert called down Mustang strikes on the town and, tiring of being on the receiving end of the Japanese 6in mortars, requisitioned the only 4.2in mortars in India. When they arrived, he used them to harass the Mogaung garrison.

In Lakum, the Chindits were able to receive regular supply drops and they built a light plane strip to fly out their wounded. From Lakum, the village of Pinmhi, where a road crossed a chaung, was seen as the next step forward. The Lancashire Fusiliers and the South Staffs attacked and overran this sizeable village, where there were substantial ammunition dumps, a hospital and several HQ units. This was a heartening success, although the brigade had lost over 200 killed or wounded since leaving 'White City'. After the capture of the village, the Lancashire Fusiliers followed through and attacked Pinmhi bridge but here, in spite of a determined attack, they sustained very heavy casualties from well defended enemy positions.

In a series of hard-fought actions along the road from Pinmhi to Mogaung, lasting from 9 to 13 June, the South Staffs, the Lancashire Fusiliers and the 3/6 Gurkhas gradually advanced, first taking the village of Mahaung, then Naungkaiktaw, then the Court House, and finally in a particularly stiff fight, the Gurkhas captured Pinmhi bridge. By throwing in swift attacks, Calvert had hoped to capture Mogaung before any reinforcements could reach the defenders, but on 10 June it was discovered that two new battalions had arrived. By 12 June the Gurkhas had advanced to a position from where they could direct machine gun fire on to the railway bridge, but it was impossible to dig-in properly in these waterlogged forward positions, and the continuous Japanese artillery bombardment was causing about 20 casualties a day. Calvert signalled for 1,000 gum-boots, but was told that the best answer to foot problems was to keep your feet dry.

On 13 June, although they had received no word of encouragement from Lentaigne, the brigade was heartened by a message from Mountbatten congratulating them 'on their splendid achievement', but on the same day the COs of the three battalions came to say that however willing they were to go on, their men were totally exhausted, and that casualties and sickness had reduced the effective strength of each battalion to one company – ie, a quarter. The South Staffs illustrate the typical level of casualties. They had 40 officers killed or wounded, and of the original subalterns, only two had survived and they had been wounded seven times between them. One of them had taken part in 14 platoon attacks and had been wounded four times. He later received the DSO and American Silver Star. A group of sergeants went to Calvert to say that they were saddened to see so many keen, young, inexperienced officers getting killed, and offered to command the platoons themselves. Calvert agreed and no more subalterns were brought in.

The Chindits now faced an added hazard. Aircraft had to be requisitioned through Stilwell's chaotic HQ and so planes no longer came so promptly, the wounded piled up, and men were left to die. In one attack by the South Staffs, Archie John Wavell, the son of the Viceroy, was wounded, and Lentaigne – as ever giving in to pressure from above – ordered that he was to be flown out at once, but he refused until other wounded men had been flown out first. One exception to the growing problem of flying out the wounded came from a USAAF sergeant pilot, who flew in and out, never turning off his engine when he was on the strip, and did 10 trips a day until the backlog of wounded were saved.

From the start of the attack, 77 Brigade had been assured that strong Chinese forces would be assisting them and as the battle continued and the casualties mounted, the need for Chinese help became more urgent. On 14 June, Calvert sent Colonel Rome to see Lentaigne and Stilwell in order to get the Chinese to advance. He also sent a Burma Rifles officer to fetch the promised Chinese battalion.

Still the Chinese did not come, and still the Japanese kept up their shelling from a small gun position near Naungkaiktaw, so Calvert planned a careful assault. On the night of 18 June, the Lancashire Fusiliers went forward to a covering position and formed up together with a flame-thrower unit (called Bladet after the officer in charge). Well before dawn the Mustangs put in a heavy attack, followed by a 10-minute barrage from the 4.2in mortars, all the 3in mortars, and all the Vickers and Brens. Then a company of the King's Liverpool – now only 70 strong – assaulted across the open paddy field and successfully drove out the Japanese defenders, who lost 150 dead and many more wounded. The King's consolidated quickly and, as they ate an evening meal, a Japanese patrol wandered in and took off their equipment, not realising the position had been taken. They were all killed. Above all, this brave and well-organised attack had silenced the gun position which had inflicted so many casualties.

On 18 June, rather to Calvert's surprise, the Burma Rifles officer reported that the Chinese 114 Regiment was on the other bank of the river, and the first battalion crossed that night. A number of Hong Kong Volunteers were serving in 77 Brigade – a link dating back to Calvert's pre-war skirmishing in Shanghai – and they were helpful in establishing a good rapport with the newly arrived Chinese. Very soon all three battalions and an artillery battery arrived and took over some of the weaker flanks. The Chinese caused problems when they refused to mount assaults, but Calvert was remarkably philosophical about this, for he realised the Chinese had a totally different attitude to warfare and had been fighting the Japanese since 1931. The Chinese rarely made a frontal assault and preferred to work around flanks, forcing the enemy to retire, thus avoiding the casualties of a direct attack. Even allowing for this, relations with the Chinese remained fairly good.

77 Brigade had been encouraged by the arrival of the Chinese and, with their help, Calvert wanted to capture Mogaung before he lost any more of his emaciated forces to sickness or battle-casualties. With the Chinese unit, there also arrived a so-called American liaison officer, whom Calvert nicknamed 'Colonel Bluster'. He appeared typical of the dishonest sycophants with whom Stilwell surrounded him-

self, and was the direct cause of a major rift between the British and the Americans.

Calvert decided to launch an all-out attack on 24 June and the Chinese agreed to take part. He aimed, as a first phase, to capture the railway line embankment from the bridge to the railway station. Prior to the infantry assault, over 70 Mustangs swept on to the Japanese positions, then at 0300 hours the 4.2in mortars and all available 3in mortars put down a barrage of over 1,000 bombs, together with support from the Chinese artillery. In spite of this heavy bombardment, the Japanese artillery replied and caused casualties among the troops forming up for the attack. They therefore moved off rapidly, trying to keep close behind their own barrage. The infantry advanced on a two battalion front, with the 3/4 Gurkhas on the right, the South Staffs on the left, with the Lancashire Fusiliers and the flame-throwers as an immediate reserve. Calvert hurried them on, because the attackers had to cross 500 yards of open paddy field and they would be very vulnerable as soon as it became light. They advanced swiftly and the Gurkhas, with sound leadership from their young officers, captured the railway bridge. Strong points in houses were eliminated by flame-throwers firing through the grills on the windows. Things went well until the South Staffs came under fire from a strong point on the flank, which had not been located in the reconnaissance. This crisis was made worse because the Chinese, who had announced that they held the railway station, had in fact withdrawn leaving the flank of the South Staffs unguarded. To save the situation, Calvert called up the King's and the flame-throwers, and directed every available weapon on to the enemy strong point. The position was captured but the troops were completely done in, so Calvert called forward literally every man who was able to walk in order to consolidate the position. The survivors hung on grimly through the rest of that day and the next night.

Then the Chinese said they would assist in an attack on the remaining Japanese positions in the town. They agreed to attack at 1400 hours, but Calvert warned the Lancashire Fusiliers not to move forward until the Chinese appeared. They arrived at 1700 hours and put in an attack, but then withdrew, again leaving the British units in a precarious position. By 27 June, after two further days of careful mopping up, the last of the Japanese had been killed or driven out. Mogaung had been captured, but at a very heavy cost. Out of 2,000 men in the brigade at the start of the Mogaung battle, over 1,000 were battle casualties and the fighting strength of the brigade was reduced to less than 800 men. Two VCs were awarded to 3/6 Gurkhas. The Japanese defenders had lost even more heavily, and those units of 18 and 53 Divisions which had been diverted to Mogaung instead of reinforcing the attack on Imphal and Kohima, were destroyed as fighting units.

The cost had been too high for any feeling of elation at what had been a significant victory, but any sense even of satisfaction was completely soured when on the BBC and world news, the signal section heard the announcement that the Chinese-American forces had captured Mogaung. This was, of course, the despicable work of 'Colonel Bluster', and the Chindits were furious. The Chinese commander came to Calvert and in the presence of the wretched American, apologised for the false statement. Later he paid a glowing tribute to Calvert's leadership and to the 'superlative bravery of 77 Brigade'. Calvert enjoyed a brief moment of revenge. He signalled to Stilwell, 'The Chinese-American forces having taken Mogaung, 77 Brigade has taken umbrage'. Further satisfaction came when it was heard that Stilwell's intelligence officer – in fact his son – said Umbrage must be a very small place because he could not find it on the map.

With the capture of Mogaung, the worst of the fighting for 77 Brigade was over, but Calvert still had battles to fight. After the victory, the inevitable reaction set in, and men who had survived the whole campaign just lay down and died. He sent macabre details to Lentaigne – fewer than 300 men were even able to walk. Calvert wrote 'I was haunted by the fact that we had been the willing horse, and I had allowed them to be flogged until they could hardly stand'. (*Prisoners of Hope*, p246) He was given the choice of taking the brigade to Kamaing or to Myitkyina. The whole brigade had a phobia about Myitkyina – were they going to be ordered to capture that too? – so Calvert chose Kamaing. Then he received a counter-order to go to Myitkyina, so he pretended he had not received the message, closed down his set and moved off to Kamaing. This in itself was an appalling journey, in which nine men dropped dead from exhaustion. Calvert later agreed that going to Kamaing was a serious mistake because, apart from anything else, it gave the opportunity to that evil man Bluster to say the Chindits 'were cowards, yellow, deserters, walked off the field of battle, should all be arrested etc'. (*Prisoners of Hope*, p247) These lies were more than compensated by a further sincere and genuine tribute from the Chinese Colonel who had fought alongside 77 Brigade.

Mountbatten went to Stilwell's HQ on 30 June, but in spite of his intervention, Stilwell still demanded more from the Chindits. Mountbatten overruled him and ordered a full medical inspection of the whole brigade and of 111 Brigade. The medical report by a team of Anglo-American doctors was decisive. It found that the men were physically and mentally exhausted, most had suffered several attacks of malaria and dysentery, but had kept fighting. Every day, more men were dying of typhus, jungle sores and cerebral malaria. When he saw the report, Mountbatten ordered 77 and 111 Brigades to go out at once. Wisely he ordered Merrill to be involved in the arrangements, for the Marauders too had been driven into the ground and it was felt that he would understand. Calvert commented 'It left a bitter taste, when the Chindit brigades were treated like malingerers by the Supreme Command, and subjected to an independent medical inspection before they could be believed'. (*Chindits*, p157)

In the final stage of this unhappy saga, Calvert, Lentaigne and a staff officer were summoned to see Stilwell. Lentaigne, tense and apprehensive, begged Calvert not to antagonise Stilwell, who sat with Boatner. This proved to be a significant moment not only for Calvert but for the Chindits. Stilwell started aggressively 'You send some very strong signals Calvert'. Calvert replied, 'You should see the ones my Brigade Major would not let me send'. In this moment of high tension, to everyone's surprise Stilwell roared with laughter, and this established a rapport which instantly wiped away the fog of duplicity and deception which had marred the whole operation. He listened carefully to Calvert's description of what 77 Brigade had achieved. Time and time again he asked 'Why was I not told this?'. Then he began to realise that he had been given false figures and false information by the toadies who surrounded him. At the end of the interview he said 'You and your boys have done a great job. I congratulate you.' He awarded a Silver Star to Calvert, with four more for the brigade.

Calvert epitomised all the best of the Chindit ethos, and was the real heir to all Wingate's aspirations. Like Wingate, he too was to suffer from envy, malice and the skulduggery of the Establishment. He had received a bar to his DSO for his leadership at the fly-in on 5 March. From then until the end of June he had been constantly in action behind the enemy lines; he had led the charge of the South Staffs at Mawlu; he had shown superb leadership through all the action at 'Broadway' and 'White City'; he prompted the remark of his Brigade

Major that he did not realise it was his job to carry crates of grenades for the brigadier to throw; he was in the thick of every action from Mawlu to the final victory at Mogaung. His brigade won three VCs and numerous other awards, but what did he receive? Many felt that, like Group Captain Cheshire RAF, he should have been awarded the VC for prolonged leading from the front in contact with the enemy, rather than for one single act of bravery. The Tulloch Papers (Rylands Library) show that a VC or a CBE were considered, but in the end Calvert received nothing for his prolonged bravery and leadership from 5 March to 30 June. Why was it blocked? Was it perhaps the petty vindictiveness of 'the excessively timid' Lentaigne, piqued by Calvert's previous insubordination, or by the certain knowledge that most of the Chindits thought that Calvert should have been the commander of Special Force? Or was it Slim, or just the Establishment? Certainly, the Chindits were sparsely rewarded compared to the units which took part in the great advance to Rangoon, but for Calvert to be ignored after all he and 77 Brigade achieved was – and is – a scandal and a disgrace.

The victory at Mogaung brought to an end the fighting of the Chindit brigades. Most Chindits had gone through such prolonged physical hardship and suffering, made worse by the stress of months behind the enemy lines, that they needed lengthy medical treatment and convalescence. 77 Brigade at Mogaung, 111 at 'Blackpool', Morris Force on the Bhamo road, 16 Brigade in its march to attack Indaw, 14 Brigade and 3 West African Brigade in the aftermath of 'Blackpool', and 23 Brigade on the fringe of Kohima, had all acquitted themselves well and fought bravely. In August 1944, when the last Chindit brigades were flown out to India, the Japanese still controlled much of South East Asia, and the Chindits, after their convalescence, were thinking and training positively for their next LRP operation.

The Quebec Conference had established a clear plan: for Wingate and the Chindits to operate behind the Japanese lines to assist the advance of 4th Corps from Imphal, of Stilwell in the Hukawng Valley, and China from Yunnan – all aiming to clear the Japanese from Burma north of the 24th parallel, and to open the land route to China. 4th Corps and the Chinese did not advance, but Wingate saw the opportunity for effective LRP activity when, instead of the British advancing, Mutaguchi used three divisions to attack Imphal and Kohima. Operation 'Thursday' conformed to the original Quebec brief, which was finally achieved after the capture of Mogaung and Myitkyina, and when the road to China was re-opened. This was confirmed in cables from Mountbatten to Roosevelt and Churchill in January 1945.

This very substantial success brought few benefits to those people and units who had fought and suffered to achieve it. The Marauders were disbanded and Stilwell, because he had spoken so openly about the duplicity of Chiang Kai Shek, was sacrificed by his political masters and sent home. On the British side, there was no-one at the highest level to argue the case for the Chindits or for the role of LRP. All the successes of the Chindits were not enough: SEAC and 14th Army decided that the Chindits must be disbanded and it fell to Mountbatten, who at least was gracious enough to say it was the hardest duty of his life, to order the break-up of the Chindits. He said 'Now the whole army is Chindit minded, there is no need for Chindits. We are all Chindits now.' These were intended as comforting words to the battered survivors of Wingate's Special Force, but as the ensuing months of fighting were to prove, they were not true.

The effectiveness of Wingate's concept of Long Range Penetration, and of the Stronghold, had been proved at 'Broadway', 'White City' and 'Aberdeen', and by Morris Force on the Bhamo road. After his death, his principles were abandoned by Slim and Lentaigne, and it is an injustice that the mishandling of the Chindit brigades after March 1944 should be used as a reason to abandon the idea of Long Range Penetration, and as criticism of Wingate.

PART TWO

WINGATE'S DEATH AND REPUTATION

9
The Public Image
1944–1951

Orde Wingate died when his B-25 Mitchell bomber crashed into a hillside jungle near Imphal on 24 March 1944. In attempting to assess the significance of his career and achievements in a dispassionate way, one factor is the impact made by the news of his death. After all, 1944 saw D-Day, the Second Front, the Russian advance from the Ukraine, and the Americans and Australians advancing in the Pacific, so the death of a relatively junior major-general in the Forgotten Army might well have passed unnoticed.

Lorna Wingate, Orde's widow, was living in Aberdeen when the news reached her. One of the first letters of condolence came from Mountbatten who wrote: 'The serious point is the loss to the nation of the most forceful and dynamic personality this war has produced. He was on the road to surpassing even Lawrence's almost mythical reputation.

'He has revolutionised jungle warfare and when Burma is reconquered – as it will be – it will be your husband who showed us how, who inspired us and drove us.' (Wingate Papers, letter 28 March 1944)

General Carton de Wiart VC, then the Military Representative to the Chinese in Chungking wrote: 'From the point of view of the nation and army, I feel his death is an irreparable loss, and I do not think I could say the same of any man'. (Wingate Papers, letter 3 April 1944) Wingate's enthusiasm was recalled by Lord Ismay who, in sending the condolences of the Chiefs of Staff, said: 'No one who worked with him on the plans for Burma will ever forget the vivid imagination, the resolute courage, and the simple faith he brought to the task'. (Wingate Papers, letter 29 March 1944)

The reaction in London can be illustrated by a letter from the distinguished academic and political figure Harold Laski: 'When I opened *The Times* today the news was like a blow. Twice in my life I have met men who embodied that kind of remarkable courage which makes one feel that the dignity of the human spirit is unbreakable. Orde was one... and hardly less than his courage I valued his superb spiritual and intellectual insight.' (Wingate Papers, letter 1 April 1944) On the same day, David Ben Gurion, later to be Prime Minister of Israel, cabled: 'Every Jewish home in Palestine is shrouded in unspeakable sorrow over the loss of a devoted friend, who inspired us by his moral courage and sublime faith, (Wingate Papers, cable 1 April 1944) The American Zionist Council (6 April 1944) wrote: 'The death of General Wingate comes as a shock to the Jews everywhere, who knew of the intense devotion to the cause of the Jewish National Home of this brilliant and fearless British soldier'.

On Friday 14 April, a memorial service to Wingate was held at Saint Margaret's Westminster, and after the hymn 'Who would true valour see', L. S. Amery, Secretary of State for India and Burma, spoke of Wingate's fundamentally religious and almost mystical temperament, and added: 'The last Chindit campaign will live in history, not only from the care and perfection of its planning and initial conception, and for the boldness of its execution, but as the opening of a new chapter in the art of war destined to effect future strategy.

'His greatness as a leader lay in qualities beyond mere intelligent grasp of war or swift daring. It lay in a deep compelling faith, faith in himself, faith in his men, faith in the cause for which he was fighting. He never asked of others what he was not prepared to do and endure himself. Orde Wingate was many things – a hard realist yet a dreamer, a tough exacting leader and a man of infinite tenderness to those in distress. A great soldier, his name will live in the history even of this vast conflict.'

Michael Foot, not renowned for eulogies to military leaders, touched on a factor which was to dog Wingate's reputation. 'I first heard of Orde Wingate about the year 1938. Rumour and gossip painted the portrait. He was a crank, a maniac, a soldier too interested in politics, a prophet in uniform, a genius perhaps, but more noticeably for the moment, a tiresome arrogant fellow with a strange obsession about the Jews.' But Foot concluded: 'A man of this calibre must be honoured not only for his spectacular achievements, but for his whole character. He must be judged by his innermost convictions which light the flame within his soul, which gives him the power to perform mighty deeds, which stamp all his acts with the quality of greatness. Wingate was not only a great soldier. He was also a great rebel, a great Puritan, a great man of God in the Old Testament sense – a great Englishman.' (*Evening Standard*, May 1944)

In 1944, as the first rumours of the Nazi concentration camps circulated, and the Jewish people looked to a bleak and daunting future, the death of Wingate, who had taught them to defend themselves seemed doubly poignant. Chaim Weizmann, the first President of Israel, Moshe Shertok and Professor Namier paid their tribute: 'The name of Wingate will be enshrined in the memory and history of the Jewish people... one of the noblest and sincerest friends the Zionist movement and the Jewish people ever had'. Wingate had made a unique contribution to Jewish hopes of independence, and at his death all the Jewish flags in Palestine flew at half mast.

Some of these tributes might have been expected, but what moved the family even more were the 2,000 letters from ordinary people all over the country. Sergeant Ainszten described how a friend, another Polish Jew, went to Palestine in the 1930s and conceived a great hatred for the British. Then he served in Wingate's Night Squads, and later he wrote: 'A people who can give birth to such a man as Wingate cannot be so hypocritical and self seeking as I imagined. He is my ideal man, in whom thought and action are so perfectly counterbalanced.' (Wingate Papers, letter 1 April 1944)

A Lance Corporal Sulzbach wrote: 'You would receive millions of letters if all men thinking of you in your deep sorrow were able to write to you. He was for us a man you admired and loved, even only reading of him... Perhaps we refugees from Germany who have the privilege to serve in the army feel still more than others the irreplaceable loss of this great man.' (Wingate Papers, letter 1 April 1944)

The wife of a Chindit quoted her husband: 'He is the only man I have known whom I would follow to the ends of the earth. He is a king among men.' (Wingate Papers, letter 3 April 1944) In 1993, a Chindit in a message to the author said: 'When you first met him you thought he was a maniac – after a week you would have died for him'.

During April 1944 the tributes continued. General Hap Arnold, Commander of the US Army Air Force wrote: 'General Wingate has for years been the outstanding example of a military commander – imbued with that imagination and daring so vital to winning this war. It was his vision that made it possible to combine the tremendous mobility of the Air Arm and the fighting quality of the ground forces into the Commando organisations.' General Stilwell, notorious for his denigration of everything British, wrote: 'Wingate was a fighter whose combative spirit was inspiring... He was co-operative, always ready to change his plans to meet those of others, and was ready to break with tradition where necessary.' (*Aberdeen Press and Journal*, April 1944) On 1 April *The Times*, after a rather dull outline of Wingate's career, added 'By any measure Wingate was one of the thrilling figures of the war'.

The Journal of the Royal Central Asian Society pointed out that it was no small honour for a young general to be commemorated at Saint Margaret's Westminster, but to that honour had been added memorial services in the Great Synagogue in London, and in Jerusalem. A fellow officer in a personal tribute wrote of Wingate as a curious mixture of scholar and man of action 'with the rather intriguing eccentricity so often associated with genius... a brilliant example of Emmerson's observation that concentration is the secret of success'. Having served in the Royal Artillery with Wingate, he recalled his restless energy which gave the impression of a caged lion, and concluded 'He possessed the courage to express unorthodox opinions, and the infinitely more valuable gift of being able to persuade others to accept his views... His death is a heavy blow not only to his country and the United Nations, but ultimately to the cause of Peace, Justice and Freedom throughout the world.' (Wingate Papers, undated MS)

On 11 May 1944, six weeks after his father's death, a son Orde Johnathan was born to Lorna Wingate. His birth was noted by the Emperor Haile Selassie, who recalled the achievements of Wingate in Ethiopia, and sent a gold chain and cross to his son. The Emperor launched an appeal for a Wingate ward in the Addis Ababa hospital, and the appeal was supported by Winant, the US Ambassador to Britain, who said: 'Few men have won more fully the ordinary man's sense that here were the gifts of a great man – high courage, intense realism, a vivid intelligence which never shrank from the difficult obligation of hard thinking. He gave all of himself to the task he sought to perform... with a magnanimity which had in it something of that instinctive generosity of heart that is the sign manual of genius.' Winant then quoted the Confederate General Robert E. Lee: 'Duty is the sublimest word in the English language' and added 'Wingate would have understood that'.

The backbone of the early Chindits had been the King's Liverpool Regiment, and on 25 April the Liverpool Branch of the Amalgamated Engineering Union wrote: 'This splendid officer endeared himself to his men, not only by his great leadership, but by the fact that he shared their life, and suffered the same hardships, discomforts and dangers. His selfless devotion to duty has been an inspiration to us all.' (Wingate Papers)

King George VI, Clementine Churchill and Edwina Mountbatten added their personal condolences, and Earl Wavell, in a sincere personal letter, wrote: 'I asked for him specially, as you probably know, for Abyssinia and again for Burma'. (Wingate Papers, letter 2 April 1944) Madame Chiang Kai Shek, writing for her husband, sent £1,000 for the Wingate memorial. Hamish Hamilton, the publisher, considered Orde's death a national calamity, and confessed to Lorna Wingate 'When I read all the tributes I am not ashamed to say they made me cry'. (Wingate Papers, letter April 1944) *Time and Tide* (22 April) stated: 'To Orde Wingate, good and evil, the forces of light and darkness, and the constant struggle between them, were as real, visible and tangible as they were to Milton, Dostoyevsky and Tolstoy: and their battlefield is the human heart'.

All of these moving tributes were capped by Churchill in the House of Commons on 2 August 1944. He said: 'We placed our hopes at Quebec in the new Supreme Commander Admiral Mountbatten and in his brilliant lieutenant Major-General Wingate who, alas, has paid a soldier's debt. There was a man of genius who might well have become also a man of destiny. He has gone, but his spirit lives on in the Long Range Penetration Groups, and has underlain all these intricate and daring air operations and military operations based on air transport and air supply.'

This should have been the climax and the conclusion to the vivid and dramatic story of a brave and controversial military leader but although, as these tributes have shown, Wingate had friends and admirers all over the world, from the highest to the lowest, he had also made bitter enemies. These men were determined to wreak their revenge and, for over 40 years, continued to wage a vendetta against the reputation of Orde Wingate, often by mean, negative and destructive criticism.

Those closest to him realised this danger more than the world statesmen and leaders. Michael Calvert, the colleague most closely attuned to him both in thought and action, heard of Wingate's death during the battles at 'Broadway', and said 'Who will look after us now?'. His fears were well founded, for from then onwards the Chindits were never again used in their proper role, they were slaughtered in their hundreds under the command of Stilwell and Lentaigne, and were then disbanded.

Wingate must clearly bear some of the blame for the intensity of the antagonism which he generated among the senior ranks in the British and Indian armies, and especially among the army staff and GHQ in Delhi. Wingate's dilemma can be illustrated by the situation he faced on his return from the Quebec Conference, with Churchill's known backing, and with a brief to set up Long Range Penetration Groups on a large scale. He had faced almost total opposition and he decided that the only way to achieve his goal was by direct attack. Tulloch, his oldest friend and loyal supporter, has described how Wingate therefore deliberately set out to impose his will by fear, and to bludgeon the staff into providing him with the supplies and equipment the Chindits required. Wingate believed passionately that there was such sloth, inefficiency and spiteful antagonism towards him, that no other approach would have worked. On the other hand many, including Mountbatten, have argued that there were many officers all over India who would have been only too willing to help.

There was understandable antagonism in the Indian Army about Wingate's dramatic promotion, and his well-known support from Churchill, whose diatribes about India and the Indian Army were deeply resented. Within army circles in India most leaders were horrified at the idea of breaking up a tried and battle-hardened British division – 70 Division – and turning it into Chindit brigades. Auchinleck, who had just succeeded Wavell as Commander in Chief, protested strongly at the orders he received from Quebec in August 1943, was voicing a very widely held view. At the same time, Wingate's tactless and insensitive description of the Indian Army as 'a system of outdoor relief', was seized upon by his opponents and repeated over many years.

Some contemporary evidence of the feelings about Wingate among senior staff in India is given in the diaries of Lieutenant-General Sir Henry Pownall, the Chief of Staff to Mountbatten at SEAC HQ. (*Chief of Staff – The Pownall Diaries*, published 1974) Pownall's caustic remarks illustrate the strong feelings which Wingate generated. 'GHQ loathed the sight of Wingate' and 'He infuriated Giffard and got his goat'. (*Pownall Diaries*, December 1943) Pownall recorded the violent upsets and antagonisms which were fuelled every time Wingate came to SEAC HQ. In February 1944, after a vigorous discussion of future strategy 'Wingate replied with a long-winded diatribe accusing almost everyone of stupidity, ignorance, obstruction and much else besides'. Pownall concluded 'At any rate he is a thoroughly nasty bit of work'. (*Pownall Diaries*, p142)

Pownall also records another aspect of the feuds in the High Command which exacerbated feelings about Wingate throughout the Army. In January 1944, there had been serious clashes between Mountbatten, Giffard, Slim and Wingate over the use of LRP Groups, and Pownall was worried that if the matter was referred to Churchill, who was critical of Giffard and Slim, he might 'Jump at the chance of breaking another general or two, and would push very hard and maybe successfully to get Wingate installed in command of the 14th Army'. (*Pownall Diaries*, January 1944)

Wingate's critics might seize on these comments as ample proof of the feelings about him, but Pownall's evidence is not entirely reliable on this issue, for he was equally and destructively critical about all the other commanders. On the crisis at Kohima, he wrote 'All the initiative came from Mountbatten — neither Giffard nor Slim had shown any at all. They just sat back, although all of us had known for weeks the Japs were going to give trouble... Giffard and Slim were not nearly quick enough off the mark mentally.' On 1 April Pownall added 'Slim and Giffard between them lost a valuable week and would have lost more if Mountbatten had not galvanised them into action... Giffard, Slim and Scoones should have managed their affairs better.' (*Pownall Diaries*, p155)

In similar vein he wrote off Stilwell as 'offensive, ignorant and obstinate' (*Pownall Diaries*, p139) and he approved the removal of SEAC HQ from Delhi because he 'Deplored the lethargic non-possumus attitude that prevailed at the Delhi HQ'. In January 1944 he expected more trouble from Churchill 'who takes his usual impossible attitude of disbelief and refusal to listen and... is at his old game of general hunting – like a pi dog'. (*Pownall Diaries*, p135)

Finally, Pownall is equally dismissive about Mountbatten, his direct superior. He 'is highly strung, inconsequential and temperamental, his tongue runs away with him... and I must read him a lesson'. (*Pownall Diaries*, 11 March 1944) As balanced evidence, Pownall's comments are seriously flawed, but they do give a vivid insight into the criticism and back-biting which took place among the higher command.

At Wingate's death, while the world recognised the loss of a great military leader, those close to him were alarmed not only that his plans for Long Range Penetration in the immediate battles would be thwarted or reversed, but that his antagonists in both the Indian and British Army Establishments would attempt to destroy all he had striven for. Unfortunately those fears were amply justified. There followed a prolonged campaign in which Wingate's achievements and his reputation were subjected to a petty and vindictive attack, which was kept up for more than 40 years.

In March 1944, while the Chindit brigades were still battling at 'Broadway', 'Aberdeen' and across northern Burma to the Chinese border, Brigadier Tulloch at the Rear Chindit HQ, quickly realised that in recommending Lentaigne to succeed Wingate he had made a grave blunder. It soon became apparent to Tulloch and most members of the HQ that Lentaigne was not up to the job and, more important, neither understood nor approved Wingate's concepts. This, and Lentaigne's clear attitude of hostility to future LRP Group plans, prompted Tulloch (fearing that Wingate's papers might be destroyed by his detractors), to gather together all his relevant papers, and take them into his own safe-keeping. Tulloch has described these distressing events in a document he later produced for General Sir Geoffrey Evans who was preparing his book *Slim as Military Commander*. In reply to a questionnaire, Tulloch wrote:

'My relations with Lentaigne deteriorated after the decision had been taken to install another "White City" block to the north in the railway valley ("Blackpool"). I told Lentaigne it was a crazy decision, and, with the monsoon approaching – plus no hope of surprise while the Block was being installed – it was bound to end in disaster. I was overruled and I resigned in protest. It was totally contrary to all Wingate's teaching and practice. Lentaigne begged me to stay on and I agreed, thinking I might be of some use, but I had no confidence in him, nor he in me, after that date. I found he was bitterly jealous of Wingate, and would denounce Wingate and his theories loudly to sycophantic staff-officers... when Special Force came out of operations I offered my resignation personally to Giffard... Slim wrote me a charming letter saying he thought I had taken the correct action in resigning.'

After some further questions on Slim, Tulloch returns to the theme of Wingate: 'I was sore with rage at all the ill-concealed feelings expressed by Wingate's many enemies... I had every reason to admire Slim immensely and so I did. When Wingate was killed he was completely confident that he had Slim's full support – and that his plans were entirely in line with Slim's wishes.' (Tulloch-Evans, August 1966. Rylands)

From May to July 1944, Tulloch had to watch in increasing frustration while Lentaigne mishandled the Chindit operation and made blunders, which led to heavy casualties among the Chindits in the series of battles from 'Blackpool' to Mogaung and Myitkyina. Tulloch was particularly concerned about sending 77 Brigade to Mogaung, and recorded that Slim shared his worry, but 'as Lentaigne had agreed it with Stilwell there was nothing he could do'. Tulloch believed that tactics were totally wrong after 'White City' was evacuated, and was completely opposed to the establishment of 'Blackpool'. On 13 June 1944, Tulloch had written that he had serious worries about the whole situation, and 'Orde's whole plan for this operation was concentrate, concentrate, concentrate, and we are dispersed to the four winds'. (Tulloch Report, CAB/106/170)

In July 1944, Tulloch had a meeting with Slim at Shillong and afterwards, knowing his resignation had been accepted, felt justified in blowing off steam and jotting down a few indiscretions. He presents another aspect of the higher command with some Pownall-type comments. Slim agreed that the Chindits had been badly let down, and then discussed Mountbatten whom he considered a bit of a playboy who tried to please everyone, particularly the last person he saw. Slim added 'The only way to get anything done is to ensure that you see him last'. Then Tulloch says of Slim:

> 'The more I see of Slim the more I like him. He is the only high-up general out here who is straight and honest and capable. If SAC and that absurd organization 11 Army Group was abolished, and Slim put at the helm we might get somewhere.
>
> 'It is a filthy business the war out here – a political racket cum squabble for notoriety and hang on to your job at all costs – revolting... Planners should be abolished, Giffard sacked, Scoones double-sacked for a start, Stilwell and Boat-

ner exterminated then we could start to get somewhere. All feel we have been let down with a bang, and also know that had Wingate lived it would never have happened.

'Unfortunately Wingates only appear every 100 years or so. He would have dealt with the altered circumstances... and Stilwell would never have had his evil way with us. J. L (Lentaigne) is so very anti-Wingate, and wants to get rid of me at the earliest possible moment.' (Paper 22 July 1944, CAB 106/170)

At the end of 1944, Tulloch returned to England with Wingate's papers in his luggage. After the war he pursued a fairly conventional army career and became a Major-General, but his whole future life was really devoted to a campaign to protect the name and reputation of Wingate against his detractors.

Bernard Fergusson (later Lord Ballantrae) took part in both Chindit expeditions and was one of the first participants to write about his experiences. He wrote *Beyond the Chindwin* (published 1945), describing the first expedition. Fergusson was to play a key role in the postwar assessments of Wingate and this book is significant evidence. It gives graphic accounts of the sufferings and the achievements of Operation 'Longcloth', but it does not pretend to be a considered historical judgement. He sums up the achievements of the operation in a fairly dismissive way: 'What did we achieve? Not much that was tangible', but he adds a comment about Wingate. 'Surely posterity will not grudge to the memory of the great leader and military genius who fashioned us, the honour that should be his if his teaching and spirit survive.' (*Beyond the Chindwin*, p241)

'Wingate may have appeared as an ogre, and was a fearsome man to cross, but he had only one standard – perfection. He seemed almost to rejoice in making enemies, but he was a military genius of a grandeur and stature seen not more than once or twice in a century. Secondly, no other officer I have heard of could have dreamed the dream, planned the plan, obtained, trained, inspired and led the force. There are men who shine at planning, or at training, or at leading; here was a man who excelled at all three, and whose vision at the council table matched his genius in the field.'

In a final moving paragraph, Fergusson praises Wingate's restless mind and spirit 'for ever growing, grafting, crossing... To keep faith with him, we must follow, spurning the pedestrian ways of commonplace thought... such is our duty and the honour which we owe him.' (*Ibid*, p242) It should be remembered that this assessment, although it described Operation 'Longcloth', was actually written after Operation 'Thursday', when Fergusson was back in Britain recuperating.

Fergusson's next book, *The Wild Green Earth* (published 1946) described the part played by 16 Brigade in the long march from Ledo to the Stronghold at 'Aberdeen', and the battles around Indaw. This book gave the first public evidence of a dispute about the action in which 16 Brigade attacked Indaw. As the brigade approached Indaw, there was a period of silence from Force HQ, and Fergusson had urgently required news of 14 Brigade which, from his final discussion with Wingate, he had assumed was coming to assist him in the attack on Indaw. He wrote 'I was damned angry. Why the silence about 14 Brigade? Why had its job been changed without warning?' (*The Wild Green Earth*, p116) Then he received news of Wingate's death and he adds, 'Had I known earlier that he was missing, I might have guessed what was in fact the case: that the plan devised at "Aberdeen" had never reached Force HQ. Wingate was dead and his plan with him.' (*The Wild Green Earth*, p117)

The role of 14 Brigade after it flew into 'Aberdeen', and whether it was intended to help Fergusson at Indaw, or to march southwestwards and attack the lines of communication of the Japanese divisions facing Imphal, became one of the prolonged and bitter arguments between those who supported Wingate and those who denounced him. The arguments continued for decades, but Fergusson's description written and published within two years of the events, do not make a great issue out of it. From his description, he had initially been annoyed at the lack of information, but that was a normal hazard of a Chindit operation, and then when he heard of Wingate's death he assumed that the plans had been lost in the crash. Reading *The Wild Green Earth* it is difficult to understand why the 14 Brigade issue became such a cause célèbre, to be argued with such venom over so many years, unless there was someone of influence who was determined that it should be so. Fergusson was disappointed at not capturing Indaw, but even so, he wrote 'If I had stuck to Wingate's original plan I might have pulled it off'. (*The Wild Green Earth*, p121)

Fergusson gives a fair appraisal of Wingate's strengths and weaknesses, criticising him for dominating wireless time with his own orders, but countering the charges of creating a private army by writing 'A good deal of venom can be infused into the phrase "private army", though if it was a private army I am proud to have been in it'. He believed Wingate's ideas on direct air support were a wholly new contribution to military thought, and then, perhaps sensing some of the troubles that were to come, wrote: 'Some of those who now whisper that he was not all he was cracked up to be, remind me of the mouse who takes a swig of whisky and then says "Now show me that bloody cat". He was hard to serve, and difficult to command, but if I had a rope around my neck, to be jerked tight unless I recanted my allegiance to him, I would still proclaim he was a great soldier. And what is more he sought battle when many others were seeking excuses for evading it.' (*The Wild Green Earth*, p146)

In October 1944, after the main Chindit operation and after Wingate's death, the SEAC newspaper produced by Frank Owen, who himself wrote widely and wisely on the Burma campaign, published a special booklet on the Chindits, with articles on many aspects of their campaigns. Slim wrote the first article – a detailed tribute to Wingate. This was written, not as an obituary just after his death, but as a more considered tribute some months afterwards. In view of Slim's role in the later development of the Wingate saga, this lengthy and thoughtful tribute is given in full, because it touches on nearly every aspect of Wingate as a personality and as a soldier.

TRIBUTE
by Lieut.-General W. J. Slim,
C.B., C.B.E., D.S.O., M.C., G.O.C. in C. 14th Army

I first met Wingate in East Africa in 1940 when he was taking a leading part in the organization and leadership of the patriot forces in Abyssinia. I regarded him then as one of the several daring young soldiers who were showing themselves to be outstanding guerrilla leaders. It was not until months later when I travelled with him on a long air voyage that I realised that Wingate was much more than that. I talked with him, and he gave me a paper he had written on the organization, control and operation of guerrilla forces.

I then learned that, added to the tactical daring of the guerrilla leader, were a wealth of vision and a depth of imagination that placed him far above his comrades.

Genius is a word that should not be easily used but I say without hesitation that Wingate had sparks of genius in him. Someone has defined genius as 'an infinite capacity for taking pains.' Genius is not that. People who have an infinite capacity for taking pains are not geniuses. They are routine men fit for minor administrative posts. Wingate was not like that. Real genius has the power to see things more clearly than ordinary men can.

This he had.

He had, too, another attribute of genius, the power to accept other people's ideas, to adapt them to his own purposes, and to give them his own individuality - a form of genius which has always marked a great artist. Thus Wingate would discuss tactical ideas with you. He would contradict, argue, make you explain and defend your methods.

When he had completely satisfied himself he would accept them and incorporate them harmoniously in his own technique. An example of this was his application of airborne methods to his own long-range penetration tactics.

But there have been many geniuses who have accomplished little. The rarer combination of vision and action is required for results. As a man of action Wingate excelled. He was truly dynamic. When he was about, something had to move.

First he had the power of imposing his view on others, not so much by argument alone as by sheer force of his own belief. To see Wingate urging action on some hesitant commander was to realise how a medieval baron felt when Peter the Hermit got after him to go crusading. Lots of barons found Peter the Hermit an uncomfortable fellow, but they went crusading all the same.

Wingate spared no one, himself least of all. He never courted popularity with those he commanded or with those who commanded him. He invited, and skilfully used, publicity in all its forms, not for his own glorification but to ensure support for his force, to increase the resources allotted to him, to sell his ideas to the people who could help them on.

For the effect on himself, I believe he was indifferent. It was the cause that mattered. As a deeply but privately religious man he had a firm belief in the justice of the cause for which we fight and his one object was to serve his country in that cause.

The number of men of our race in this war who are really irreplaceable can be counted on the fingers of one hand. Wingate is one of them. The force he built is his own; no-one else could have produced it. He designed it, he raised it, he trained it, he led it, inspired it and finally placed it where he meant to place it - in the enemy's vitals.

In all this he would have been irreplaceable, but he has accomplished his greatest work. He has forged the weapon; others may now wield it. From the force itself come his successors, imbued with his will and his vision.

We are proud to have Wingate's force as part of the Fourteenth Army. The men he led, his Chindits, know that the finest tribute they can pay to the great leader is to complete his work and to perpetuate in themselves his courage and his determination to strike to the utmost in their country's cause.

Fergusson with his background of Eton, the Black Watch, Sandhurst and the Scottish aristocracy had a polished turn of phrase and an outlook different from others who started writing about the Chindits when the war was over. W. G. Burchett, who wrote *Wingate's Phantom Army* in 1946, stressed that Wingate brought out the best in men, 'He was not only a fine leader, but a good kindly, generous hearted man, who felt the rebuffs of his trade more than most people realised. He left us richer in faith, strength of purpose and in ideas for the future, as well as in military knowledge.' Burchett refers, as many have done, to Wingate's amazing attention to detail, and how he was proved right time and time again, but his was no uncritical assessment. He argued that Wingate was an able advocate, but that his best friends could not call him diplomatic. He got impatient and irritated if he did not get his way, and he could be outrageously rude, but he introduced a totally new concept of war. In similar vein, Charles Rolo in *Wingate's Raiders*, published 1944, referred to the phenomenal thoroughness of Wingate's training, but recalled too the views of 'the Brass Hats, that this young puppy would come to a bad end' and that 'he was a young upstart, a madman, and certainly this (Operation 'Longcloth') was not pukka war'. (Rolo, p23)

The first overt signs of official disapproval of Wingate came indirectly as a result of an article in *The Observer* of 16 April 1944. The military correspondent had referred to the solid opposition of India Command to Wingate's expedition, and concluded 'It would be sad indeed if Wingate's death should lead to the shelving of his ideas because they were not liked by Official Delhi'. Immediately after this article appeared, the correspondent was told clearly by W. W. Astor MP that it was the opinion of the Secretary of State for War that Wingate was no longer sane at the time of his death, and his short-comings should be listed for the record. (See Mead, *Orde Wingate and the Historians*, p142)

The Wingate saga is given an ironic twist by his old school Charterhouse, when in 1951 a memorial was erected in the school chapel. At what was virtually a national occasion, Churchill sent a message to be read at the service of dedication by, of all people, General Pownall: the message referred to Wingate as 'one of the most brilliant and courageous figures of the Second World War, and hoped that the memorial would stir and inspire future generations of young men to defend the cause of freedom, for which he so heroically fought and died'. Churchill then described how he met Wingate. 'We had not talked for half an hour before I felt myself in the presence of a man of the highest quality. It was his genius of leadership which inspired all who served under him. Here indeed is a name which deserves lasting honour.' How unfortunate that Pownall who during the war recorded his acerbic comments every day in his diary, did not record his thoughts on that day!

Before a congregation which included L. S. Amery (Former Secretary of State for India and Burma), the Ambassadors of the USA, Abyssinia and Israel, former colleagues including Earl Wavell, Baldwin, Carton de Wiart, Scoones, Fergusson, Tulloch and many others, Mountbatten gave the address. He referred to the inspiration Wingate exerted over everyone, with his fiery desire to get to grips with the enemy in a part of the world where the enemy had had it all his own way. Then, describing the work of the Air Commando, he added 'I do not suppose there has been a finer example of Inter-Allied, Inter-Service co-operation than between the Chindits and the American Air Commando'. Wingate proved that ground forces could operate while supplied entirely by air and 'As we got more transport aircraft, so we ended up with practically the whole of the 14th Army on air supply, of which Wingate was the pioneer... He was a great fighter, a fearless leader of men, a brilliant originator, and a deeply religious man.' Mountbatten recalled that Wingate had refused promotion for himself until after Operation 'Thursday' was over. He was a fiery tempestuous character but with a sly sense of humour. On one occasion Mountbatten sent him a message urging him to be more diplomatic in dealing with Generals who were senior to him. Wingate replied that he would be 'wise as a serpent and harmless as a dove'. Mountbatten had checked up on this statement of Jesus and found it was advice given to his disciples when he sent them forth 'as sheep among wolves', and he concluded 'And so we see the secret of Wingate's character. Behind the burning fiery desire to fight, and a corollary his deeply religious senti- ment, he had that niceness of spirit, that balancing sense of humour which made him human.' (*Carthusian*, June 1951)

These tributes from Churchill, Wavell, Mountbatten, Slim and many others, over the period 1944-1951, have been given at some length because they provide a detailed and balanced assessment of Wingate's whole philosophy, his achievements and his character, and it is from this year that his detractors begin their campaign of denigra- tion.

10

Kirby, Slim and the Official History

I t is not surprising that Wingate had his enemies and detractors. His close friend and confidant Tulloch has already described how, in the period after August 1943, when Wingate had just returned from the Quebec Conference, in response to an attitude of almost total opposition in GHQ Delhi, he was deliberately aggressive and offensive, and purposely used the threat of his direct access to Churchill in order to get things done. From this period he made a particular enemy of Major-General Kirby, who had been Director of Staff Duties at GHQ. Kirby – also a product of Charterhouse – was commissioned into the Royal Engineers in 1914, won an MC and bar, and then had steady promotion until he was Deputy Chief of the General Staff in Delhi in 1943. As a regular officer holding a very senior post, he was certainly among those who regarded Wingate as an upstart. He and Wingate had a severe clash over supplies for the Chindits (Wingate Papers, Memo, November 1943) and from then onwards he harboured a strong resentment against Wingate. In 1951, Kirby's opportunity came. As a senior officer who knew the Far East but had not actually served in the campaign, he was appointed to write *The Official History of the War against Japan*.

Criticism of Wingate spread at other levels. Because of the extremely tough and severe training of the Chindits, a large number of both officers and men were returned to their units (RTU) because they did not meet the high standards which were demanded. Having been proved inadequate, when they got back to their units, some tended to be critical of Wingate and all he stood for, and to exaggerate all his un-military eccentricities, which are now a part of military folklore.

At the top, there was serious and genuine resentment from August 1943 onwards that 70 British Division had to be broken up to form Chindit brigades. Further resentment erupted when the Chindits appeared to receive priority over material and equipment in short sup-ply. Mrs Kirby, the widow of General Kirby, has explained that strong resentment was caused by Wavell, who laid down rules about supply priorities, but then broke his own rules to supply the Chindits. Wavell also overruled decisions made by the Director of Staff Duties in order to favour the Chindits. (Interview with the author, February 1993)

In the long-running dispute, both sides have tended to exaggerate and to belittle the arguments of their opponents, and it is necessary to sift the valid and sustainable arguments from prejudices carefully fuelled by resentment. The Chindits have always maintained that they used normal units and were not an elite force, but there were certainly strong appeals for volunteers for the Chindits from normal infantry units, who often lost key NCOs even when the unit was in the front line. For example the 4/10 Gurkhas, the leading unit of 20 Division in the Kabaw Valley, lost several experienced NCOs who left to join the Chindits, just before the Japanese attack in March 1944. (Interview, Major M. Roberts MC, February 1993) Gurkha units suffered particularly when experienced officers and NCOs who knew Gurkhali went to the Chindits, and replacements came who could not communicate effectively with their troops.

After his appointment in 1951, Kirby produced five large volumes over the next 15 years, including Volume III, which deals with the battles of Imphal, Kohima and the Chindit issue. He had no training as an historian, but proved to be masterly in assembling facts for the massive work, but his judgement and opinion on a number of issues – particularly the Chindits – has been seriously called into question, as has his professional integrity in the way he handled historical evidence. Kirby led a team of officers representing the three services, together with a Japanese expert and a number of researchers who wrote the 'Narratives', ie the basic details of each campaign. Brigadier Michael Roberts who had commanded a brigade in the campaign and had held staff appointments in 4th Corps, became Kirby's assistant and wrote some of the narratives. Kirby and Roberts clearly shared a highly critical view of Wingate. Roberts was an ex-Gurkha and an old friend of Slim, and through this link they were soon involved in another aspect of the Wingate saga.

In 1956, the London publishers Cassell brought out Field Marshal Lord Slim's book *Defeat into Victory*. Correctly considered one of the most distinguished books on the Second World War, it told the story of the Burma campaign from the time when Slim was flown in to take charge of the two battered divisions during the retreat of 1942, until the final defeat of the Japanese and the capture of Rangoon by the 14th Army. Through this book, Slim, who as a junior officer had done quite a lot of writing under a pseudonym, endeared himself to generations of readers by his modest and self-deprecating approach. He was particularly generous to other commanders and frequently shouldered the blame himself when something went wrong. In a well-known case, the withdrawal of 17 Division from Tiddim in March 1944 was fatally postponed and the fault clearly lay either with Cowan, the Divisional commander, or with Scoones the Corps commander, but Slim generously took the blame himself. In admitting his errors, he always maintained that he was rescued from the effects of his mistakes by the valour of his troops. Serious blunders were undoubtedly made during the 1942 retreat, but Slim made no word of criticism of the commanders involved.

Slim's generosity of nature is also shown on the two occasions when he faced the difficult situation of being told he was to be sacked. The first of these involved General Irwin who tried to get rid of Slim in May 1943, but then sent him the cryptic message 'You are not sacked. I am.'. This incident is told in other books, but Slim, showing great restraint, does not even mention it. Similarly, after the great victories of Imphal, Kohima and Meiktila, General Oliver Leese came out to the Far East and tried to get rid of Slim. Again, Slim hardly mentions this incident in *Defeat into Victory*, and his unselfish and perhaps over-generous restraint colours most of the book.

In view of this, it was a matter of incredulity and amazement to the Chindits and to all admirers of Wingate, when *Defeat into Victory* put forward not the detailed and well-known assessment Slim had made in 1944, but a highly critical and dismissive description of Wingate and what he and the Chindits had achieved.

In referring to the first Chindit expedition, Slim explained that the Chindits had blown up some bridges and cuttings, and had then broken up into small parties, and he added 'As a military operation the raid had been an expensive failure. It gave little tangible return for the losses it had suffered and the resources it had absorbed. The damage it did to Japanese communications was repaired in a few days, the casualties it inflicted were negligible, and it had no immediate effect on Japanese dispositions and plans... if anything was learned of air supply or jungle fighting it was a costly schooling.' (Slim, p134)

Slim then compares Operation 'Longcloth' to an old-fashioned cavalry raid on the enemy's communications, but declares it was ineffective because the planned advance never took place. This is hardly a fair statement of the strategic significance of Long Range Penetration, but Slim did conclude this section by saying that the effect on the morale of the troops in Burma was worth the hardship and sacrifice Wingate's men endured. (Slim, p135) He then describes the problems of morale among troops in India in 1943, and referred to 'The somewhat phoney propaganda that followed Wingate's raid'.

When planning the campaign for 1944, Slim had lengthy discussions with Stilwell, Scoones and Wingate, and agreed many things, but he wrote 'It was impossible not to differ from a man who so fanatically pursued his own purposes without any regard to any other considerations or purpose'. (Slim, p187) This matches almost word for word the sentence of Kirby in the Official History (Vol III, p220). Were they Slim's words or Kirby's? This view also contrasts starkly with that of Stilwell – covering the same period – when he said that Wingate was always co-operative and ready to change his plans to meet those of others.

In describing the preparations for Operation 'Thursday', Slim makes it clear that he disapproved of private armies and private air forces, and maintained that it was Mountbatten who persuaded General Arnold to provide the Air Commando to support the Chindits. This view directly contradicts American reports on the Quebec Conference which attribute Arnold's generous act directly to Wingate, not to Mountbatten.

Slim's account continues by describing how, over the use of 26 Division, he virtually dared Wingate to write to Churchill and then, in another dispute over the provision of aircraft, threatened him with court martial if he did not obey his order. Slim continued this generally dismissive and disparaging description, by saying that Wingate had never experienced a real fight against the Japanese, and he would find them very different to the Italians in Abyssinia. Some Chindits argued that, since the end of the 1942 retreat, Wingate was the only British general who had had a successful fight against the Japanese.

Even more surprising than Slim's generally destructive attitude towards Wingate, is his inaccurate and damaging references to particular detail. For example, he stated that for the fly-in of Operation 'Thursday', with two gliders towed by one aircraft, 'Never before had these aircraft towed more than one'. This statement is categorically untrue, since prolonged and exhaustive trials had been carried out without one failure. (Tulloch report, Rylands) Wingate was the most meticulous planner, yet Slim seems to suggest that the launch of Operation 'Thursday' was just one of his madcap schemes. Similarly, referring to 'Broadway' and 'Piccadilly' he said they were just fancy names written on a map, within striking distance of Indaw, but in fact every site had been personally reconnoitred by Tulloch and General Old.

Slim's description of the start to the fly-in of Operation 'Thursday' was at odds with every other eyewitness statement. He now added another dig at Wingate by saying that the publicity for Operation 'Thursday' would be more effective if the Japanese thought it was Wingate and 'a repetition of his minor and ineffective raid of 1943'. (Slim, p231)

In describing Wingate's death only days after the fly-in, Slim recalled the impact of the news on his HQ where it struck like a blow. 'He had stirred up everyone with whom he came into contact. With him contact too often had been collision, for few could meet so stark a character without being either violently attracted or repelled... Wingate always regarded himself as a prophet, and that always leads to a single centredness that verges on fanaticism with all its faults. Yet had he not done so, his leadership could not have been so dynamic, nor his personal magnetism so striking'. (Slim, p234)

The Chindits – like most veterans who read a book about a campaign in which they took part – looked first at descriptions of the battles in which they had actually fought, and in their case at the description of the commander whom they revered. When they read Slim's narrative they were horrified and faced an acute dilemma. They had the highest regard for Slim – 'Uncle Bill', the man who had led them to ultimate victory – yet here he was deprecating and belittling their own leader who was killed at the height of the battle, and for whom they had an equally high regard. They asked how could Slim, who had written such sincere and moving tributes to Wingate in the SEAC publication in 1944, which most of them possessed, now run him down, belittle his achievements and impugn his character. They even noticed that in Slim's index Wingate was referred to as Brigadier, and not as Major-General. Was this just carelessness or another attempt to belittle? Their dilemma has never been entirely resolved, though there is some explanation.

While Slim was writing *Defeat into Victory*, he was already Governor General of Australia and busily involved with his duties and responsibilities in Canberra. In such a situation, where would he be likely to turn for help over detail, but to the officers in the Cabinet Office writing the Official History of the war in Burma – namely Kirby and Roberts. Churchill College Cambridge has a military archive which contains the Churchill Papers and several other collections of military documents, including the Slim Papers and the Roberts Papers, which complement each other in an interesting way. Slim and Roberts had served together in the Gurkhas in pre-war days and shared the warm family feeling of all Gurkha officers, which transcends rank or eminence.

The major interest in the Slim Papers lies in the files of letters from Slim to Roberts, and from Slim to Kirby. The majority of these are from Government House Canberra, written in the early morning, sending Roberts each chapter of *Defeat into Victory* as Slim wrote it, and asking him to correct it and add comment wherever necessary. Slim and Roberts correspond as old friends, their letters relaxed and informal, but Kirby's letters appear obsequious and sycophantic. There was clearly some tension between Kirby and Roberts because, in a petulant outburst, Kirby complained about Slim writing directly to Roberts. (Slim Papers)

In a letter of 8 October 1954, Slim wrote to Roberts: 'I herewith inflict on you another chapter (XIII) of the book, in the hope that you will repeat your kindness in dealing with its predecessors... I would be most grateful if you would, from your much greater resources, correct me where I need it. I fear it will be in several places.' He then goes over the controversial description of the Chindit fly-in – virtually as it appears in his book – and concludes, 'I am as usual immensely indebted to you for all your help. You have seen quite a bit of the book and you might have some general criticism of its content, style, method of presentation etc. Please let me have them, and don't spare my feelings. Yours ever Bill.' (Slim Papers)

The correspondence over the fly-in continued over several months, and the letters show clearly that Roberts put forward a highly critical view of Wingate. Slim had written 'I have toned down in several places what I might have said about Wingate's methods and character, as I don't want to hurt anybody, but he was not a reliable chap'. (Slim Papers, letter 3 March 1954) Roberts then replied, sending copies of letters from Air Marshal Sir John Baldwin, and saying 'They in fact bear out your account... and Calvert's account in *Prisoners of Hope* corroborates your version very clearly. There is no cause for you to revise the account you give.' (Slim Papers) This is a totally misleading comment, since Baldwin and Calvert both gave detailed descriptions of the start of the fly-in which completely contradict Slim's version. Roberts then continues his comments, 'I think you give Wingate all the credit due to him, and you have been much kinder to him than I have in my narratives'. He then dismisses Baldwin's contribution as 'It demurs rather half-heartedly and is inclined to be self-contradictory'. These letters are a good illustration of how Roberts tried to impose his prejudiced views on Slim, and there is a strong feeling that this is an army matter and the RAF ought to keep out of it.

Roberts, clearly representing the feelings of the Indian Army about Wingate, and the resentment of the regular units which assumed the Chindits had been given priority in supplies, wrote, in reply to a query of Slim, 'I can't see the Chindits were value for money. Vast expenditure on special everything, including its own admin base, and they did three months hard fighting.' (Slim Papers, undated report)

A close perusal of the correspondence in the Slim Papers between Slim, Kirby and Roberts makes it clear that Kirby and Roberts were highly critical of Wingate and did their best to influence Slim both on detail and on general assessment.

An interesting comment on Slim's changed attitude towards Wingate comes from Sybil Wingate, Orde's sister. Naturally, the family were extremely upset when *Defeat into Victory* was published. She wrote to Tulloch 'As to the reason for Slim's change of front, I suspect my brother Nigel is right in attributing it to Churchill's publication of the fact (Churchill, *Second World War*, Vol 5) that he had contemplated putting Orde over Slim's head. Wounded vanity is one of the strongest of mortal feelings.' (Letter Rylands)

The links between Slim, Roberts and Kirby continued long after *Defeat into Victory* was published (1956). Kirby and Roberts, then busy working on the Official History, submitted each of their chapters to Slim for comment, so that there is no doubt that Slim saw and vetted all its chapters before it was published in 1962.

Volume III of the Official History which covered Operation 'Thursday' appeared in January 1962. Before considering its assessment of Wingate in any detail, it is important to recall the tributes which were paid to him in the 10 years after his death by the world's leaders, by other commanders and by humble privates. The contrast is surprising. The Official History disregarded any favourable comment, and launched into a destructive attack on Wingate both as a character and as a soldier. It made a series of unsubstantiated criticisms which are clearly designed to destroy his reputation, and it made no attempt to give a balanced view.

This critical tone appears in a reference to Churchill 'who claimed he was a genius' and 'took him, a junior and relatively unknown officer to America'. Referring to other commanders, Wingate is described as missing 'few opportunities of belittling them and questioning the value of orthodox forces'. (p220) Wingate's concept of Stronghold is dismissed in favour of 'The pivot of manoeuvre'. It was grudgingly admitted that he raised 'what can only be described as a private army' – a doubtful compliment from the army Establishment, but it argued that 'Special Force was formed only at considerable cost to the army in India'. (*Official History*, p221)

Kirby claimed that 'Wingate's fertile imagination would form an interesting psychological study' and then quoted, out of context and with no background detail, Wingate's memorandum of February 1944, and added the comment 'Wingate was already concerned lest the Combined Chiefs of Staff's global strategy should interfere with his own fast developing plans of reconquest'. It continues, 'He was so obsessed by his theories that he entirely forgot that victory in Burma could only be achieved by the defeat of the enemy's main force'. (*Official History*, p222)

This petulant and destructive tone of criticism continued with the allegation that he was unwilling to co-operate with anyone not directly under his command, and as his ideas developed he was driven into using his formations as conventional forces. This totally inaccurate criticism is matched by another which argued that the qualities which enabled him 'to win the support of the Prime Minister and create his own private army, reduced his value as a commander in the field'. A more illogical comment it would be hard to imagine, and it was followed by another criticism that 'He had neither the knowledge, stability nor balance to make a great commander'. In the final paragraph of the assessment came the most disgraceful and unprofessional statement: 'Just as timing played so great a part in his rise to prominence, so the moment of his death may perhaps have been equally propitious for him'. (*Official History*, p223) When the Official History virtually says it was just as well an officer was killed, it cannot claim to be a fair or balanced assessment.

Such views were certainly held by senior officers in the Indian Army. Some said officially that Wingate was just a bloody nuisance, and Michael Calvert recalled that in an Officers' Club in Delhi in 1944 a Lieutenant-General remarked that Wingate's death was the best thing that had happened to the British Army. Later that night a fully clothed general was hurled into the club fountain, and his assailants were never discovered. Elderly generals are entitled to prejudices which are unacceptable and out of place in a serious historical assessment. This is where Kirby is gravely at fault.

The Official History makes such detailed, inaccurate and often vituperative criticism of Wingate, that it is necessary to consider the main aspects individually. On strategic issues the main thrust of the criticism comes from the memorandum, already referred to, which Mountbatten requested from Wingate after they met with Scoones on 8 February 1944. They discussed Operation 'Thursday' and the strategic and military background, which at that time was so uncertain that they had wondered whether the whole operation should be called off. As a result of this discussion, Mountbatten had requested Wingate's views on the whole future strategy of the war in the Far East and he replied with two appreciations within three days. Considering Fergusson's brigade was already marching from Ledo, and Operation 'Thursday' was due to start in a matter of days, this memorandum showed a remarkable grasp of the wider strategic issues. These included the role of China, plans for an advance to Bangkok and Hanoi, and the role of Long Range Penetration Groups in that move. Yet, Kirby has published it, with no background information, and he uses it to suggest that Wingate was unbalanced and fanatically ambitious, and that he was so obsessed with his theories that he would consider nothing else.

The Official History also criticises a memorandum of Wingate, dated 13 March 1944 (PRO WO 172/1708), which suggested that with a major advance by 4th Corps, there should be a Chindit operation at Pakkoku, lying to the west of Meiktila and Mandalay. Kirby argues that this would have been an incorrect use of LRP forces. In fact it could have been a classic Chindit operation, linked to Wingate's stronghold concept. This proposal has another interesting off-shoot. After the battle at Meiktila in February 1945, when Slim moved a whole Corps under cover of the jungle to Pakkoku, when questioned about the origin of the idea he maintained that his staff alone had produced the idea and worked out the detail, yet we know that the idea of cutting off the Japanese at Pakkoku originated with Wingate's memorandum of 13 March. Again, both Slim and the Official History either ignore this or put a wrong interpretation on it.

Next, the Official History criticises Wingate for abandoning his Chindit principles and for using the Chindits as conventional forces. It quoted the example of the attack by 16 Brigade, which found Indaw held by the Japanese. Wingate had laid down that LRP Groups should not be used to attack prepared positions because they did not have artillery and armour support. The whole point of the Indaw attack was for 16 Brigade to occupy Indaw before the Japanese did. This again appears as deliberate misrepresentation.

The Official History criticises the concept of the Stronghold and alleges that Wingate established one of his main Strongholds, 'White City', in a place that was accessible to enemy armour and artillery. This is another inaccurate allegation and suggests clearly that Kirby was deliberately misrepresenting Wingate's idea. The essential for a Stronghold was a base where there was water, where there was sufficient flat land for a Dakota air-strip, but was remote from main roads or rail so that enemy tanks and artillery did not have access. The real significance of this comment – as Kirby must have known – was that 'White City' was not a Stronghold, but a temporary base astride the road and rail to Myitkyina. The Stronghold which met Wingate's criteria in every way was 'Broadway', and this totally vindicated Wingate's idea. 'Broadway' fought off all Japanese attacks and, with 'Aberdeen', was the only Stronghold established according to Wingate's principles. This again calls into question Kirby's integrity as the Official Historian.

In the later Chindit campaigns there were several instances where Wingate's principles were ignored – the most obvious being the establishment of 'Blackpool', which flouted all the basic rules for a Stronghold, and the attack of 77 Brigade on Mogaung. But these took place after Wingate's death and were the responsibility of Lentaigne, who rejected most of Wingate's philosophy. Kirby levelled no word of criticism at Lentaigne.

After dealing with Stronghold, Kirby reverts again to the attack on Indaw by Fergusson's 16 Brigade after their arduous march from Ledo and he makes a major issue of this, although Fergusson in *The Wild Green Earth* does not do so. Kirby's argument centred on the allegation that, at a meeting on 20 March 1944, Wingate promised Fergusson that 14 Brigade would fly into Aberdeen and would assist in the attack on Indaw. The allegation continues that, after a meeting with Slim on 21 March, Wingate changed his plan and gave orders to 14 Brigade to fly in to 'Aberdeen' (23/24 March), and then march south of Pinlebu. The Official History concludes 'He did not tell Fergusson of his change of plan, a very serious omission, and as a result the attack failed'. This is clearly a serious criticism of Wingate's integrity, but how valid is it?

In December 1957, well before the Official History was published, Fergusson wrote to Tulloch: 'I am appalled at the things I have forgotten about the second expedition. General Kirby has been trying to get out of me details of my talks with Orde at "Aberdeen", and I am still vague about them even after seeing the War Diaries.' (Ryland) It must be remembered that Fergusson was the key witness in Kirby's allegation of Wingate's deception about 14 Brigade.

It has already been seen that Fergusson thought his last meeting with Wingate was on 23 March, but during the 1950s Kirby was in frequent contact with him and finally convinced him that his last meeting was on 20 March and not the 23rd. This suited Kirby's allegation of Wingate's deception, although there is very strong evidence that 16 Brigade did not expect the help of 14 Brigade in the attack on Indaw. For example, Fergusson's deputy, Colonel Cave at the 16 Brigade Rear HQ, came to see him on 23 March to confirm orders, and no mention was made of 14 Brigade. Similarly, Cave's private diary (Imperial War Museum) makes no mention of any involvement of 14 Brigade in the Indaw attack. On 24 March Fergusson gave his orders and Brigadier Wilkinson, then CO of the Leicesters, and the Leicesters War Diary (PRO WO 172/4899), confirm that no mention was made of 14 Brigade sharing in the attack, and in any case they had not at that time completed their arrival at 'Aberdeen' and could not have helped Fergusson's attack on Indaw.

Fergusson's letter to Tulloch shows that Kirby badgered him about the date of his last meeting with Wingate until he changed his mind. This action damages Kirby's integrity as an historian, but far greater damage is done to Kirby by a comment made by his close colleague Roberts who, some years later, corresponded with Ronald Lewin who was writing the biography of Slim. Lewin sent each chapter to Roberts for his detailed comment. Roberts replied 'You quote extensively from Slim's letters to Kirby. His letters to Slim contain "loaded questions". As he had done with Percival (the commander at

Singapore), Kirby was trying to catch him out. In regards to Percival I remember being horrified when Kirby exclaimed "Now we've got him", over an answer Percival gave to one such loaded question.' (Roberts to Lewin 7 October 1972, Roberts Papers Churchill College) This damning indictment of Kirby has never before been published. If, as Roberts confirms, Kirby tried to catch out Slim and Percival, his other evidence must be open to serious doubt.

One of the key pieces of evidence in the Indaw dispute is the War Diary of 16 Brigade, which Kirby used extensively in the 1950s. Strangely, this diary is not now available, having apparently been 'lost'. Peter Mead, who thoroughly investigated this matter, found that the War Diary of the 16 Brigade Rear HQ under Colonel Cave was still in existence (PRO WO 172/4396), and this makes no mention of any promise by Wingate that 14 Brigade would assist in the attack on Indaw. This shows that Kirby's thesis is seriously flawed.

On 21 March 1944, Wingate had seen Slim at Comilla and Slim had agreed that 14 Brigade would fly in to 'Aberdeen', though it was understood that the urgent move of 5 Indian Division to Kohima would have priority. Wingate returned to his HQ and on 23 March, the day before he died, ordered 14 Brigade to fly to 'Aberdeen' and then move south-east of Pinlebu; ie, it would not assist 16 Brigade at Indaw. This was close to Wingate's Plan B, to attack the communications of the three Japanese divisions approaching Imphal and Kohima. On 3 April, one week after his death, there was an important conference at Jorhat, attended by Slim, Mountbatten, Stilwell and Tulloch. Slim proposed, and it was confirmed, that 14 Brigade should be used in the way he had agreed with Wingate at their last meeting. This detail is confirmed by Tulloch who discussed it with Wingate during their last day together, and who was present at the Jorhat conference. In contrast to every other description of this incident, the Official History states 'Wingate either once again misinterpreted Slim's wishes, or deliberately decided to carry through his own plan'. (*Official History*, p212) This is an absurd charge which ignores all the evidence.

On 19 March, Mountbatten wrote to Wingate saying that he had just seen Slim and Baldwin, and was 'surprised and delighted by the spontaneous tribute which they both paid to the way you have been working with them... both said you had been first class to deal with, very reasonable, very sensible, and they had been delighted to give you all the backing they could. They were enthusiastic about the way your operation had started off, and full of praise for you and Cochran personally.' (PRO WO 172/1709) This well-known letter was ignored by Kirby, who wrote, referring to Wingate, 'instead of co-operating wholeheartedly with the army and air force commanders for the public good, he missed few opportunities of belittling them'. Nor did the Official History quote Mountbatten's judgement that Operation 'Thursday' with the Chindits and the Air Commando was the most superb example of Inter-Service and Inter-Allied Co-operation in the Second World War. (Mountbatten at Charterhouse 1951) Both of these were omitted because they would have refuted the adverse image of Wingate which was being sedulously built up. Thus Kirby is guilty, on a large scale, of using selective evidence and ignoring evidence that does not fit his own thesis.

After considerable specific criticism, the Official History proceeds to a more general attack. It starts by giving some faint praise – that Wingate offered a plan of action where there had been retreat and defeat, that he inspired others with a sense of mission, that he raised and trained a private army, and made a valuable contribution to the development of air supply. (*Official History*, p217-222) This is followed by other more serious criticism: that he had an extraordinary degree of furtiveness; he faced problems which from lack of experience he was not equipped to solve; he rejected advice from those more experienced than himself; he committed errors of judgement in tactical and technical matters as well as planning; he 'Tended to react too easily to the enemies' movements and at times laid himself open to the charge of order, counter-order, disorder'. (*Official History*, p222)

After the war, the Japanese commanders were interrogated and a leading figure in this process was General Symes, formerly GOC 70 Division, and second-in-command to Wingate. Symes became GOC Burma and provided interrogation reports on many of the Japanese leaders including Mutaguchi. In a lengthy report Mutaguchi made one particularly important statement. He said 'The Chindit invasion did not stop our plans to attack Kohima BUT they had a decisive effect on these operations, and they drew off the whole of 53 Division and parts of 15 Division, one regiment of which would have turned the scales at Kohima'. This is a crucial statement in any assessment of the Chindit operations and has been quoted in a number of books. The real significance of the sentence is that the Official Historian, Kirby, omitted the whole sentence after BUT. In other words, he deliberately reversed the meaning of Mutaguchi's statement. (See Calvert, *Prisoners of Hope*, and Tulloch, p269) This is a clear case of distortion of evidence in order to support a biased view of the Chindits, and must finally demolish Kirby's credibility. It must be added to his rejection of any favourable comment about Wingate and the Chindits from other sources; to his attempts to mislead Slim and other commanders; to his prolonged efforts to force Fergusson to change his evidence; and to the careful selection of evidence to suit his biased view. Such actions are unacceptable in a responsible historian, and their effect was prolonged and maximised because Kirby and Roberts were in a privileged position, and had access to material denied to other genuine researchers for 30 years or more.

Volume III of the Official History came out in January 1962. At the front, in 'The instructions to the Authors', there is an ironic comment on the whole Wingate controversy. The instruction states: 'There is an obligation on authors to avoid personal bias or perverse interpretation'. (CAB 103/34) Kirby must have been generally pleased with its initial reception because many of the reviewers, unable to grasp such a huge and complex subject, tended merely to quote occasional sentences without attempting to make an overall analysis, but some gave a more thorough assessment. Norman Scarfe in *The Birmingham Post* (20 February 1962) pointed out that although the writers were professional soldiers 'There is no reason why they should be exempt from the disciplines of professional historians'. He noticed that Operation 'Longcloth' was considered 'Of little strategical value', yet it changed the whole Japanese strategy. *The Times Literary Supplement* (16 February 1962) criticises the dull reading, the flat style clogged with detail, and considered that as a history it is seriously incomplete. Strong controversy followed the early reviews. *The Sunday Telegraph* asked 'Will none of the eminent commanders of the last war who worked with Wingate, defend him against the outrageous conclusions of the Official History?'. It added 'Reading Major General Kirby's edgy judgement it seems that the anti-Wingate party at the War Office was determined to have the last word'.

Fergusson, about to become Governor General of New Zealand, wrote to *The Scotsman* (14 February 1962) that the recent criticism of Wingate cannot be allowed to stand. In contrast, *The Economist* wrote (3 February 1962) 'Wingate is finally devalued by the publication of his insulting, self-ambitious and often false forecasting memorandum'.

The Jewish Observer (2 February 1962) deplored that 'There appears to be no end to the official vendetta against Wingate', and added that his ideas were used in planning Israel's Sinai campaign, and *The Jewish Chronicle* regretted that it seemed Wingate would be honoured in every country but his own. A major in the Burma Rifles summed up some of the feeling: 'The great difference between Wingate's critics and Wingate is that they are so very wise after the event and he was so very wise before the event'.

Much of the venom in the attacks on Wingate seem to stem from his critical attitude towards the Indian Army, and therefore the *Official History of the Indian Armed Forces* could be expected to throw some light on this issue. Volume I, *The Reconquest of Burma* (published 1958) deals in considerable detail with the Chindit operation and with Wingate's death. It records that when he heard of Wingate's death, Mountbatten wished to fly in to 'Broadway' and address the Chindits personally, but was dissuaded by his Commanders in Chief. Instead he issued his moving Order of the Day. There is no adverse criticism of Wingate in the Indian Official History and the chapter on Operation 'Thursday' ends with Mountbatten's tribute. The detached and scholarly Indian Official History – written by distinguished historians who consulted the generals and sought their advice, but did not ask them to write the history – was published four years earlier than the British, and makes it clear that it did not share Kirby's unbalanced obsession about Wingate. It also makes another interesting contrast. While Kirby devoted several pages of destructive criticism to Wingate, he made no attempt to consider or discuss Wingate's theory of Long Range Penetration Groups, whereas the Official Indian History gives a detailed and sympathetic assessment which recognises that Wingate's theory was a significant contribution to the development of modern warfare. Thus the Indian Official History is another balanced source of evidence which Kirby ignored.

11
Redressing the Balance

Many Chindits, although alerted to some extent by Slim's criticisms in *Defeat into Victory*, were outraged by what they read in the Official History. This was particularly true of General Tulloch who, from 1944 onwards, had become Wingate's main protagonist. Kirby had corresponded with Tulloch for nearly 10 years in an amicable way when they were discussing detail and facts about the Chindit campaign, but at no stage did Kirby give him an inkling of the destructive comment he was going to make about both Wingate and the Chindits. (Tulloch Papers, Rylands)

After Tulloch read the Official History he determined to write his own account in order to refute the official version, and he devoted much of the rest of his life to this task. From this time forward the military Establishment went to extraordinary lengths to prevent Tulloch from presenting his case, and to ensure that nothing favourable to Wingate was published. They attacked anyone who wrote anything supportive of him, but if an author criticised him (eg, Masters) this was latched onto and exaggerated. Perhaps the best immediate example of this treatment is Air Marshal Sir John Baldwin, who commanded the 3rd Tactical Air Force, and who played almost as significant a role as Slim in the great Burma victories.

Baldwin wrote to Tulloch in the late 1950s, when the Official History was being prepared, explaining that as early as 1953 he had given the Cabinet Office Historical Section his detailed notes about the situation when it was discovered that the 'Piccadilly' landing ground was obstructed. He agreed that Tulloch's account of the incident was almost word for word the same as his, and he considered Slim's version 'was decidedly inaccurate'. (Slim's version was contradicted by every other eye-witness, yet it appeared in *Defeat into Victory* and in the Official History.) Baldwin continued, 'I feel it is most unfair that an incorrect version should appear in the Official History'. He also added 'I got a caustic answer from the Secretary of the Historical Section in the Cabinet Office saying "Slim's account written at the time is quite definite", in other words he did not believe me'. (Baldwin–Tulloch 28 February 1957, Rylands)

In 1962 Baldwin again wrote to Tulloch 'I feel the Official History is most unfair to Orde... and is very scathing about the tactical results of the Chindit operations. Yet it makes no mention of what a valuable exercise the airlift and the supply of the Chindits proved to be. It enabled the Army and the Air Force to iron out many snags, and if it had not been for the experience gained in air supply to the Chindits, the RAF air supply would not have been as efficient as it was when the dash for Rangoon was on... Chindit expeditions brought home to senior Indian Army officers how air supply could be used for ground forces – they had little appreciation of army-air co-operation. I was hopping mad when I read the extracts of the Official History.' (Baldwin–Tulloch, 13 February 1962, Rylands)

After he had made it plain that he was going to write a book, Tulloch was called to the War Office in March 1962 and given a fierce grilling by one of Kirby's team, a Brigadier Latham, who warned him that if he wrote a book using Wingate's Papers he would be court-martialled, could lose his pension, and could be imprisoned in the Tower of London. This threat may sound ludicrous or even laughable, but it haunted Tulloch for the rest of his life, and after his book came out in 1972 he had a nervous breakdown. Again it has to be asked why the military Establishment was so determined to prevent anything favourable to Wingate from being published? Frequently, the answer seems to point to Kirby.

Tulloch received strong support from his friends including Calvert, Fergusson and the Wingate family. An indication of the atmosphere and of the intensity of feeling is given by a letter from Wingate's sister Sybil: 'I would trust the War Office custodians of the documents as far as I could throw them. I think they are perfectly capable of destroying or tampering with original documents of whose existence there is no external proof and whose evidence is inconvenient to them.' She concluded 'If you put on record what documents exist, you will have rendered a priceless service both to Orde and to history. That will deter the forgers and the evidence burners if nothing else does.' (Letter, Sybil Wingate–Tulloch, 22 February 1964, Rylands)

The threat by Latham of court martial, imprisonment and loss of pension, raises a much wider and graver issue in terms of historical evidence. If the detail and the views expressed in the Official History were all open, honest and above-board, the authors would presumably be perfectly happy for all available evidence to be made public. Why then did they go to such lengths, and by the use of dire threats, attempt to suppress one of the most significant sections of evidence? The answer can only be that they were determined to muzzle any point of view that did not fit in with their own view.

When the Latham threat is added to Kirby's actions in altering, losing or suppressing evidence, it amounts to a very serious assault on the reputation and integrity of a brave officer killed on active service.

When the Official History was published, it appeared that the military Establishment were determined to ensure that the reputation of Wingate would for ever be besmirched. For their part, while nearly all the Chindits were outraged by the Official History, there were many who were prepared to assist Tulloch in his efforts to put the record straight. Considerable support came from Scotland where Lorna Wingate was living. Her mother, Alice Hay, wrote a book *There was a Man of Genius*, and she encouraged Tulloch in his task. She, like the Wingate family, expressed her fears of evidence being suppressed or destroyed. She wrote 'Have several copies done and leave them in different and safe hands'. (Hay–Tulloch, undated letter, Rylands) Her book, in the form of letters to Orde's son, was well received and brought her many letters, 'Some wonderful, (Lady Churchill's) others less nice, (Like John Connell's), and from enemies of Orde and friends of Sykes'. (Hay–Tulloch, undated letter, Rylands)

Christopher Sykes, whose biography of Wingate appeared in 1959, did not please the family. They had hoped that after Slim's criticism in *Defeat into Victory*, Sykes would put the record straight, but when the book appeared they were seriously disappointed. One possible reason for this has emerged quite recently. Mrs Kirby has confirmed that Sykes submitted his whole script to Kirby who 'Found his draft was full of inaccuracies, but he managed to put most of them right'. When the biography appeared, Sykes sent a copy to Kirby with the enigmatic inscription 'To General Kirby with much gratitude for the help that regrettably the author cannot acknowledge'. (Interview, Mrs Kirby, February 1993) So Kirby's influence spread still further.

As Tulloch started to write his book, he too contacted Sykes. After discussing some detail of SEAC policy and agreeing that Kirby's assembly of facts was masterly, Sykes wrote 'Kirby's ideas are shamefully biased on many matters... and his turgid unreadability is appalling... It looks as if the papers are too embarrassing to be published until a lot more people are under the sod.' (Sykes–Tulloch, 26 December 1964, Rylands) Sykes does not emerge creditably from this, with his two totally conflicting statements.

Tulloch's labours included correspondence with many veterans of the campaign. Mountbatten wrote in a supportive and helpful vein, and totally refuted the allegation of the author John Connell that he and Slim would have resigned if Wingate had become a Lieutenant-General. Mountbatten, in rejecting other allegations about Wingate's ambition, added that he personally had offered that promotion to Wingate who had refused it, preferring to wait until Special Force had proved itself. (Mountbatten–Tulloch, 6 April 1965, Rylands)

From the Japanese side General Tanaka wrote from Tokyo 'It is an undeniable fact that the Wingate operation is one of the principal causes for the fall of northern Burma; the 18th Division fighting in the Hukawng Valley was forced to retreat from there because their route of communication had been cut off by Task Force Wingate'. (Tanaka–Tulloch, 27 February 1964, Rylands)

Mutaguchi also wrote in detail about the Chindit operations and concluded 'Wingate's airborne tactics put a great obstacle in the way of our Imphal plan, and were an important reason for its failure'. (Mutaguchi–Tulloch, 1 February 1964, Rylands) The continuing Japanese interest in Wingate is illustrated by a TV film on the Burma campaign (1993), which featured Wingate and posed the question whether such an outstanding leader could have emerged in the rigid hierarchy of the Japanese army.

Wingate's supporters have maintained consistently that his opponents, including the Official History, never seriously evaluated his military ideas. This is supported by the military historian Otto Heilbrunn in his book *Warfare in the Enemy's Rear* (1963) in which, having dealt with the Waffen SS, the Chindits, and the SAS under David Stirling, he argued that warfare behind the enemy's lines is as important in the nuclear age as before, but it needed the coherent doctrine which Wingate tried to give it.

In a review of Heilbrunn's book, the *Times Literary Supplement* (26 December 1963) made a comment which applies to many aspects of military history and may account partly for the lengthy Wingate saga: 'Of the many prickly feuds that bedevil the profession of arms, the most irreconcilable is that between the advocates and the opponents of Special Forces – those elite troops designed for unconventional operations, who infuriate the orthodox professional soldier by wearing funny hats, by adopting an idiosyncratic approach to the generally accepted customs of discipline and dress, and by getting themselves a reputation for panache and gallantry'.

This shrewd comment touches on a question that goes back at least as far as Sir John Moore and the Rifle Brigade in the Peninsular War, and comes forward to the role of the SAS in the Gulf War. It was certainly brought up in 1969 when Brigadier Calvert wrote to the author of the Official History *Victory in the West*. He protested that one of the most successful parachute operations in the European campaign, carried out by French parachute troops under his command in the SAS, had been omitted altogether from the Official History. After the Chindit operations, Calvert had returned to Europe to command the SAS and in his letter he queries the attitude of the military Establishment towards irregular forces and especially the Chindits. He described an incident when he was on Lord Montgomery's Planning Staff in 1947, and came across the minutes of a meeting of the Army Council in which they discussed the future line to be taken about Wingate and the Chindits. He wrote 'Although the Air Force rep differed strongly with the final line to be taken, it was in effect "We know these units fought very bravely and successfully, and the Japanese have a very high opinion of them and the decisive results they achieved, but Wingate was a divisive influence in the British Army, and we do not want every company commander thinking he is a Wingate. We don't want any more Wingates in the British Army. Therefore we must write down Wingate and the Chindits".' (Calvert–Ellis, 21 September 1969, Rylands) Calvert also corresponded with Tulloch and encouraged him to go ahead and write his book, despite the threats from Kirby's team and the Establishment.

Just as the opponents of Wingate manipulated witnesses and distorted evidence, so Tulloch, perhaps understandably, became obsessed with the feeling of persecution, but as he laboured on, he received positive encouragement from a number of disinterested sources. Colonel Barker, who wrote *The March on Delhi* (1963) and who produced much new evidence from the Japanese side, wrote 'What never ceases to amaze me, is the Official Historian's smug claim to infallibility – a sort of divine right to pronounce the verdict of history without question'. (Barker–Tulloch, 29 December 1966, Rylands) Barker also criticised Roberts as a pompous ass.

Tulloch received powerful and unexpected backing from people who could give unbiased testimony. Basil Liddell Hart, the distinguished military historian, wrote to say that the criticism and opposition Wingate met came as no surprise. (Liddell Hart–Tulloch, December 1965, Rylands) In similar vein the historian Arthur Bailey wrote that Tulloch was not alone in his criticism of the authors of the Official History. 'John Grover (GOC 2 Division) said they would not listen to him; Stopford (GOC 33 Corps) said they were a waste of time; and Richards, who commanded the garrison at Kohima and claimed to be able to put the record straight, was told to fuck off.' (Bailey–Tulloch, 21 January 1964, Rylands)

The most remarkable and telling evidence in this long-running dispute came from Colonel Barton, who had been employed under Kirby in the 1950s in writing the Narratives of the Chindit campaign for the Official History. He wrote: 'I am tremendously impressed by your loyalty and the courage with which you are tackling this job of vindicating Wingate, and correcting the vile accusations emanating not only from the Establishment, but also from high ranking officers in all branches of the services. Although one was forbidden as a narrator to make comments, it soon became pretty clear that Wingate was having a raw deal, and not getting the backing to which he was entitled. It is a mournful revelation that those who did give him this backing ranged from the Prime Minister (Churchill) and most of the American Chiefs of Staff on the one hand, and those who served him in the field down to the humblest soldier – not to mention his Japanese opponents. The document found on the body of a dead Japanese officer (Tulloch, p266) is surely a complete justification for all that Wingate stood for and did. Whereas those who came in between – and these included, alas, even Mountbatten and Slim at times, and of course GHQ India all the time – were out to put every obstacle in his way. It makes Wingate's steadfastness of purpose all the more praiseworthy. But the sequel is even more staggering, and I was astounded to read of the viciousness of Kirby and the Official Historians, who more than any others should try to keep a balance in assessing the pros and cons.' Barton then refers to the threats made against Tulloch and adds 'Pretty obviously because they don't like the idea of the truth being told, and the Official History, which I suppose they regard as sacrosanct, being shown for the biased document it is.' (Barton–Tulloch, 28 September 1970, Rylands)

Tulloch completed his labours and his book *Wingate in Peace and War* was published in 1972, but it had cost him dear and he died two years later. Although Tulloch's book was well received, Wingate's supporters still felt that injustice remained and while Brigadier Peter Mead and Sir Robert Thompson were preparing to challenge the Cabinet Office, the Chindit Old Comrades Association (COCA) combined together to present an appreciation. Some opponents have tried to write off the Appreciation, but while obviously presenting Wingate in a favourable light, it is a remarkable and moving tribute to a general 40 years after his death.

Brigadier Scott, DSO, MC, President of COCA, introduced the Appreciation by reminding members that Earl Mountbatten had agreed to support their document, which attempted to redress the impression given in the Official History.

One of the most effective and moving tributes came from a private soldier, Mr Allmont, who served in the 2nd Leicesters in 16 Brigade, and had joined up as a drummer boy aged 16. He was not surprised at the Establishment writing off the achievements of the Chindits, or at its portrayal of Wingate as a half-mad visionary, since in the past they had tried to do the same to Wellington 'The Sepoy General', and to Nelson. Allmont argued that fighting men do not wish to be cosseted, and they have no time for a man who is profligate with their lives, but they will lay them down for a good or brave officer. Wingate taught them everything – even to splitting bamboo to make a noiseless fire – and he was a hard taskmaster demanding perfection. The men often felt the lash of his tongue, but so did the officers.

> 'Above all General Wingate told us of his plans as far as was reasonable, remembering we faced a savage and barbaric enemy... and he shared the same discomforts and carried the same numbing burden... Rough and cussed as we soldiers were, we only asked for someone over us who was a craftsman at his job... if he was hard in his demands for perfection we did not mind. The perfection he demanded lay in our unique Chindit skills, not in bull and shining parades.'

Reading through more than 50 tributes in the Appreciation, a clear picture emerges: a consistent refrain of integrity, inspiration, the force of his personality uplifting men as if by magic, but, above all, from brigadiers to privates 'He would never ask you to do anything he would not do himself'. A Captain quoted from his diary entry on the day he heard of Wingate's death, 'We have lost a courageous leader, a great man, may his spirit carry us through our task'.

Post-war detractors have sneered at Wingate's classical and biblical messages, but a trooper recalled the inspiration which came to 16 Brigade from the message 'Hannibal eclipsed'. Colonel Cane MC recalls joining a unit in 1943, with senior officers in pre-war mess kit, who 'instinctively disliked the brusque, harsh and impatient ways of that young upstart Wingate', and he added that Wingate's mind was always running at full speed and driving his body to the limit. Wingate's subsequent detractors have claimed that he was brutal and inhuman, and squandered men's lives. The very opposite view comes from those who served in the Chindit campaigns. Major Dunlop MC wrote of his great kindness and humanity, and his consideration for all his men.

A particularly sensitive comment comes from Brigadier Walter Scott who served as Column Commander and Battalion Commander in the two Chindit expeditions. Scott was in the command tent at the start of Operation 'Thursday' when Cochran's dramatic photographs arrived and he described that scene in detail, and then the start of the fly-in: 'As my glider rose into the purple dusk above the mountains to the east, I was not thinking what lay beyond them, but rather of General Wingate's unforgettable demonstration of cool, determined and inspired leadership. I believe that if ever I saw greatness in a human being I saw it in General Wingate that night.' Scott adds that Wingate's greatest achievement was to give faith, confidence, pride in themselves, and to raise the morale of every serviceman in India, and 'to give us all hope'.

Many recalled that he was a hard taskmaster, that he was often downright unreasonable, but withal, there was nearly always a strange sort of affection for him. To the many wartime soldiers – who perhaps hit on why he was so unpopular with the Establishment – 'He was a completely irregular regular soldier'. Mr J. J. Lindo who served in the 1st King's Regiment in 77 Brigade wrote 'God dammit, we were proud of him, proud to be part of him. Let the historians denigrate him, let the chairborn wallahs scoff. We knew him.'

One of the most distinguished members of the Chindits was Sir Robert Thompson, who served in both campaigns as an RAF Liaison

Officer and who later became a world expert in counter-insurgency. He was on the staff of Templer during the Malayan emergency and then advised on South Vietnam, and the American presidents Nixon and Ford. Thompson's view on the Wingate controversy was clear and unequivocal. Of the assessment in the Official History, he wrote 'It was intended as a hatchet job by little men who could not have competed with him either in military argument or in battle. It has misfired.' (Quoted Mead, p9) Thompson considered that of all the British generals of the 20th century, Wingate's reputation would steadily increase and probably last longest.

Although Thompson was heavily involved as adviser to Nixon and Ford during and after the Vietnam war, he enthusiastically supported Brigadier Mead, himself a Chindit, who took on the struggle after the death of Tulloch, and who worked meticulously to obtain the true background to the attack on Wingate in the Official History. Thompson concentrated his argument on the brilliance and originality of Wingate's strategic and tactical concepts: the basic idea of supplying major forces by air behind the enemy lines; the direct link between ground forces and aircraft both in supply and in close support bombing; the masterly concept of Strongholds behind enemy lines; and Wingate's passionate belief that boldest measures are the safest. Thompson emphasised that all Chindit operations were geared directly to Japanese lines of communication – a point marginalised by the Official history – and he asked 'What would the effect have been, if two days after the D-Day landings in Normandy in 1944, two German airborne divisions had landed in central southern England and blocked several of the main roads to the south coast ports? No analogy is exact, but this is roughly what Wingate did.' Thompson concluded 'Every time I look at the picture of General Slim and his Corps Commanders being knighted by the Viceroy Lord Wavell on the field of battle after Imphal, I see the ghost of Wingate present'. (Quoted Mead, p10)

Thompson and Mead produced a carefully researched document, which argued that the treatment of Wingate by the authors was hostile and prejudicial to objective study. They asked that certain allegations which were not supported by the balance of evidence should be withdrawn. These included: that his concept of future operations was unsound and prompted by personal ambition; that he used his LRP Groups in conventional operations; that he deceived the commander of ·16 Brigade (Fergusson); and that he disregarded the wishes of Slim over the use of 14 Brigade. Thompson and Mead presented the document to the Cabinet Office in April 1977, and had further correspondence prior to a meeting with Sir John Hunt, Secretary of the Cabinet in December 1977. No comment was made about the arguments put forward, and all their requests were rejected. They had demanded that slips detailing the inaccuracies should be issued and placed in all known copies of the Official History. This was a blunder, for it was quite impracticable, and it is not surprising that this request was refused.

Their rejection prompted them to continue their research and this led to the publication in 1987 of Mead's book *Orde Wingate and the Historians*. The book outlined in considerable detail the evidence in the Public Record Office and other archives which was relevant to Wingate and the Chindits. It showed how the image of Wingate put forward in the Official History had been accepted, copied and enlarged upon, over a period of more than 20 years.

While the Official History remained unchallenged, its influence spread widely through the military Establishment. Kirby and Roberts had clearly touched a chord with a large number of senior officers in both the Indian and British Army who had been offended by Wingate, and this helped to proliferate their views. Training briefs and precis at Staff College and Sandhurst repeated the general line of the Official History, and this was reinforced in the 1960s by Roberts who, with all the authority of a brigadier who had taken part, lectured at Staff College on the subject of the Burma campaign. In this context, Roberts had full scope to put forward his own view of Wingate and he made the most of this opportunity. Making little attempt to discuss Wingate's ideas or military thinking he concentrated, as the Official History had done, on the allegations made about the attack on Indaw. He repeated that Wingate, without getting Slim's approval, had ordered 14 Brigade to move south and not to help Fergusson as promised. 'Slim did not know of it, but what was worse nor did Fergusson who took a beating.' (Roberts Papers) Although he had all the available information, Roberts made no attempt to give a balanced view of Wingate or the Chindits, and thus these prejudices were perpetuated through new generations of Staff College students. These prejudices were reinforced officially by the 1961 Staff College Paper on 'The Problems of the Burma Campaign'. Referring to the Stronghold concept, it said 'LRP Columns were called on to do things for which they were never intended'. It repeated Kirby's unsubstantiated criticism by saying 'Wingate became obsessed with the capture of Indaw, and abandoned his own precepts', and it concluded – against all the Japanese evidence available by that time 'Chindit operations did not deflect any troops earmarked for Imphal except for two battalions'. That statement is categorically untrue.

Another aspect of this controversy is given by the publication in 1980 of *Chindit* by Richard Rhodes-James, who had been a cipher officer in 111 Brigade. After the disasters of 'Blackpool' he, like most of the survivors, had spent many weeks recuperating, and during that time he wrote a description of his experiences. More than 30 years later he decided to publish it. He described vividly the rather futile meanderings of 111 Brigade – 'After two exhausting weeks we had blown one bridge' and 'We were still fumbling in the jungle seeking a role'. (*Chindit*, p88) The early chapters illustrate above all that, even after a few days, Lentaigne had completely lost his nerve and would have had to be removed if he had not been taken out to succeed Wingate. Rhodes-James gives a candid view of Wingate and recorded the deep antipathy between Wingate and Lentaigne, who thought Wingate's ideas 'were dangerously unsound and totally unproven'. Rhodes-James considered that Slim and Mountbatten protected Wingate from those who tried to frustrate his plans, and 'they also protected him from himself when he did and said things he should never have done or said'. (*Chindit*, p89) There were a distinguished few who saw he needed special protection and encouragement: 'Churchill, Wavell, Mountbatten and Slim. What a bodyguard!' (*Chindit*, p89) Rhodes-James concludes: 'The strange man we followed because he had ideas and because for a brief moment in our lives he made us bigger than ourselves'. (*Chindit*, p206)

This honest and reasonable assessment prompted a review in *Newsweek* (1 September 1980) entitled 'Debunking the Chindit Legend'. This stated 'Now a book by a veteran charges that Wingate was a failure', and it describes Wingate's guerrilla war as 'a bloody and pointless failure'. The review was by an officer who had served in Morris Force, who said that Morris told him 'If Wingate had not already died he might have been tempted to murder him'. (That comment has a quiet irony; see page 154.)

The reviews of *Chindit* illustrate the strange and continuing controversy over Wingate. The reviews of the book were almost entirely favourable, but their titles varied from 'Wingate the Wizard', 'God or

Oddball', 'Appalling Truths', to the destructive review in *Newsweek*. Rhodes-James felt that *Newsweek* totally misrepresented what he had tried to say. Referring to the other reviews he wrote 'Most reviewers have used their review as an excuse to unload their views on Orde Wingate, and the arguments are as furious as ever'. (Interview, April 1993) In another review Philip Warner in a shrewd comment wrote 'The misfortunes of the second expedition provided ample material for the wholesale condemnation of anything except traditional methods and conventional leaders'. In contrast Ronald Lewin, by that time the author of biographies of Slim and Wavell, referred to Wingate's megalomania and asked 'Whether the Chindit myth is not blown apart by this chronicle of suffering and sacrifice?'.

Many of the reviews quoted at length from Shelford Bidwell's book *The Chindit War* which came out in 1979. Bidwell, a retired Brigadier, had written a number of books in the field of military history, and wrote *The Chindit War* as a comparative study of Wingate and Stilwell. In a long and detailed book, he tends to be highly critical of Wingate and, while ignoring most favourable comment, quotes the destructive criticism of other people. One example may illustrate this. Bidwell, on the testimony of one staff officer, wrote that at the news of Wingate's disappearance, the officers in the HQ Mess brought round after round of drinks, and 'There was no indication of gloom, let alone dismay'. (Bidwell, p157) This view did not accord in any way with other descriptions of that moment, which were known to Bidwell, yet he allowed it to stand. Significantly, the officer he quoted later maintained that Bidwell's implication was erroneous and he yielded to no man in his admiration of Wingate. (Mead, p171) Bidwell also pursued a fairly consistent theme that Wingate was mentally unbalanced. He tended to use pseudo-medical language and claimed that Wingate was 'Undoubtedly a paranoid manic-depressive whose mental processes were not analytical or intellectual'. Continuing this theme, Bidwell even wrote an article for a medical journal, *The Practitioner*, entitled 'Wingate: A Diagnostic Problem'. He tended, too, to make sweeping generalisations of a generally critical nature. He denied that Wingate had any influence over the Burmese people and added 'He did not know a Burmese from an Arab'. (Rhodes-James Papers) Similarly, the *Newsweek* review quoted Bidwell as saying: 'The irony of the Chindit War lies in the fact that the whole enterprise was a waste of human effort and sacrifice.'

Many of Wingate's detractors, including Bidwell, have been criticised for failing to discuss or consider Wingate's highly original tactical and strategic ideas, on which his reputation as a military leader must depend. This point was made in a review of Bidwell's *The Chindit War* by M. Elliott-Bateman at Manchester University. He wrote 'One would expect a book entitled *The Chindit War* to be based on some analysis of this form of warfare, its historical evolution, the stage reached by 1944 in Burma, and its continued development in such places as Vietnam and the Middle East. One would hope to find sufficient of Wingate's writings to make his concepts intelligible to the layman, and perhaps a brief outline of the development of his ideas from Palestine through Abyssinia to Burma. Alas this book contains none of these aspects which are essential to anyone trying to make sense out of the second Chindit expedition, let alone understanding or evaluating it.' (Rylands)

Probably the final contribution to the Wingate debate by anyone who actually took part, came from Sir Robert Thompson in his autobiography *Make for the Hills*, published in 1989. As a counter-insurgency expert, and as an adviser to governments from Malaya, Vietnam and Washington, his views deserve consideration. Because of the demands of his career he came late into the Wingate controversy, but then actively supported Mead's protest.

Thompson described Wingate's physical and moral courage; his vision and determination; how 'mediocrity was stripped bare in his presence', something which upset his lesser contemporaries. Wingate, among the defeatism of 1943, saw that by harnessing wireless communication to air power and air supply, the Japanese could be defeated; that the answer to penetration was counter-penetration; and that aircraft could replace artillery for LRP Groups. Wingate's technique of close support bombing by Mustangs was years ahead of its time and if it had been developed could have helped at Arnhem. His strategic concepts, including Stronghold, based on his belief that boldest measures are the safest, were equally advanced. Thompson rejects Bidwell's slur on Wingate as a butcher and argues that Wingate, alone among commanders, insisted on light aircraft to bring out the wounded.

Thompson refers to Kirby's action in putting Wingate's Memorandum on future operations in an appendix in full. 'This was designed to show Wingate's wildness, but instead it showed an offensive vision which was way beyond the grasp of more conventional minds.' (*Make for the Hills*, p72) Thompson noted, too, that Slim may have mentally filed away Wingate's idea of a thrust to Pakkoku and Meiktila, and he then concentrates on the way the Official History dismisses the contribution of the Chindits to the battles of Imphal and Kohima. He argues that at least one and a half divisions were diverted from the initial attack towards Kohima, when one additional regiment could have overrun the desperate defence of the Royal West Kents in Kohima and would have had the ill-defended base at Dimapur at their mercy. 'The Chindit landings were an essential factor in the defeat of the Japanese and in the saving of Imphal'. Finally, Thompson quotes the Japanese evidence of the disruption caused by the Chindit landings, and Mutaguchi's words 'Wingate the man in whom I met my match'.

Of all the commentators on the Burma campaign, the most revered and respected is Louis Allen, whose book *Burma The Longest War* (1984) was the product of a lifetime's scholarly devotion by someone uniquely well-qualified; who fought in the campaign, spoke Japanese, interrogated Japanese prisoners after the war, and spent nearly 40 years sifting Japanese and British evidence. Allen who is critical of some of Wingate's actions, wrote that after the defeats of 1942, the Army 'Needed an immense uplifting of spirit. It needed Orde Wingate... On the other hand the animus Wingate aroused in fellow commanders and distant staffs has also led to determined efforts to denigrate him and to reduce the impact of what he did.' (*Burma The Longest War*, p116) Allen quite rightly made the point that it was the Indian divisions at Imphal and Kohima which broke the Japanese but, referring to Wingate's plans, wrote 'Devotees of the dull and staid will decry his flamboyance, histrionic procedures and the publicity which attended them. They miss the point. What the press and world opinion made of Wingate's initial exploits, infused a new spirit into the affairs of Burma; whatever the strategic upshot, whatever Wingate's psychological faults – on a les défauts de ses qualités – that renewal of spirit cannot be gainsaid.'

In attempting an objective assessment of the achievements of Orde Wingate, it has to be said that the protagonists on both sides have exhibited bias, prejudice and exaggeration. His supporters, stung into action by what they saw as Slim's inexplicable change of view, followed by the unjust and destructive criticism of the Official History, tended to over-react and to play down different and perfectly justifiable criticism of aspects of Wingate's stormy career. On the other hand, although Kirby and his assistant Roberts articulated the antagonism felt by senior staff officers and much of the Indian and British Army Establishments, they used their privileged position in an unprofessional way to put over their own biased view. This has been copied and elaborated – often in all innocence – over the last 30 years. Much of the feud which followed, stemmed from Kirby's dishonest handling of historical evidence. Understandably, other writers repeated these views and so the momentum continued, but the attitude of antagonism and acrimony created by Kirby often resulted in other writers accepting his prejudices and copying his loaded evidence. Even Bidwell – certainly no champion of Wingate – referring to Kirby's view of Wingate in the Official History wrote 'He took his revenge'. (Bidwell, p40)

Having as far as possible sifted the facts from the prejudices, and in the process uncovered a story of deplorable conduct by officers in positions of authority, the summing up must be that Wingate was often a difficult, prickly, contemptuous, outrageous and impossible colleague, but at the same time was one of the ablest and most dynamic military leaders of the Second World War, with a brilliant, original and incisive mind. As Fergusson said 'There are men who shine at planning, or at training, or at leading; here was a man who excelled at all three, and whose vision at the council table matched his genius in the field'. The views of serious military historians recognise that his concepts of Long Range Penetration and of Strongholds were years ahead of any contemporary thinking. In the face of deliberate and powerful opposition in the Indian Army, Wingate mounted two Chindit expeditions – at a time when from the myriad forces in India, no successful attacking action had been carried out in the Burma theatre. Such achievements never arise from mild consensus, especially not in the atmosphere of lethargic defeatism which brooded over India in 1942. His demand for perfection meant that many officers were RTU and they frequently carried with them bitter criticism which did not diminish in the telling. His unwise and often unnecessary criticism of staff officers and the staff system resulted in many acrimonious disputes, and created numerous enemies with long memories, who rallied to the opposition when Kirby emerged to give a lead.

Tragically, Wingate died before the success of his theories could be fully proved, and before he had time to develop and publish a detailed thesis of all his ideas. Another drawback, stemming from his death in March 1944, was that no one else in top command positions really believed in the Chindits, and the costly battles at 'Blackpool', Mogaung and Myitkyina, under the inadequate leadership of Lentaigne, have been used by Wingate's subsequent detractors to argue that his concepts did not work. Had he lived, 'Blackpool' would never have been established – it offended every principle he had enunciated for a Stronghold – and the Chindits would have been taken out after the great success of Calvert's 77 Brigade at 'Broadway', and used again in their proper function. In all the wrangling which followed Wingate's death, Calvert stood with complete integrity as the brave leader, who had proved the validity of Wingate's theories, and then remained loyal both to Wingate and his philosophy.

The role of Kirby in this regrettable saga needs to be spelt out. After his clash with Wingate in 1942, as Bidwell says, he waited to take his revenge, and then with all the power of the Official Historian he set about his task. If a group of professional historians were asked to list the cardinal sins of a historian, they would probably include: using selective evidence; suppressing evidence contrary to their thesis; altering original documents; misquoting statements to alter or reverse their meaning; asking loaded questions to trap witnesses into misstatements; manipulating witnesses to withdraw previous statements; and destroying documentary evidence. There is now incontrovertible evidence that Kirby did all of these, and through the Official History did grave and lasting damage to the reputation of Orde Wingate and the achievements of the Chindits.

Instead of the petty, destructive and dishonest commentary of Kirby, which has had so much influence since it was written, Wingate should now be remembered as an outstanding wartime leader, a brilliant and original military thinker whose reputation spanned the world, a meticulous planner and organiser, and a fearless and inspiring leader.

Select Bibliography

For a brief introduction to the military background of the Chindit campaign, readers are referred to my book *Burma Victory – Imphal, Kohima and the Chindit Issue* (1992). All books listed below were published in London unless stated.

Allen, Louis, *Burma, The Longest War* (Dent 1984)
Baker, Alan, *Merrill's Marauders* (Ballantine 1972)
Barker, A. J., *The March on Delhi* (1963)
Beamish, John, *Burma Drop* (Bestseller Library 1960)
Bidwell, Shelford, *The Chindit War* (Hodder and Stoughton 1979)
Bond, Brian, *Chief of Staff – The Pownall Diaries* (1974)
Bond, Brian, *Fallen Stars* (Brassey 1991)
Burchett, W., *Wingate's Phantom Army* (Muller 1946)
Calvert, Michael, *Prisoners of Hope* (Cape 1952)
— *Fighting Mad* (Bantam 1964)
— *Slim* (Ballantine 1973)
— *Chindit* (Ballantine 1973)
Cane, Peter, *Chinese Chindits* (1948)
Carfrae, Charles, *Chindit Column* (Kimber 1985)
Connell, John, *Wavell* (Collins 1964)
Cross, J. P., *Jungle Warfare* (Arms and Armour Press 1989)
Fergusson, Bernard, (Lord Ballantrae)
— *Beyond the Chindwin* (Collins 1945)
— *The Wild Green Earth* (Collins 1946)
— *The Trumpet in the Hall* (Collins 1970)
Fraser, George Macdonald, *Quartered Safe Out Here* (Harvill 1992)
Halley, David, *With Wingate in Burma* (Hodge 1945)
Hay, Alice, *There was a Man of Genius* (Spearman 1963)
Jeffrey, W. F., *Sunbeams Like Swords* (1951)
Keegan, John, *A History of Warfare* (Hutchinson 1993)
— *The Face of Battle* (Cape 1976)
— *Churchill's Generals* (Weidenfeld & Nicholson 1991)

King-Clark, R., *Free For a Blast* (Grenville 1988)

Lewin, Ronald, *Slim* (Leo Cooper 1976)

Machorton, Ian, *Safer than a Known Way* (1958)

Masters, J., *The Road Past Mandalay* (Joseph 1961)

Mead, Peter, *Orde Wingate and the Historians* (1987)

O'Brien, Peter, *Out of the Blue* (Collins 1984)

Official History of the Indian Armed Forces, *The Reconquest of Burma* (Delhi 1958)

Official History, *The War against Japan*, Vol III (1961)

Rhodes-James, Richard, *Chindit* (Murray 1980)

Rolo, Charles, *Wingate's Raiders* (Harrap 1944)

Rooney, David, *Stilwell* (Ballantine 1971)

— *Burma Victory* (Arms and Armour Press 1992)

Shaw, James, *The March Out* (Hart-Davis 1953)

Shaw, Jesse, *Special Force* (Sutton 1986)

Slim, Field Marshal Viscount, *Defeat into Victory* (Cassell 1956)

Tripp, Alan, *Codebreaker in the Far East* (Cass 1989)

Sykes, Christopher, *Orde Wingate* (Collins 1959)

Thompson, Sir Robert, *Make for the Hills* (Cooper 1989)

Thomas, Lowell, *Back to Mandalay* (Greystone, New York 1951)

Towill, Bill, *A Chindit's Chronicle* (1991)

Tulloch, Derek, *Wingate in Peace and War* (Macdonald 1972)

Tuchman, Barbara, *Sand against the Wind* (New York 1970)

Warner, Philip, *Auchinleck* (Sphere 1981)

Ziegler, Philip, *Mountbatten* (Collins 1985)

Sources

The Wingate Papers – by kind permission of Lieutenant-Colonel Wingate.;

Churchill College Cambridge, Military Archive: Slim Papers, Roberts Papers;

Public Record Office (Abbreviation PRO): see *Guide to Documents in the PRO* by J. D. Cantwell; CAB files especially;

Imperial War Museum;

John Rylands Library, Manchester (Abbreviation Rylands): Tulloch Papers, Auchinleck Papers.

Index

Main units involved in the different campaigns are mentioned at the start of each chapter or section.